# FORGOTTEN
## VOICES

Also available in the Forgotten Voices series:

*Forgotten Voices of the Great War*
*Forgotten Voices of the Great War* (illustrated)
*Forgotten Voices of the Somme*

*Lest We Forget: Forgotten Voices from 1914–1945*

*Forgotten Voices of the Second World War*
*Forgotten Voices of the Second World War* (illustrated)
*Forgotten Voices of the Blitz and the Battle for Britain*
*Forgotten Voices of the Holocaust*
*Forgotten Voices of the Secret War*
*Forgotten Voices of D-Day*
*Forgotten Voices of Burma*

*Forgotten Voices of the Falklands*

# FORGOTTEN VOICES
# OF THE
# SOMME

THE MOST DEVASTATING BATTLE OF THE GREAT WAR
IN THE WORDS OF THOSE WHO SURVIVED

IN ASSOCIATION WITH THE
IMPERIAL WAR MUSEUM

## JOSHUA LEVINE

EBURY
PRESS

7 9 10 8

First published in 2008 by Ebury Press, an imprint of Ebury Publishing
A Random House Group Company
This edition published 2009

The Random House Group Limited Reg. No. 954009

Addresses for companies within the Random House Group can be found at
www.randomhouse.co.uk

A CIP catalogue record for this book is available from the British Library

The Random House Group Limited supports The Forest Stewardship Council®
(FSC®), the leading international forest-certification organisation. Our books carrying
the FSC label are printed on FSC®-certified paper. FSC is the only forest-certification
scheme supported by the leading environmental organisations, including Greenpeace.
Our paper procurement policy can be found at www.randomhouse.co.uk/environment

Printed and bound by CPI Group (UK) Ltd, Croydon, CR0 4YY

ISBN 9780091926281

To buy books by your favourite authors and register for offers visit www.randomhouse.co.uk

I, that on my familiar hill
Saw with uncomprehending eyes
A hundred of Thy sunsets spill
Their fresh and sanguine sacrifice,
Ere the sun swings his noonday sword
Must say goodbye to all of this:–
By all delights that I shall miss,
Help me to die, O Lord.

**Lieutenant William Noel Hodgson, MC**
**9th Battalion, Devonshire Regiment**
**(January 3, 1893 – July 1, 1916)**

# Contents

# Acknowledgements

Once again, I would like to thank everybody at the Imperial War Museum Sound Archive, Photography Archive and Photo Studio. Margaret Brooks, Peter Hart, Richard McDonough, John Stopford-Pickering and Richard Hughes have all been generous with their time and their knowledge. Their infectious enthusiasm for the treasures that they hold in their collection fills me with admiration.

I would also like to thank Liz Bowers, Terry Charman, Abigail Ratcliffe, Madeleine James, Ken Barlow, Jake Lingwood, Jim Gill, Barbara Levy, Alan Wakefield, Ian Procter, Dave Parry, Andrew Margerison, Jason Strange and Kiran Patel. My thanks also to Max Arthur, Sam Crew and Claire Price.

Most of all, I pay my respects to the men who raided, dug, wired, advanced and died ninety-two years ago in Picardy.

*Joshua Levine, June 2008*

# Author's Preface

The influence of the Battle of the Somme on the psychology of subsequent generations has been so great that it now invites trite modern comparisons. It has become a lazy way of alluding to fear, danger or horror. I once sat listening to an actor as he described the courage necessary when stepping out on stage in front of a packed audience. 'It must be rather like,' he said, 'going over the top at the Somme.' Or perhaps not. Perhaps going over the top was nothing at all like appearing in weekly rep, but was, rather, an experience that can only be described by the men who did it: the men whose voices appear in this book.

This is a book about individuals, and individual experiences. These men are not historians. They are not generally interested in conclusions, nor do they seek out the 'bigger picture'. Occasionally, they question the ethics of an action, sometimes they challenge the judgement of those higher up the chain of command, but, for the most part, they tell us about what they – and they alone – did at a time when the rules of civilisation were suspended. The Battle of the Somme threw hundreds of thousands of men into a world beyond morality and this book is a record of their reactions. These reactions can – and should – be used in evidence when framing conclusions. Nevertheless, these men are entitled to stand alone as witnesses to an event that is difficult for us to imagine truly.

This book is dedicated to the men who fought on the Somme, those who lived and those who died. They were asked to make sacrifices that we can barely comprehend in our modern, rights-driven society. It is the least that we can do to read their stories, and try to understand why, and how, they did what they did.

*Joshua Levine, June 2008*

# Introduction by
# Professor Richard Holmes

There is an ineluctable poignancy to the battlefield of the Somme, although time has healed most of the damage that man inflicted on this rolling downland. Those little villages that meant so much in 1916 have reverted to somnolent type; broadleaved trees have replaced their shattered predecessors in big woods like Mametz and Delville, and the Albert-Bapaume road still slashes busily across the battlefield. The Somme meanders its gentle way just south of the British sector, and its tributary, the little Ancre, curls in behind the old front line just west of the Thiepval ridge, crowned by the memorial listing over 70,000 men missing on the Somme between the arrival of the British Third Army in the sector in July 1915 and March 20, 1918, the eve of the great German offensive.

The visitor to the Somme needs real determination not to have his interest wholly fixed by the cemeteries and memorials scattered across these haunted acres, for they help chart the impact of the most costly battle in British history. Its first day was the army's bloodiest, and the total of 415,000 British casualties – to which must be added the 200,000 French and upwards of 600,000 German – make it one of the deadliest battles in world history. However, the memorials post-date the battle, and it is all too easy to let them detract from the militarily crucial details of the landscape (a gentle declivity here, a concave slope there) which meant so much to men who lived and died upon it. What matters is less the view *from* Thiepval memorial than the view *of* Thiepval ridge from the uplands across the Ancre, whence British artillery observers did their best to batter German trenches before the first attack on July 1, 1916. To understand the microterrain of the Somme we must, in our mind's eye, strip the landscape of precisely those symbols which give it such an enduring appeal.

In very much the same way it is easy to study the Somme through the thick prism of hindsight, and to superimpose our own view on its events, just as we have planted our own memorials on the landscape upon which it was fought. The great strength of this remarkable book is that it tells the story of the Somme in the words not of professional historians, but of the men who fought the battle. These men came from a world in which 'you could get nicely drunk on a shilling', farm work went on from 'four o'clock in the morning to seven o'clock at night', many families got through the week by pawning belongings on Monday mornings, and village policemen spanked naughty boys. Many young men were 'full of patriotism and the *Boy's Own Paper*', and came from a background where they had had 'a certain amount of discipline' so that army life was less of a shock. Several of the 'Pals' battalions, formed in response to Lord Kitchener's appeal for volunteers in August 1914, were filled with 'a splendid lot of men . . . university students, doctors, dentists, opticians, solicitors, accountants, bank officials, works directors, schoolmasters, shop owners, town hall staff, post office staff – you name it'.

Neither patriotism nor the strong bonds forged within units made men immune to the shocks of war. One was struck by seeing a convoy of wounded leaving Rouen as he arrived, and another saw 'a mangled body blown to bits on a sack' on his first trip to the front, and a third remembered the jam-like consistency of the French corpses that made up the rear wall of his trench. Some remembered the weight they carried in battle – 'I could have been a mule . . . not a human being' – and others the sheer impatience – 'browned off with the waiting' – of wanting to get on with the attack. One officer suggested that most people had a breaking point, although there were a few actually who '*liked* it'. An experienced private went to the heart of the matter when he affirmed that: 'Bravery is shown when a man is fearful but continues to carry out his obligations . . . Fear becomes cowardice when one withdraws oneself from one's moral obligations.' However, even the well-motivated might relish a wound serious enough to get him home, 'a Blighty one', in the jargon of the day.

Too many accounts of the battle focus largely on its first day, but the accounts here take us across the knife-edge of that terrible summer, from the mid-July attack on Bazentin Ridge, through the first tank attack on September 15, to the final autumn battles as the weather closed in. One officer remembered that the attack on Beaucourt on November 13, at the very end of the battle, took place in 'frightful' conditions. 'There was so much water, everywhere,' he wrote. 'I remember a broken-down railway station, shelled for months, and it was one of the most unpleasant times in my experience. The terrain was simply a mass of shell-holes.' He took about seventy men into the line, and brought out thirty-six a week later.

Men remembered the battle in many ways. One officer thought that 'people just don't want to know' about the real war, and another gruffly opined that war poets 'wrote nonsense. Writing poetry about horrors. No point. It goes without saying'. 'I didn't deserve to get through it all,' admitted a private touched by the guilt that afflicted many survivors. 'I look upon the war as an experience,' reflected another. 'I got just as much pleasure out of it, as I did the bad times. When I came back, I was no different from when I went.' In contrast, a comrade admitted that the war had never really left him. 'I can only remember faces and first names. I can remember them one after another . . . It's a thought that's in my mind all the time. Has been for years.'

This is not a book which seeks to rule off a historical balance-sheet that will always haunt us, but to let those who fought more than ninety years ago tell us about a piece of France that is for ever British.

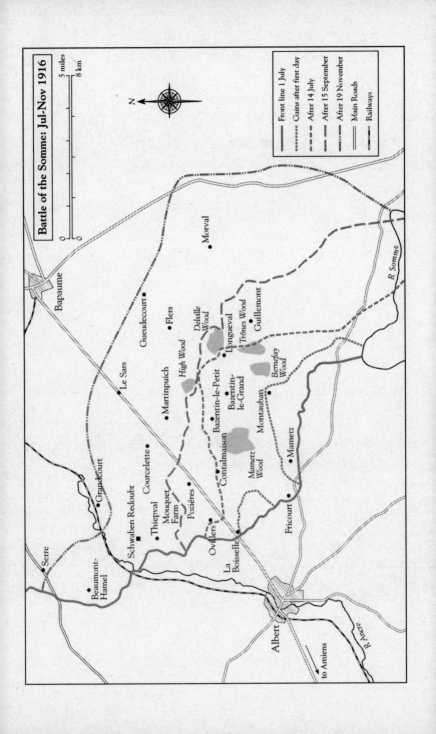

Battle of the Somme: Jul–Nov 1916

5 miles
8 km

N

Front line 1 July
Gains after first day
After 14 July
After 15 September
After 19 November
Main Roads
Railways

Bapaume

Morval

Gueudecourt

Flers

Delville Wood

High Wood

Longueval

Trônes Wood

Guillemont

Le Sars

Martinpuich

Bazentin-le-Petit

Bazentin-le-Grand

Bernafay Wood

Montauban

Contalmaison

Mametz Wood

Mametz

Courcelette

Grandcourt

Schwaben Redoubt

Thiepval

Mouquet Farm

Pozières

Ovillers

La Boisselle

Fricourt

Serre

Beaumont-Hamel

Albert

to Amiens

R Ancre

R Somme

Many events in British history have come down to us with received wisdom firmly attached. The signing of the Magna Carta embodies the birth of liberty, the Battle of Agincourt represents the flowering of patriotism, and the Battle of the Somme evokes futility, flawed leadership, and the snuffing-out of public innocence. Yet received wisdom can owe a great deal to the tastes and prejudices of those who come after. Where the opportunity exists to view events through the eyes of those who experienced them – as it does here – the opportunity should be taken. The men who fought the Battle of the Somme may have their own prejudices, and their observations limited perhaps to a single corner of a foreign field, but they are first-hand witnesses to the facts. They return us to a point before legend and received wisdom took hold. We are fortunate that their voices can still be heard above all the ensuing noise.

The battle in which these men fought arose out of a desire to break the existing deadlock. Since the winter of 1914, a continuous line of trenches had stretched from the Belgian coast to the Swiss border, creating a war of attrition amid the wire, mud and trenches. The Gallipoli campaign of 1915 had been an attempt to outflank the Western Front, but it had failed. At the Chantilly conference of December 6, 1915, Allied strategy for the coming year was agreed upon: large-scale offensives would be carried out on every front.

This plan pleased the British Imperial General Staff, eager to mount a push to break through on the Western Front. The Imperial General Staff feared that a defensive strategy would ultimately weaken the Allies, allowing the Germans – who were already in possession of economically valuable swathes of France and Belgium – to make peace on their own terms. Such a strategy would also increase the vulnerability of the Allied-held Channel ports, exposing Britain to the threat of invasion. A decisive attack was considered necessary.

The next question was where the attack should take place. On December 19, Sir Douglas Haig took over from Sir John French as Commander-in-Chief of the British Expeditionary Force. Haig believed that the British should attack in the Belgian Ypres salient. Britain had, after all, entered the war to protect Belgium, the majority of her troops were in the northern part of the line, and clear strategic goals existed in the region. Britain was France's junior partner, however, and Joseph Joffre – the French Commander-in-Chief – was adamant that a combined attack should be mounted in Picardy, to the south. Haig had little say in the matter, and a plan was formulated: a joint British and French offensive against German positions on both sides of the River Somme.

The area had already seen fighting in August 1914, during the initial advance of the German army, and again in September, as the Germans fell back in the face of resistance. The subsequently formed line of trenches passed through the region, where it was defended by troops from Brittany. In August 1915, they were replaced along a fourteen-mile sector by British troops.

And so, in early 1916, preparations began for an Allied push along the Somme front. These preparations did not, however, take into account the possibility that the Germans might be making plans of their own.

# Young Lions

*I couldn't get into the army quick enough.*

The British Expeditionary Force that sailed for France at the outbreak of the Great War was made up of four infantry divisions, a cavalry division and an independent brigade. This was a meagre force with which to confront the German army of a hundred infantry divisions. The British Army had long been little more than a means of policing the Empire and deterring potential aggressors. Britain's world supremacy depended not on its army, but on its navy, which continued to rule the waves. A European war presented quite different challenges, and although men of the Territorial Army and soldiers from the dominions and colonies were available to fight, a call to arms was urgently needed.

The problem was addressed promptly by Lord Kitchener, the Secretary of State for War, who set about creating a 'new army'. Adhering to the idea that men would be more willing to enlist if they knew those with whom they would be serving, he mounted a nationwide drive to encourage cities, towns, villages, factories and groups with shared interests to raise their own battalions, which would then be attached to existing regiments. They would consist of men between the ages of eighteen and thirty-nine, who would join up for three years, or the duration of the war, whichever proved the longer. Posters of Kitchener with his steady gaze and pointed finger went up across the country, and patriotic fervour ensured that half a million men had enlisted by the end of 1914. These were men with no experience of soldiering, who were joining the army in a spirit of adventure.

Regular soldiers, Territorials, dominion soldiers and men of the 'Pals battalions' were to fight in close proximity on the Somme. As members of the British Army they shared an enemy, but as individuals they might have little else in common.

## Corporal Don Murray
### 8th Battalion, King's Own Yorkshire Light Infantry

I remember my first day at school. It was a terrifying experience. My sister took me, and we had to walk through the door into this big building – but I dug my heels in and refused to go in. So my sister went into the school alone, and she came out with the headmistress, Miss Phillips, who took me by the scruff of the neck and the seat of my pants. I was jet-propelled into the school. The lady who took me into her class was Miss Kane. I thought she was very, very beautiful. She smelt very strongly of carbolic soap – it's always stuck in my memory.

I can remember the end of the Boer War. We were all allowed to go out into the playground, line the railings round the school, and we all waved little Union Jacks as the soldiers were marching back from the war, to the barracks at the top of the road. I remember one soldier in particular, who had a bandage round his head. We cheered him madly. I expect he had a boil or something; still, we thought he was a hero.

And I remember, we used to go round by the girls' school, and watch them come out and make fun of them. But the girls had a way of joining together, and instead of going home separately, they used to go home in groups, singing a song that's quite popular now, 'Strawberry Fair', and they used to do a little dance with it, and each lot branched off as they got to their home.

After that, I went to Usher Street School, where I did very well. I did what became known as the 'Eleven Plus' and failed it purposefully, because I didn't want to leave the school. I was wrong – but that's what I did. Whilst I was there, I joined the church choir. My father and brother were also in the choir, and we used to go two nights a week and three times on a Sunday. And at the end of the morning service, all the choir men would march out, straight across to the pub, and they'd all go in together. It seemed so *wrong*. But that's what they did. And there was a big, roaring fire in one of the rooms of the pub, and the wall on the street outside was hot. I used to stand there, and warm my hands in the winter. It always seemed to be winter – I don't know why.

There was no television, or radio, in those days, and we used to make our own fun. We all used to get round the piano and sing; but there was a queer custom that Sunday was a day when you couldn't enjoy yourself in any way whatsoever. You couldn't sing, unless it was a hymn. If you were whistling, you were reprimanded: 'Do you know what day it is?' There were no toys on a Sunday; it was a miserable blooming day.

My dad was very funny. He was always in trouble. No matter what he did, it went wrong. If he went into a public lavatory, he'd lock himself in and somebody would have to let him out. He was too fond of his booze; that was his biggest fault. In those days you could get nicely drunk on a shilling. He was a very good singer. He used to sing in the pubs on a Saturday night, and mum would go down there to listen. That was the night when they used to come home and quarrel. I used to lay in my bed, shivering, dreading them coming home. One weekend, he went to a cricket match with the choir men. He wasn't to play, but they were a man short, so they decided that he should keep wicket. He had no flannels, and he was wearing his bowler hat. As the ball went past, he stuck the hat out, and the ball went right through it. He came home that night, and he'd bought some sausages, as a gift offering to keep mum sweet. He was as drunk as ever he could be, and he stood in the doorway with these sausages hanging out of his coat pocket, and a little lid sticking up on top of his hat, and he was saying, 'What have I done wrong now, my dear?'

There was a scheme in those days called the half-time system, so you could work in the morning, go to school in the afternoon, and the following week it would be reversed. It didn't matter which you did, you couldn't win – if you worked in the morning, you fell asleep at your school desk in the afternoon, and got a clout from the teacher; if you went to school in the morning, you got a clout in the afternoon from the overlooker. And in those days, every class had at least three or four children who were either knock-kneed, bow-legged, or hump-backed. There was something physically wrong with them.

When I was fourteen, I left school. I went to work in the office, at the dye works. I was nearly bored stiff with the job. I wanted to be apprenticed to something that would give me a trade. I eventually went to a seven years' apprenticeship, at a firm of printers called Woodits. I was there when the war started. Everywhere you went, there were huge posters – 'Your King and Country want you!' There were patriotic slogans, pictures showing German soldiers marching through Belgium with babies on the end of their bayonets. We were young, impressionable, and we hadn't had a war since the Boer War, when we were children, and every apprentice went straight to the recruiting office and joined up. We thought we'd have to be sworn in, individually, but they just lined us up, told us to lift our shirts, drop our trousers, and that was it. Then we all swore obedience to the King, with our hands up. They gave us a shilling, one-and-six ration money, and we were soldiers.

### Corporal Jim Crow
### 110th Brigade, Royal Field Artillery

I was born in Hardwicke, Manchester, on November 5, 1893. My father moved to Manchester from Lincolnshire, because the money was better. He'd started as a drayman on the railway, and then worked as a greengrocer in Salford. On his first day in the shop he only took seven and sixpence, but by the time Mother died in 1906, he was taking more money than that in a minute. By then, there were five people working in the shop: my father, my elder brother, two ladies, and the man who used to deliver stuff with his horse and lorry.

I was delicate when I was born. I had scarlet fever, and the doctor said that if they could send me into the country, it would be an advantage to me, so I moved down to live with my grandparents in Lincolnshire, where my grandfather had a smallholding. They were very good workers, and they taught me how to do things as they should be done. When I do things, they should be *exact* – or else I have to do them over again.

I was at a very small school with thirteen of us in one class. We were all ages, from the children starting school, to the thirteen-year-olds who were leaving. I only remember having one lesson in grammar, and none in algebra. When my mother died, my father got married again. That was disastrous. The second wife drank like a fish, and he came up to Lincolnshire, bringing her with him. We were in the sitting room, having lunch, and my grandfather said to my father, 'Jack! I don't think much of your choice!' They had one child, but my father ran out and left her in the end.

When I left school, I started work for a blacksmith in the village. I would milk four cows at six in the morning, then go in the shop, and then at night time we'd go back in the shop, and, many a time, my grandmother would fetch me home at nine o'clock. The waggoners from the local farms would congregate in the shop, and we used to lay the implements for them. It was a nice warm place for them to meet. When I had flu I was off for a week, and when I went back to the shop I'd barely taken my jacket and waistcoat off, when they had me swinging a ten-pound hammer. My grandfather came in, saw this, played merry hell and he sent me home. That was the end of my blacksmithing. I was very sorry. He was a wonderful blacksmith. He taught me a lot in the eleven months I was with him.

After that I worked on various farms in the village, and in 1910, a cousin of mine, who'd been helping my grandmother in the house, got married – and my grandfather told me to clear out too. I took him at his word and went to the May Fair, and I took a situation at Waterloo Farm with a man called William Busby. I was there for a year, and then I went to a farm in the village at home. My duties were ploughing, looking after the horses, and anything else that was required.

At Christmas 1911, I went with a lad from the next farm to join the armed services, the Lincolns. We never thought anything of war: we were just a bit browned off with farm work, working four o'clock in the morning to seven o'clock at night. It was a bit deadly. We made an agreement that if one of us didn't pass, the other wouldn't stay. We spent the night in Lincoln Barracks, and he didn't pass, so we both came home. I carried on as a labourer and I moved to a farm where my boss was deaf, with a short tongue, and his brother was deaf and dumb, and there was only the three of us on the farm. I don't know how I stuck it. Between Sunday night and Saturday night, I never spoke to a soul.

When war was declared, I was a bit uneasy. I wanted to go but it was harvest time, and I was up to my neck in it. I suppose we were doing more benefit to the country by staying on the farm. Later in the year, the Germans came over in a ship and they shelled Scarborough. We were so incensed that five of us met in a public house, and arranged to go down to Lincoln and join up. The brother of one of the lads working on the farm with me was in the Coldstream Guards, and he'd been wounded. He went with us to Lincoln, and he said, 'Whatever you do, don't go in the infantry! Go in the artillery! You'll be on horses, and not on foot!'

**Private William Chapman**
*3rd Stationary Hospital, Royal Army Medical Corps*
I was born in a mining village called Easington Lane in the county of Durham. We had a one-bedroomed cottage with only one other room. That was the

beginning of it. My parents met in a very singular way. When Mother was about fourteen, my father was seventeen, and at that time he was driving his father's pony trap. And the pony took fright at some paper that was on the road, and it ran over my mother's leg and broke it. That was their introduction. A few years after that they married and set up home.

And they had to take a very small cottage in order to get started. And the first three children were girls, two of whom had to be adopted so that the rest of the family could get in the cottage. One was adopted by Grandmother, and another by a doctor who lived nearby. They simply went out of the home, and visited when they could, of course.

My father became manager of a grocery business. But he died within a year and there was I at seventeen, head of the family. Mother had a small stationery shop but she knew nothing about business. She would sell exercise books and slate prints and that sort of thing, without replenishing, and things went down and we made very little out of that.

So I began to look out for another job and got one not three miles away. And while there, the war started. I had made my mind up to be a Methodist minister and it was confirmed one Sunday evening – I'd been to church, I'd been there all day long. And the minister was a real beautiful man, not very scholarly, but very mystic and a very charming personality. He came from the minister's vestry with his wife who had led the service, and he put his hand on my head and said to his wife, 'You know, William's going to be a minister one day.' That's just what I'd been thinking myself but he confirmed it. That was really my ordination.

I went to theological college when I was twenty-one. I remember news came through that Parliament had said that theological students were not going to be called up. And we were very delighted. But then one day, three of us – we called ourselves a clan – went into Manchester for what we called a 'fuddle'. We went into Lyons café for a good tea, and started back to college on the tram. And about half a dozen new recruits in their khaki got on. They were obviously just in the army, you could tell by their uniform and bearing. We were very frisky and happy. We'd just been out for tea and been joking. And one of these boys turned round and said, 'You fellows ought to join the army – and then you'd have something to joke about.' We didn't answer back. Within a few days we were allowed a half-term break, and most of the boys went home for a long weekend. I went home and joined the army. I couldn't go back to college. Nobody else left the college, and I never gave any notice: I simply joined the army. I was told to report back in two days. And two of us were placed in the charge of a sergeant. We went by train as far as Sheffield and, strangely, also on the train was our village policeman. When I was a boy I was terrified to death of him. Twice he spanked me, once for playing in a haystack and making a mess of it. Another time I managed to dodge him. But he was in the same boat as we were now. He was going to Aldershot to join the military police. And I was as good as he was. He was a private and I was a private.

Anyway, we got out at Sheffield and went to Hillsborough Barracks, a very old barracks indeed, containing hundreds and hundreds of recruits. And we were there about a week, getting fitted up with a uniform and learning how to form fours and how to salute. The next day, a sergeant-major and a sergeant were in command. And their purpose was quite a noble one – to find out what we had been in civil life, so that we'd be fitted in if possible. 'And what were you in Civvy Street?' 'Oh, I was a butcher, sergeant-major.' 'Sergeant, send so-and-so to the quartermaster's stores.' 'And what were you?' 'Well, I was a clerk in an office, sergeant-major.' 'Send him to the orderly room.' And so on.

The sergeant major came to me and he said, 'What were you in Civvy Street?' 'I was a theological student, sergeant-major.' 'What?' 'A theological student.' 'What's that?' he said. 'Well, I was just a theological student,' I said. He called his sergeant over. 'Sergeant, come and ask this fellow what he was.' I was beginning to enjoy it. 'What were you in Civvy Street?' 'I was a theological student, sergeant.' So they walked away and had a little conference. And I had to follow the sergeant to the operating theatre. They didn't know the difference between theological and biological.

This was a Sunday morning, and there was an operation taking place. And the sergeant put me in the scrubbing-up room and I just stood there waiting. Eventually a sergeant came from the operating theatre itself. 'What are you doing here?' so I told him, and he took me into the theatre. It was a strangulated hernia, and when I went in there, there were half the man's innards right out. I stood looking at this new sight, and I began to feel rather strange. The sergeant had his eye on me. He said, 'Get out, get out!' I went out for a breath of fresh air, and ducked my head to get my blood circulating, and went back into the theatre within three minutes. I never turned a hair after that. I've seen hundreds of operations, and the worse an operation was, the better I liked it.

My experience in the theatre was an important phase of my life. I saw all kinds of surgery and met all kinds of people. The surgeon was a Major Ritson from Sunderland. He was a brilliant surgeon but very asthmatic. There was a Sister Brook and a sergeant. The sergeant was a very lovely fellow, but he was too fat to be much use at the operating table. Once, when the Sister became faint, the sergeant had to take over. He couldn't do the retracting. It was an operation on the carotid artery, and there was a great deal of retracting to do. I have a thin arm and a thin hand, and I was put on to that job in place of the sergeant. I was thinner so I could do it and he couldn't. I gained a lot of experience in that theatre, and I realised what surgery was about. And many an amputated arm or a leg I used to cart away and put in an incinerator.

**Private William Holmes**
*12th Battalion, London Regiment*
When I was a little boy of seven, I was taken to St Thomas' Hospital, in a special carriage with rubber wheels – because they thought I was dying. I had peritonitis. My sister carried me in, and they took me up to the top of the building, where they gave me an enema – but not an ordinary enema. It was done with a stirrup pump! You can imagine the state I was in. For two nights, my life was in the balance. I got over it, but I spent the next six weeks on milk alone. I was as close to death as I could have been.

When I was fourteen, my father died. He'd been getting blind for some time, and he died at the age of sixty. In the latter part of his life, he'd worked at the Army & Navy Stores as their chief detective. And then the Army & Navy Stores wrote to my mother, and asked if she had any boys available for work. I was sent straight up for an interview with him, and he said, 'You can start here, on Monday morning, as a cashier.'

I started off in the department with the ladies' big clothes. I might only take three or four bills a day, but I might take a couple of thousand pounds. As I progressed, they sent me on to busier desks, so that after three years I was put in the dress department, at Christmastime, where I was so busy that I couldn't be relieved for half an hour to have my dinner. They'd fetch me twenty-five bills, and we didn't have time to write them down; we had to add them up as we turned them over.

After that, they sent me across the road to the offices, where they put me in charge of what they called 'the passenger train accounts'. In those days, I was living on the Battersea Bridge Road, and I used to walk to the stores in Victoria.

I had no idea that the war was coming. It came as a bombshell to me when it started. No one was prepared. Everywhere, posters were put up telling us to fight for our country. It was a patriotic thing, so about fifteen of us from the Army & Navy Stores went to the Horticultural Hall in Vincent Square, where there was a notice asking for volunteers to relieve the regular troops in Malta. There were about 250 men there, and we all lined up in two ranks. They only wanted twenty, and they picked the tallest. The rest of us were sent home and told to wait for another chance. When I got home, I found out that my young brother had joined up under age. Another brother, John, had signed up for ten years, before the war, and was in the 17th Lancers, in India. My eldest brother was a taxi driver, and he joined up and was sent to the Australian supply column – because he could drive cars. The other brother, Alf, wasn't fit for the army, but he was married. My mother was a widow, and my other brothers said to me, 'Bill, you stop at home and look after Mum as long as you can.' I felt it was my responsibility. I wasn't given a white feather. Right down my road, everybody knew the situation.

### Private Basil Farrer
#### 3rd Battalion, Green Howards

You have heard of Nancy Mitford? One of her characters is referred to as 'the bolter'. That was in my nature. I had run away from home as a small child – as children do. Then, when I was fourteen, I ran away to London. I had my train fare down to London, but not my fare back home to Bradford. I finished up in some doss-house somewhere in London, but the next morning I looked around and noticed I was at York Road station. I thought I had better go back home, but I hadn't my fare so I decided to walk. I started walking – and I did walk as far as Leicester, where I was picked up by a gentleman. He had seen me in the morning, and then again at night, coming back in his trap. He asked me what I was doing. I told him I was walking home and he took me home, and gave me a meal. He said, 'Why don't you stay for a drink?' I said I hadn't got enough money, and I was using what little I had for food. So he took my money, added to it, and put me on the train for Bradford and home. I was always a bolter, and people said I would make a good soldier.

**Sergeant Jim Davies**
*12th Battalion, Royal Fusiliers*

People used to pawn everything in those days, and I was a warehouseman for a pawn shop in Ladbroke Grove. I slept over the top of the warehouse. Everything that had been pawned was kept in the warehouse. I worked twelve hours a day and fifteen hours on Saturday, and half a day off a week. For five shillings a week. We used to take five hundred pledges on Monday alone. You would come in there with a suit, say, and ask for ten shillings. I'd look at it and see it was a bit worn and offer five and we'd agree on six. So then, you'd get a 'low ticket' for which you'd pay a ha'penny and you'd get your six shillings. The interest was a ha'penny on every two shillings per month. So if you redeemed it on Saturday, that would be three ha'pence interest and you'd pay back five shillings and three ha'pence and you'd take your pledge. If it was over a pound, generally jewellery, you paid a penny for a ticket instead of a ha'penny. After a year and seven days, if it hadn't been redeemed, it became the property of the pawnbroker. But it was kept for another month after that and it was still redeemable. After that, the pawnbroker could do what he liked with it.

Then, I moved to a pawnshop on the Fulham Road near South Kensington where I became a ticket writer. Whilst a manager and a 'second' were busy taking in the pledges, I would be busy writing out the tickets. All types of people used to come in. People working in the museums, the school of mines, drunkards, actors, artists and the usual clothes from the poorer people. Whilst I was there, I met an actor and we used to talk about it. He told me that he knew the man who was running a particular show and that I could go in as 'utility' and learn the acting trade. So I gave a fortnight's notice in and I went and became an actor.

I started work in a 'fit-up' company which was almost the lowest form of company. It played anywhere – institutes, halls and the lower-class theatres. The scenery we travelled with was only twelve feet instead of eighteen feet, which was normal theatre size. We used to play 'stock'. That meant that we had a stock of plays that we performed. It wasn't called repertory in those days. We spent all our time rehearsing for the next play. I did props, played parts when necessary. I was the general help. We had about ten members. A juvenile lead, lady juvenile, heavy man, heavy woman, two comedy actors, a manager. People would always play similar roles. These people taught me quite a lot. I used to study them. We performed all the old standard melodramas. We never played anything high class because we had to pay licences to Samuel French. At that time, I was only playing walk-on parts. I was getting £1 a week but I could get full board and lodgings for ten shillings. We dried up in Dorchester when the manager disappeared. He couldn't meet his obligations so we had no money. So we paid a guinea for a hall and we did a concert to raise money. I got three and sixpence for my share – having been out selling tickets all day.

After that, I walked to London and I met a clown called Bonzo and he took me on at five shillings a week. That's how I joined Lord John's Circus. I used to march round the town in the parade and I was an 'Auguste' – a white-faced clown. I did a lot of little routines with the team – I used to be slapped up the backside with the slapstick. Circus life was a bit rough but I managed to get myself another five shillings a week by helping with the seating and loading up.

Then I came back to London and talked myself into a musical comedy because I could do a few tap-dancing steps. I was the second juvenile in *The Dairy Maids* and we played town halls and places like that. I was learning all I could. Then I got a job as an understudy in a play called *The White Man* at the London Palladium. I talked my way up the ranks and after a while, they gave me the part. The chap playing Black Eagle got pissed and I took over. By then I was living in Chelsea and earning £3 a week. There were eight or nine of us in the dressing room. The social life for a two-bit actor like myself was non-existent.

On the day war was declared, I hurriedly took off my make-up, left the theatre and I rushed down to Big Ben. As Big Ben struck eleven, everybody cheered because we were at war. We all sang 'Rule Britannia' and somebody suggested we go to Buckingham Palace so we all marched up Whitehall and down the Mall. It was late now, getting on for midnight, and we stood outside Buckingham Palace shouting for the king. I met a couple of medical students and we climbed up the gates and we stood there saying we were going to join the army the next day. We were full of enthusiasm. The king and queen came out and we cheered and sang. I was young and stupid, full of patriotism and the *Boy's Own Paper*. That's what my childhood was based on. I couldn't get into the army quick enough.

## Corporal Tommy Keele
### 11th Battalion, Middlesex Regiment

I found myself a job in the theatre, in a show at Drury Lane, called *The Whip*. Everyone knew that the Drury Lane Theatre was putting on these big racing shows using mechanical horses. Ex-jockeys used to ride the mechanical horses on revolving tracks and I thought that I'd like to do that.

*The Whip* was the story of a famous horse that was sabotaged as it was travelling across the country. In the play there was a most frightening train crash that could only have been done at Drury Lane. The stage was equipped for that sort of business. It had hydraulic lifts so that part of the stage could go up and part could go down and it could also revolve. The race scene was wonderful. They set up six tracks on stage. Each horse had its own individual track that was eight foot long and two foot six wide. There were three hundred-odd wheels inside each horse and they were all harnessed on to the track by little wire traces and a steel bar on the offside. It was often a job to get the horses started.

One day, something went wrong with the horse at the back and the stable lads couldn't get it going. The curtain stayed down while they struggled with it and I was on the horse at the front so I turned round in the saddle to watch them. I was an agile little geezer. Suddenly, they got the horse going and the curtain went up and the audience saw me riding my horse backwards. They must have been a bit confused.

I was always in trouble at Drury Lane. *The Hope* was a similar sort of racing show to *The Whip*. The big thing in this play was an earthquake. It was terrifying. All these houses tumbled down and people were shouting for help from windows and falling to the ground. They were acrobats, of course. It was a ghastly sight. The race scene was at the end but there again, silly little Tommy Keele got into trouble. I was supposed to come second in the race but something went wrong on the first night. All of us jockeys had been issued with riding whips over a foot long. On the first night, my whip got caught and it bent and flew out of my hand.

But after the play, there was a big knot of people around my track and I elbowed my way through. The producer was standing there looking black as thunder, with my riding whip in his hand. I wasn't listening to what he was saying and eventually, I said, 'Excuse me, sir, may I have my whip back, please?' He looked at me. '*Your* whip?' 'Yes, sir.' '*Your* whip?' 'Well,' I said, 'if it comes to that, it's *your* whip, isn't it?' He stared at me. 'You little bugger!' he said. 'I'll kick your arse out this theatre!' What had happened was my whip had flown up in the air, came down through an inch-wide slot and landed across the track of the horse that was supposed to win the race. It acted as a chock and stopped the 'winning' horse from moving forward. So by accident my horse won the race. It changed the whole play, and I didn't even know it had happened.

I used to get twenty-five shillings a week, which was quite good for those days. I was living at home in King's Cross. If we were touring, which a lot of the shows did, we could get into professional digs, which meant bed and full board for twelve shillings a week. If you paid thirteen shillings, you expected them to do a little bit of washing as well. So twenty-five shillings a week was quite good.

When we declared war on Germany, I was told 'Your country needs you!' I didn't even know what a soldier was. My idea of the army was from pictures of glamorous soldiers in tight-fitting uniforms with gold braid across the chests and a lovely hat with a feather in the top. I wandered down to Whitehall where all the recruiting activity was. I hadn't been there five minutes before I was grabbed by a recruiting sergeant. 'Hello, sonny,' he said, 'you going to join the army?' 'I've come down to have a look at it. I might join,' I said. 'What do you want to join?' he asked. 'Light Infantry,' I said. So he told me to follow him, and I was about to sign when I said, 'This is a horse regiment, isn't it?' 'Oh no,' he said, 'this is a marching regiment!' So I left him. I wouldn't sign the paper.

But I was grabbed very quickly by another recruiting sergeant. I told him that I'd been a jockey and a trick rider and a show jumper and I wanted to join a horse regiment. 'Horses!' he said. 'The Middlesex Regiment has lovely horses!' So I joined them and for my first year in the army, I never saw a horse. It was a foot regiment.

**Sergeant Frederick Goodman**
*1st London Field Ambulance, Royal Army Medical Corps*
I went to Latymer Upper School in Ravenscourt Park, and after that I worked at Chiswick Council until war came along. I had no idea what war would be like, except the odd bit that I'd learned about at school. I'd heard a bit about Winston Churchill during the Boer War, and I knew about the relief of

Mafeking, but I'd never been in the Officer Training Corps. But we were all very patriotic. We thought we would do something about this fellow, this Kaiser. We weren't going to stand any nonsense! Of course not! We weren't going to have it! Why should we? And if I'd heard of someone who didn't want to fight, I shouldn't want to know him!

We expected the war to last until Christmas, and we had a special council meeting on October 4, at which each member of staff who'd expressed a wish to join the forces was interviewed by the full council. We were told that our jobs would be kept open, and we would be paid £5 per month for the duration.

I joined the 1st London Field Ambulance, Royal Army Medical Corps, in October. My father and mother thought this was a very good thing. Training was essential for the particular work we would have to do in France. We had time before we went over, and we were sent to the Royal College of Surgeons, where we were lectured by very eminent people in the medical profession. We saw many parts of the body pickled in jars, which had to be seen, even if I didn't relish them.

Our training camp was at Crowborough. We had a number of fellows detailed off to be 'patients'. They had a number of things 'wrong' with them, written on paper pinned to their tunics, and we were expected to bandage them up and give them first aid. Then the treatment we had given these chaps was examined by the doctors. If we had made a mistake, they would put us right straight away.

And we had basic drill. Forming fours. Our sergeant major was a splendid fellow, in every possible way. I'd been used to a certain amount of discipline for my early days, and I saw what had to be done. I didn't altogether like early morning square-bashing – a bit early for that sort of thing – bit I didn't adjust at all badly. We had a little fellow who would take us for physical jerks at half past six, and then he would run us for ten miles before breakfast.

One day, a fellow joined us. He was a clergyman, and he had decided to join the army. Fine. So he arrived at the local hotel with three or four great parcels of luggage, and we were tickled pink. Anybody would have thought he was going on a cruise. But he turned out to be a good chap eventually.

Our headquarters were at the Ipswich workhouse. We didn't like the workhouse master. We didn't approve of the way he treated the inmates. Their accommodation was grim – even for those days. And the food was not good. It was an awful life for these people. They were divided up with men on one side, women on the other, and they all had to wear an awful uniform. We didn't like this, and we got hold of the workhouse master, and he found himself in the workhouse pond. Bit unfortunate, wasn't it?

The nurses in Ipswich were a very fine lot. We had dances to keep us going. We had to have something to keep us going, didn't we? We had one lady – her father and mother kept the Cross Keys pub in Henley – and I got to know her. She used to invite me to lunch at the pub on Sundays. *One certain officer* tried to pinch her from me. He wanted to dance with her. She said she was very sorry, but it couldn't be – she had arranged it with Freddie Goodman. Pleased me no end. And when I was in France, she kept me going with letters. She knew how to write the right sort of letter to keep my morale going. It meant an awful lot to me.

## Lieutenant Duce
### 1st Battalion, Royal West Kent Regiment

I was in India with one of the merchant banks before the war, and during my five years there, I had joined the equivalent of the Territorial force. We were fully trained, to the extent that we were better armed with the Lee-Enfield rifles than the British Army in England.

When the war started, after a little while a notice came in the clubs from the Inns of Court Officers Training Court, asking if we would come home and join, and be commissioned into the British Army. I asked the bank if I could go, and they told me that there were other people, senior to me, who should have choice before me. I pointed out that these people weren't going. They said that I couldn't go, but I was going to go, anyway.

I didn't expect to come out of the war alive. I had been living on the north-west frontier, up near the Khyber Pass, and I had a lot of nice books and various other things, and I gave them all away. I had the idea, as did a lot of my friends, that I shouldn't come through it, but I was of a very religious turn of mind, so it didn't bother me.

I went down to Karachi, and I shipped on board a Japanese boat as a purser. There were forty-nine Chinese crew, six Japanese officers and an English captain. I paid the captain six shillings a day for my food, and I got one shilling pay when I got to England. The bank sent my resignation after me. Just after I arrived in England, I was stopped, and asked, 'What about joining up, young man?' I said, 'I've just come six thousand miles! Give me a chance!'

In the end, I didn't join the Inns of Court: I joined the Artists Rifles. I was fully trained, so myself and three others, one from India and two from South Africa, were put on as orderlies in the sergeants' mess. We waited so well on the sergeants that they were delighted. But we wouldn't take that on permanently. Next, I was made an officer's servant. Considering that I'd come from India where I'd had eleven servants myself, it was rather amusing. In due course, I was commissioned into the Royal West Kent Regiment.

### Private Thomas McIndoe
#### 12th Battalion, Middlesex Regiment

I used to see that picture of Kitchener – from any position that you took up the finger was always pointing to you. It was a wonderful poster really. And I think it assisted recruitment very much. I went to the recruiting office at Harlesden. And when I confronted the recruiting officer he said that I was too young, although I'd said that I was eighteen years of age. He said, 'Well, I think you're too young, son. Come back in another year or so.' He didn't believe what I said.

I returned home. I never said anything to my parents. And I picked up my bowler hat which my mother had bought me, and which I was only meant to wear on Sundays. And I donned that, thinking that it would make me look older. And I presented myself to the recruiting officer again – to which, this time, there was no queries. I was accepted. My mother was very hurt when I arrived home, that particular night, and told her that I had to report to Mill Hill next morning.

### Private Frank Lindlay
#### 14th Battalion, York and Lancaster Regiment

I have a watch that was presented to my brother by my father and mother. It says on it, 'Harry Lindlay, 19th Year, 1910. From Father and Mother, with love.' My brother Harry, nine years older than me, was an able seaman. He went out to the Mediterranean with the fleet for several years. When he came back home on leave he'd got the watch twisted, so we put it in a shop to be repaired. He'd only been home a few days when the war started. He went back to his depot and he was put on a cruiser, and dispatched to the North Sea. His cruiser was torpedoed, and he went down with it in October 1914. I got this watch, and it's been with me ever since. It cut us up, I'll tell you that. It broke our family up, and I was so incensed that I thought I'd do something about it. I shot off, gave a false name, and I joined the artillery at the age of fourteen, but that wasn't a fast enough job for me; I wanted to get somewhere, so I deserted and joined the infantry. I joined the 2nd Barnsley Pals Battalion.

**Private Donald Cameron**
*12th Battalion, York and Lancaster Regiment*
Our Pals battalion was formed as a result of an appeal from the Mayor of Sheffield, Lieutenant Colonel Branson. Colonel Hughes was our first commanding officer, and by God, what a splendid lot of men he had to command. University students, doctors, dentists, opticians, solicitors, accountants, bank officials, works directors, schoolmasters, shop owners, town hall staff, post office staff – you name it. Professional men, not professional soldiers, but when they got in the trenches, they behaved like professional soldiers.

**Private A. A. Bell**
*17th Battalion, Manchester Regiment*
I felt it was my duty to join up. We hadn't been the ones that started the war. Before I joined up, I undertook one or two long walks, of six miles each way, thinking that as 'an army marches on its stomach', we would be required to do a lot of marching. Then, on September 1, 1914, a pal from my office and myself went down to the town hall, where we were told that they'd filled their requirements, but they were forming another battalion, and if we liked to go down the following day, we might be enrolled. So we duly went down, and we found that there were quite large numbers from the big firms in the town, like CPA and Tootals. But we were the only two representatives of our firm, and there were a lot of other little firms like us. The big firms were taken first, and they were stood in ranks and formed into companies. 'A', 'B', 'C' Companies were formed from the big firms, and then the riff-raff – as you might say – were put into 'D' Company. But a strange thing happened. We were all given the order, 'About turn!' So what would have been 'D' Company became 'A' Company; the riff-raff – like us – became 'A' Company.

**Corporal Harry Fellows**
*12th Battalion, Northumberland Fusiliers*
Three of us made up our minds to join up at the end of August 1914. We went

Young men enlisting with the Leeds Pals in 1914.

to the Drill Hall to join up, and there were seven hundred people outside. They were only letting in twelve men at a time. The three of us wanted to join the cavalry, even though we'd never been near a horse in our lives, but they told us there was no vacancies in the cavalry. So we asked what vacancies they had in the infantry, and they said they'd got the Notts and Derbys, at Normington Barracks, Derby. We could have bloody well walked there, and we wanted a long ride in a train. None of us had ever had a holiday in our lives. We wanted an adventure, and they offered us either the Duke of Cornwall's Light Infantry, or the Northumberland Fusiliers in Newcastle. We knew that Newcastle had a good football team, so we decided to join the Fusiliers.

When we got on to the barracks square at Newcastle, there were at least two thousand men standing around, tossing pennies and all that. We asked which way to go, and we were pointed towards a window at the far corner of the square. We went there, handed our papers in, they gave us a blanket – and that was that. We were on our own. All we knew in Newcastle was the railway station, and we went back down there. On the way, we clubbed together some pennies, and we bought half a pound of cheese and a loaf. In the booking hall of the station, there were sixty men walking about, just like us, with blankets over their shoulders. We thought we'd sleep that night in the booking hall, but a porter came to one of us and said that there were some empty carriages in the siding, and we could sleep there if we liked. So that was how I spent my first night in the army. Sleeping in a railway carriage.

After that, they sent us down to Aylesbury for a fortnight, until they found out that we should have been in Tring. So we were sent there, and we were trained on the Dunstable Downs, round Coombe Hill. We were trained in open warfare, wearing civilian clothes. The first thing that I was given was a change of underwear – long johns and a thick vest. They drove me mad, because I'd never worn underwear before in my life.

**Private Ralph Miller**
*1/8th Battalion, Royal Warwickshire Regiment*
I joined up at Witton barracks in February 1915, at the back of the Aston Villa ground. At school, there was a clique of us lads who formed a football team, and when we'd finished schooling we kept the same little clique. Teddy Deacon and Roger Walker, other members of the team, joined up that day as

well. We went in, and there was a medical officer. We took our trousers down, coughed. They tested our chests, and asked our trade of calling.

### Corporal Wally Evans
### 8th Battalion, King's Own Yorkshire Light Infantry

On September 7, 1914, I walked round to New Scotland Yard, to enlist in His Majesty's Forces. They offered me the artillery, the lancers, but when I found that these played around with horses, I said, 'No thanks!' and I enlisted in the King's Own Yorkshire Light Infantry. On September 9, with two hundred others, I entrained at a London railway terminus, *en route* to Pontefract, to join the regimental depot. We detrained at Wakefield and were told there was an hour to spare, so we walked up the cobbled streets and found a fish shop, where we had a meal.

But it was a strange new world for me; there were reflections in the sky from the blast furnaces of the factories, and there were lights from the mines. There was an autumn mist, that was more like a shower of rain, dampening my clothes and making me cold. We went on to Pontefract, where we arrived at around 11.30pm, and there we found absolute chaos. Nobody had been advised that we were coming, and there were no arrangements made for our reception. Many walked the streets at night, and some went home in disgust. But more and more volunteers kept arriving, and the streets of Pontefract echoed with their footsteps, and we all added to the chaos. After two weeks, they formed the 8th Battalion, King's Own Yorkshire Light Infantry. Its composition was rather unique: two companies of Yorkshiremen, one of Welshmen and one of Londoners. At last, we felt that some order had been made out of chaos, and soon we would be on our way to France.

### Private Basil Farrer
### 3rd Battalion, Green Howards

I wouldn't say we (as regular soldiers) ridiculed the Territorials, but we did refer to them as 'Saturday night soldiers'. We thought they were amateurs. They were a selective crew, and they were enthusiastic, but we as professionals thought ourselves superior. Naturally. We were serving soldiers, and when we went out to France, we were doing the job we were trained to do. Some of the men had done the South African War, and knew what war was about. We were going out to fight – I didn't care if it was the French or the Germans.

Lions led by monkeys; an Australian mascot on the Somme.

We had been instilled in our regimental history, and the glory of it, and you didn't know the carnage until you met it. So at the beginning we were really enthusiastic. We thought ourselves very superior too. The British soldier *did* think himself superior to any continental soldier.

We were issued with a leaflet that Kitchener had printed. It was Kitchener's advice, to remember we were British soldiers, and how to act, and that we were ambassadors representing our country. At the time I took no notice. I was too young to bother. I just read it and that was all. In parts, it read like a parson's advice to a party going off on a weekend binge to Paris. It referred to the temptations of wine and women. The ordinary soldier didn't expect to find wine and women. Kitchener might have been used to that kind of thing in Egypt, but we were not going to Egypt. We were going out to fight. There was not much hope of women and wine – or temptations, in any event. Kitchener could have been more inspiring to the troops going out.

# Into the Trenches

*I saw a mangled body blown to bits on a sack. I was scared stiff.*

The majority of the men who went out to France had never been abroad before. These men were to become used to a strange world of traverses, funk holes and parapets. Trenches had long been used by the British Army in wartime, but the static nature of the Great War was turning these from temporary earthworks into elaborate, semi-permanent constructions.

**Corporal Hawtin Mundy**
*1st Battalion, Oxfordshire and Buckinghamshire Light Infantry*
We left Burnham-on-Sea and went to Southampton. It was two days before we went from Southampton to France, and we were allowed out from Southampton into the town, and it was my birthday. I went and got myself a bottle of whisky to celebrate. We travelled to France on an old cattle boat, and we had to wait on board while they loaded it up with horses. Eventually, as it got dusk, we left Southampton. Naturally, we were all supposed to be down below, but I had my bottle of whisky, and I didn't want to take it down below. So I crawled along the deck towards the centre and I crawled under a sheet of tarpaulin, all by myself. I lay quiet, and the boat started to 'chook, chook, chook . . .' I had a tot or two, started enjoying myself, and I fell asleep. When I woke up, the engines had all stopped, and I thought we'd arrived. I shook the tarpaulin back – it was covered with snow. One of the deck hands saw me. 'What are you doing here?' he said. 'Have we got there?' I said. 'No!' he said. 'We're back where we started. We got out of the Solent, some U-boats

spotted us, and we turned round and came back. But we're going again in a few minutes and they're going to send an escort with us.' I asked him if he'd like a drink, and he had a good old swig out of the bottle. 'I'm frozen with cold,' I said. 'Come with me!' he said, and he took me down along the side of the boat, opened a door and led me into a small kitchen with a stove in the corner. 'You'll be lovely and warm in here,' he said, and I sat on top of the stove, and I went fast asleep again, and next thing I knew, he was shouting at me, 'Come on then! We're at Le Havre!'

**Private Reg Coldridge**
*2nd Battalion, Devonshire Regiment*
The first shock I had: when we went from Southampton to Le Havre and then up the river to Rouen, we saw a convoy of wounded coming in. Thousands of them. It was my first sight of war – and it took away the glamour of what we were doing.

**Private Reginald Glenn**
*12th Battalion, York and Lancaster Regiment*
We could see a lot of German prisoners working on the quay at Marseilles as we arrived. They were singing, and grinning, as happy as can be. You could see what they were saying: these poor beggars are going up to the firing line, *but we've finished*. We're prisoners until the end of the war.

**Private Ralph Miller**
*1/8th Battalion, Royal Warwickshire Regiment*
When I got to France, there was four inches of snow on the ground, and we marched from Le Havre to Harfleur. It was a nasty bloody march with full pack. A slog all the way. The little French kids shouted '*Chocolat!*' at us.

**Private William Holbrook**
*4th Battalion, Royal Fusiliers*
As we were marching to the Somme front, we passed a paper boy. He had bundles of French newspapers under his arm, and he was shouting, '*Le Journal!* Germany buggered up!'

Smiling German prisoners.

**Bombardier Harold Lewis**
*240th Brigade, Royal Field Artillery*
We rode forward into the lines. The drill for a mounted officer was that if he turned his head, you came up on one side and took his rein. I saw the captain's head move, and I moved up, but he said, 'I didn't mean that. Listen!' And we heard the first rumble of guns. We were in the war.

**Private Albert Day**
*4th Battalion, Gloucestershire Regiment*
When I first got up to the front line, I was frightened out of my life. I saw a mangled body blown to bits on a sack. I was scared stiff.

**Major Alfred Irwin**
*8th Battalion, East Surrey Regiment*
I was second in command of the battalion, and the commanding officer wanted to have some responsible person in charge of his advance party to come over and make arrangements. So I had been sent a few days before the battalion, to Dernancourt, where I had been able to get a *particularly* comfortable billet for the commanding officer, who appreciated it.

**Private Harold Hayward**
*12th Battalion, Gloucestershire Regiment*
As we were going up to the front line, we got to one corner of the communication trench, and everybody was held up. We waited for half an hour, and got fed up. I said, 'Give me a rifle – I will get around!' So I charged around – and my gumboots got stuck in the bottom of the mud and I just couldn't move them. I cut the straps on my braces and stepped out into my stockinged feet. The trench was six feet deep, of which two foot six was mud. There was no way out except to get out in your bare feet and leave your boots behind.

**Private Frank Lindlay**
*14th Battalion, York and Lancaster Regiment*
As we walked into the front line, one of the Germans shouted over, 'When are those Yorkshire bastards coming?'

## Major Alfred Irwin
### 8th Battalion, East Surrey Regiment

Officers and NCOs from new battalions coming out were always given a run around the line by people who'd been there long enough to be able to teach them. We had the same experience, and I think we were all equally frightened. The first time I heard a machine gun, I fell flat on my face in the trench, as did everybody round me. That was a normal experience.

## Major Murray Hill
### 5th Battalion, Royal Fusiliers

A young company commander, only twenty-one, was taking over a trench from another commander, aged over forty. 'It's been awfully awkward,' said the older man, 'there've been two men buried here, and they've been groaning. But it's all right now. They've stopped.' When the younger man heard this, he got to work with his men, and they got the bodies out in ten minutes. Those men could have been saved. I told that story at divisional headquarters, and everybody roared with laughter.

## Captain Philip Neame VC
### Headquarters, 168th Infantry Brigade

Trench design before the war would have been, generally speaking, considerably shallower than what we had to develop during the war. If ordered to dig in, before the war, you might make a trench three foot deep with a parapet outside eighteen inches high. Well, that wasn't good enough in the face of shelling, and what developed during the war were trenches over six foot deep with a fire-step to stand on, so as to be able to shoot over the parapet, and very deep, narrow communication trenches which would give you cover from shellfire and from air observation, and zigzagging trenches, so that you don't get enfiladed by fire. These were developments which hadn't been foreseen to any great extent before the war.

## Sergeant Charles Quinnell
### 9th Battalion, Royal Fusiliers

It was a good thing we had a guide when we arrived at the front, because the trenches to the uninitiated were a maze, but the guide knew the way. Before you entered, you got the order 'Load'. You put nine in your magazine, one up the spout, and put your safety catch on, prepared to use your rifle immediately without having to load. Then the guide took us into the communication trenches, which passed through the support line, the reserve line, and into the front line. These communication trenches were straight for a hundred yards, and then there would be a traverse of maybe five yards. That would be to break up the shellfire; if a shell fell in one stretch of trench, the traverse would stop it spreading right along the trench. And the same applied to the front line when we got there. The front line consisted of bays about ten yards in length, and then there would be a traverse and then another bay, and so on, right the way along on either side.

Each bay would hold three men. At night-time those three men would be close together, one standing up looking over the top – he was sentry. He had a box periscope, which was about two feet in height with a mirror at the bottom set at an angle of forty-five, and a mirror at the top facing outwards, so that one reflected on the other and he'd simply hold that up. The next man would be sitting next to him, close up to his leg, so that if anything was suspicious out in front, the sentry could just kick him, and they would both get up together and have another look. And the third man was allowed to lie out on the fire-step and sleep.

Life in the trenches was absolutely new to us, and the first impression that we got – at least I got – was they were very much lived in. You would see an overcoat hanging from a wooden peg on the side of the trench; you'd see a mess tin with some tea in it; a dugout which had an overcoat or a piece of blanket in it; a bed made of sandbags; and it looked very much lived in.

**Major Alfred Irwin**
*8th Battalion, East Surrey Regiment*
We took over from the French, who were a bit casual about their trenches, but they'd been there long enough to leave some fairly good ones. It was rolling chalk country, easy enough to dig, but very difficult to keep clean in wet weather, because chalk develops into a sticky mud that sticks everything together.

**Private Reginald Glenn**
*12th Battalion, York and Lancaster Regiment*
We had good, solid trenches, but the chalk that we threw up when we dug in showed the Germans where we were, because it was white. We had duckboard

to walk on, but if it was raining, the duckboards were under water, so we were walking in wet, and sleeping in wet. The trenches were tall enough for a six-footer to stand up in, and they were three feet wide so you couldn't pass one another without scraping. There was a trench bottom, then a firing step on which sentries would stand, looking out with a periscope. There was a lot of barbed wire in front. Wiring parties would put it out at night. But it was made in sections, so that a section could be moved to the side for our troops to go through when we were making an attack.

## Sergeant Charles Quinnell
### 9th Battalion, Royal Fusiliers

Our dugouts were simply holes in the side of the trench, about three feet in height from the floor, and about three or four feet in depth – and they were very primitive affairs. The Germans had dugouts that were thirty feet deep and you could shell them till the cows came home – and they would laugh at it.

## Rifleman Robert Renwick
### 16th Battalion, King's Royal Rifle Corps

When we went to sleep, we used to dig in, at the back of the trench. We called these 'funk holes', and they weren't very deep. Just person-sized. We would lie on a groundsheet.

## Lieutenant James Pratt
### 1/4th Battalion, Gordon Highlanders

In trench warfare, it was important to have trench experience to survive. A young lad would come out, and, on his first day, he might find everything peaceful and quiet; not a shot being fired or anything. He'd start looking around, over the top of the trench and he'd think, 'This is all safe.' And the next thing, he'd have a bullet through his head. You had to keep under cover all the time – the Hun was always watching. For example, once I went round behind our support line, and found some fellows busy building a dugout and a fellow was on top of the dugout, putting down sandbags. I said, 'What the hell are you doing up there?' 'Making a machine-gun dugout,' he said. 'But you're in view of the German trenches!' I said. 'Yes,' he said, 'but nothing's happening.' I looked over the dugout and I could see three lines of German trenches half a mile away. I said, 'Well, by God, the Germans are doing nothing at the moment but they've spotted you and you'll be for it later on! You'll have an artillery bombardment!' 'Anyhow,' he said, 'I'm going to finish the job.' So I left him. That evening they copped it. The first shell fell short and he remembered my warning and started to run. The next shell landed slap bang on top of the dugout.

**Lieutenant William Taylor**
*13th Battalion, Royal Fusiliers*
The general instruction, when you went into the line, was to keep your head down the whole time. In other words, if you wanted to see what was going on, on the other side, you got on to the fire-step, looked over the top and withdrew hastily. If you stood there, you would attract fire. We were under shellfire every day. There was always odd artillery burst from both sides. Occasionally just one single shot – one howitzer with shrapnel, other times four- or five-minute bombardments. They could take place at any time of the day. We weren't very frightened, because it seemed to be very inaccurate. Dropping well beyond or well in front of our trench. Occasionally, there was a shrapnel burst above us.

**Sergeant Charles Quinnell**
*9th Battalion, Royal Fusiliers*
One of the very, very important things that you learned was you could tell by the sound whether a shell was going over you or whether it was meant for you. If that shell was coming for you, you'd flop down and, believe you me, a man lying down on the ground wants a lot of hitting, because a shell when it lands penetrates the soil, and the explosion goes like that, so if you're lying down it's got to be very, very adjacent to you before it hits you.

When a trench mortar came over, you heard a plop. Everybody's head would be up – and you could see it coming towards you. It was one of the sentry's jobs that if a trench mortar was active, he'd have a whistle and he would blow his whistle as soon as he heard the plop. In the daytime, we had very, very few casualties from trench mortars – but at night-time you couldn't judge where they were coming, and you just prayed.

**Private William Hay**
*1/9th Battalion, The Royal Scots*

My pal Alec went down to HQ, and halfway down the communication trench, one of these blasted *minenwerfers* [heavy trench mortars] dropped where he was. One or two of us ran down to see if he was all right. When we got there he was lying at the side of the trench; another chap was blown to bits, his kilt was hanging in the trees for weeks afterwards. Alec was very badly mutilated, and we had a bit of a pact between us that if I was wounded, he would tell my mother, and if he was wounded, I would tell his mother, a kind of a schoolboy pact.

So anyway he died. I will always remember when he was dying, he said to me, 'You will tell my mother – won't you?' And I said, 'I will.' I was devastated. I had lost my pal. I didn't care what happened to me then, whether I lived or died. If you lose somebody that is very close to you, you've lost something of yourself. It's not possible to describe what has happened to you. You're really not in your right senses.

Anyway I went home on leave to see his mother. She wasn't married and I told her about how Alec died, and she said, 'You're not telling me the truth!' I told her he was shot through the heart you see. I couldn't tell her he was . . . I said, 'I am telling you the truth!' I said I was with him when he died. So she accepted that, and she gave me a great big bag of cakes. She worked in a baker's shop. And she said, 'God bless you, son!' I thought it would be my luck next time round.

**Private Frank Lindlay**
*14th Battalion, York and Lancaster Regiment*

As a signaller, I had a phone in my little dugout in the front line. A *minenwerfer* dropped on the top and scattered everything. It threw me and the telephone about, and it damaged the tapping key. It also busted the wire, and I climbed on top of the parados [the bank of earth above the rear wall of the trench] to repair it. When I got up on to the parados, I was walking on a load of dead 'Froggies' – all decomposed. They'd just been covered with a bit of soil, and the shell had uncovered them. They were just like jam. My puttees were sodden. And I got in awful trouble over the whole thing – 'What do you have to say for yourself? Shut up!' You couldn't explain.

**Corporal Harry Fellows**
*12th Battalion, Northumberland Fusiliers*

We were going into the line, and I was the corporal in charge of the two Lewis guns in the company, and I had four men on each gun, when I ought to have had six. I went to the company sergeant major, to ask him if I could have four more men. He said that I could have two. Anyway, we got into the front line, and one of the new lads found out that his mate was in the next fire bay, so he asked me if he could go and see him. I said yes, and as he went down the traverse, two shells fell on to the trench, one on the front and one on the back, and he was buried. All we could see of him were his legs kicking. I got hold of one leg, my mate got hold of the other, and we pulled as hard as we could, but we couldn't move him. We started scrabbling away with our hands, but by now, he'd stopped kicking. When we eventually got him out, he was dead. The strap of his steel helmet was under his chin, when it should have been on the chin. The helmet had trapped in the earth, and in pulling his legs we'd pulled his neck out. The lad who'd pulled the other leg said, 'My God, we've strangled him. We've murdered him.' We never even knew that lad's name.

**Private Basil Farrer**
*3rd Battalion, Green Howards*

In one trench, there was an arm protruding, which we used to shake every time we went by, going, 'Cheerio chum.' I have been in trenches where you thought, 'Hello, there's a body here.' The ground would be soft and smelly, and there would be a nasty sweet smell. You became acclimatised to it.

**Private Thomas McIndoe**
*12th Battalion, Middlesex Regiment*

One particular morning, I was in the corner of a traverse, and I thought, 'Hello! I just heard a high-calibre shell being discharged!' There had been one or two over beforehand, and this one was coming a bit close. And I thought, 'Good heavens, yes it is, it's on its way!' Instinctively I got down under the parapet. Sometimes you wish the earth would shrink, so as to let you get in, you know. The shell landed – but no bang. And it covered me with dirt. I wouldn't be here if it had gone off. It was a calibre 4.7 shell which is round about the size of a jug.

In my excitement, I scooped it up in my hands, and brought it down to the

An unexploded German shell. Not to be moved …

fire-step. It was still warm, see, and I thought, 'Oh yes, it's a cracker. I'm glad you didn't go off, old man!' Some ten minutes afterwards my platoon officer came round. He was a nice chap and he said, 'What have you got there, mate?' I said, 'Well, I'll tell you what I've got here, sir. It's one that dropped right on the parapet where I was standing.' He said, 'Yes?' I said, 'It buried itself in that sandbag there.'

So the officer got on the phone to an artillery officer from a battery, who came up later that morning. I explained it to him. And he said, 'And when did you take it from the sandbag?' I said, 'Oh, when it landed.' And he called me a bloody fool. And he said, 'The mere fact of you touching it and disturbing it, it could have gone up. You're lucky! You're very lucky!' I said, 'I know. I realise I'm lucky. It should have gone up when it landed.' So he said, 'I want you to put it back exactly where it was.' So I did. And before I had done it, he said, 'If I had seen that *when* it landed, we could have located that battery within twenty yards.' So I expressed my regret and promised to be more careful in the future.

**Corporal Harry Fellows**
*12th Battalion, Northumberland Fusiliers*
Artillery fire was spasmodic – but machine-gun fire was deadly. With a machine gun, men could be mown down, like mowing a field of standing corn.

**Sergeant Ernest Bryan**
*17th Battalion, King's Liverpool Regiment*
The Vickers machine gun was water cooled, and the water was contained in a jacket. Providing you had been continuously firing, you could take the tube away that led from the jacket and you had enough boiling water to make a cup of tea. Or a pot.

**Private Tom Bracey**
*9th Battalion, Royal Fusiliers*
They couldn't get anyone to go on the machine gun. People thought the machine-gunners only lived a month. We were respected by the rest of the company, though.

**Sergeant Ernest Bryan**
*17th Battalion, King's Liverpool Regiment*
The Lewis gun was an air-cooled machine gun. This had advantages and disadvantages. The advantage was that you could cover ground that couldn't be covered by the Vickers machine gun. You could sling it on your arm, and drop it down in another portion of the trench, just like a rifle. And it had terrific firepower – it could fire at between seven and eight hundred rounds a minute. Of course, that doesn't mean you could get that off – because there were only forty-eight rounds in a magazine, and unless you had a tremendous target, you wouldn't fire a full magazine.

**Corporal Harry Fellows**
*12th Battalion, Northumberland Fusiliers*
There were only forty-eight rounds in each Lewis gun magazine. It was a very delicate gun. You only had to have the slightest bit of dirt in it, and you had a stoppage. In our training, we were shown a drill to run through, 'Number One Stoppage, Number Two Stoppage, Number Three Stoppage' and so on. I went on a course with about forty other NCOs, and the instructors were members of the Honourable Artillery Company. They were going through this drill, when suddenly an NCO jumped up, and he said, 'I want to ask my friends a question. When the Germans are coming at you, and your gun has seized up, have you ever gone through this drill?' Not one NCO said they had. The gun had a little wooden handle, called a cocking handle, and when the gun stopped, you put this handle in, and you pulled it back to reload the gun. You fired again, and if it didn't fire this time, you dumped the bloody gun. That was all there was to it. When the Germans were attacking you, and you were looking into their eyeballs, how could you start doing a drill? It was the last thing you were thinking of.

**Private Ralph Miller**
*1/8th Battalion, Royal Warwickshire Regiment*
The finest hand grenade of the war was the Mills bomb. It had a pin to pull out, and then you held the lever down, and when you loosed it, it flew up, shook the detonator, and the bomb exploded about three or four seconds after you threw it.

A Lewis gun in action in a front-line trench.

British machine-gunners wearing gas helmets.

### Second Lieutenant Tom Adlam VC
*7th Battalion, Bedfordshire Regiment*

Certain people were frightened of Mills bombs. I was teaching one fellow, and he was absolutely shaking. I knew he was a good chap. But he was so afraid, you see. 'Take the pin out of the bomb,' I said, which he did, 'and while you've got it in your hand, don't let the spring go off and you're all right.' Then I said, 'Now, now, hold yourself. Nothing can happen while you've got hold of it like that. Now, just put your arm back and throw it over there.' But he hung onto it until the last minute, and he brought his arm down and let go. And it lodged in the parapet he was supposed to be throwing it over. I shouted, 'Run, you silly . . . !' We both ran back and got behind the traverse. And it blew the parapet down. He was a grand chap really – just frightened of bombs.

### Private Basil Farrer
*3rd Battalion, Green Howards*

I was in a bay, once, and a Royal Engineer came along the trench, and he had got one of these bombs in his hand. He was playing with it – and he was drunk. I shouted to him, 'Hey! Be careful, chum!' He went around the next traverse, and 'BANG!' I looked around, and it stank of rum. He was dead, in absolute pieces.

### Sergeant Ernest Bryan
*17th Battalion, King's Liverpool Regiment*

The Mills bomb could be thrown twenty-five yards – quite accurately – by the average man. If you were throwing it a short distance, you had to be very careful, because the enemy could pick it up and chuck it back at you.

### Corporal Frederick Francis
*11th Battalion, Border Regiment*

The part of the line I was on was just fifteen yards from the German line. We were so near that every morning, a German used to shout to me, 'Hello, Tommy!' and I would reply, 'Good morning, Fritz!'

### Corporal Jim Crow
*110th Brigade, Royal Field Artillery*

One of our infantrymen was on the German barbed wire, badly wounded. We could see him moving every now and again. In the end, Major Anderton

A soldier cleaning Mills bombs. These were hand grenades, serrated like a pineapple on the outside, which exploded to form shrapnel.

pulled his revolver out, climbed over the parapet, walked straight to this man, picked him up and carried him back. He walked as though he was on parade. The Germans never fired a shot at him as he went, they never fired a shot as he went back, and they cheered him as he lifted the man on to his shoulders.

## Corporal A. Wood
### 16th Battalion, West Yorkshire Regiment

There was something very strange about our sector. Every time the battalion was changed, the Germans knew who was coming in. How they found out, I don't know. But this footballer, Dickie Bond, a right-winger who played for Bradford City, came into the front-line trenches. And the Germans called out to us, 'We know Dickie Bond's in the front line!' Not long after that, he became a prisoner of war. And we heard later that he was playing football for the German army.

## Sergeant Charles Quinnell
### 9th Battalion, Royal Fusiliers

Every morning in the front line, everybody 'stood to' – from half an hour before dawn, until half an hour afterwards. The sentries would be looking through periscopes, and everybody was prepared in case there was an attack – because the favourite times for attack were dawn or dusk. That was because, at dawn and dusk, nobody could get a sight on you with a rifle. After 'stand to', if nothing untoward had happened, the order came to 'stand down'. And then instead of a sentry to every bay, there would be perhaps two or three sentry groups in the whole company's front, and the rest of the men would see about having their breakfast.

Each man prepared his own breakfast. You'd go along to the sergeant, and your mess tin would be three parts filled with water. You put that on the hob and then you would light your chips of firewood under it, and boil your water. When the water was boiling, you'd put your tea and sugar in that, and you'd go along to the man who had the milk. You'd never open a tin of milk or a tin of jam fully because the rats would get to it: you'd simply punch a hole on either side of the lid, and blow on that one and it would squirt out the other. Primitive Methodists we were!

Now you've got the glowing embers of your fire and with your mess tin lid which had a folding handle, you'd open that, you'd put your rasher of bacon in there and put a few more sticks on your fire, and you would fry your bacon, and in the fat you would put a slice of bread, or perhaps a piece of biscuit to soak up the fat – and there you are with a breakfast.

Well now, you always left a little of your tea in the bottom of your mess tin, and you would dip a corner of your towel in the tea and wipe round your face, and that was your morning ablution. Then there'd be a little tiny drop of tea still left – and you put your shaving brush in that and you would lather your face and you would have your shave. We had to shave in the front line, otherwise – especially the dark chaps – we'd look like brigands.

**Sergeant Frederick Goodman**
*1st London Field Ambulance, Royal Army Medical Corps*
We had always used cut-throat razors, but it was just about this time that Gillette brought out the first safety razor. And on the Somme, we'd only have to put our safety razor down for a moment or two, and when we came back to pick it up, it would be gone.

**Corporal Jim Crow**
*110th Brigade, Royal Field Artillery*
You got a wash when you could. Six of us would wash and shave in a pint pot. We had to keep shaving.

**Private Reginald Glenn**
*12th Battalion, York and Lancaster Regiment*
For a proper wash, you had to wait until you got back out of the line. We used to use a sugar factory's vats for bathing. There'd be twenty of us in these vats, twenty feet in radius. We had soap and towels, and they filled them with lukewarm water.

**Private Victor Fagence**
*12th Battalion, Royal West Surrey Regiment*
All the water used in the trenches was chlorinated – and it tasted of chlorine. It was carried from one place to another in old petrol tins, and you could still taste the petrol. With the combination of petrol and chlorine, it wasn't all that pleasant. We had strict orders to boil water before it was used.

Q 4559

A sergeant cooking his dinner.

## Sergeant Charles Quinnell
### 9th Battalion, Royal Fusiliers

After breakfast, there would be inspection of the trench and also rifle inspection. Although you were in the line, you had to keep your rifles spotlessly clean and always ready for use. The inspection of the trench became necessary because the rats and the fleas in summer were really a nuisance. For instance, if you threw your empty bully beef tin over the top, that would attract the attention of the rats so in every bay would be a sandbag pegged on to the wall and in there would be the empty wrappings and empty bully beef tins and such stuff as that. Now these sandbags were collected every night. Every company had a sanitary man and it was his job to come along and take them to a shell-hole, tip the lot out and then cover that with earth. And his job was also to empty the buckets, which were biscuit tins, from the latrines. Everybody hated this job and it was given to some men as punishment. Actually, one or two men preferred it, because they could do the job in about an hour, and that was their only duty for the whole twenty-four hours.

## Private Reginald Glenn
### 12th Battalion, York and Lancaster Regiment

There were certain sections put out for latrines. The latrine was a hole in the ground with a piece of board across. You squatted on the board, but there was no paper. You used the earth and the sand. There was a 'sanitary squad' who used to come along and bury the stuff. Very often, the Germans could trace where our latrines were, by seeing people going backwards and forwards, so they got them well taped with *minenwerfers*. You'd be sitting there, and you'd see one of these come over, and you'd run with your trousers down.

## Second Lieutenant W. J. Brockman
### 15th Battalion, Lancashire Fusiliers

The smells in those trenches were terrible. It's stayed with me all my life. Excreta, urine, cordite from exploding shells.

## Corporal Percy Webb
### 7th Battalion, Dorsetshire Regiment

There were always rats in the trenches. I wouldn't say as big as cats – but as big as kittens. They were enormous. I've never seen any rats in England like them. They used to feed on anything we threw away, or garbage, or on dead bodies. There were plenty of bodies about. We used to put a pole across the trench, and the rats were very tame, they would run across that pole, and we would punch them off with our fists. Kill them. That was one of our pastimes.

## Rifleman Robert Renwick
### 16th Battalion, King's Royal Rifle Corps

The rats were worst in the trenches we took over from the French. The French were a little bit careless in leaving food lying about. The rats were terrific. We spent most of the daytime putting a bit of cheese on the end of our bayonets. They would come to the end of the bayonet, and then we'd shoot them. We couldn't miss them from there. They were very annoying. Filthy. They'd get at the rations. In one part of the line, we were sleeping in wire beds in dugouts, and the rats were seizing our haversacks with the food in, so we hung the haversacks underneath the bed, and the rats were still trying to get at them.

## Private Victor Fagence
### 12th Battalion, Royal West Surrey Regiment

After being in the trenches for a very short time, every individual became verminous. Lice. Body lice. Getting rid of them took part of our time. Usually, when one got back behind the line, in a comparatively quiet place, one would take off one's shirt, and crack the lice between our thumbnails.

## Sergeant Charles Quinnell
### 9th Battalion, Royal Fusiliers

The favourite way of getting rid of the lice – or trying to – was to take your trousers off, turn them inside out and run the seams of your trousers over a lighted candle, and you could hear the eggs going, pop, pop, pop... You'd put your trousers on but next day you had just as many lice. There were various powders sent out from England, from relations and so forth, and also there was a lice belt. That was a piece of thick angora wool which you tied round your waist and it was impregnated with something, but the only thing it did was to give a demarcation to the lice. Those above didn't mix with those below the belt.

**Private Thomas McIndoe**
*12th Battalion, Middlesex Regiment*

I had a very sensitive skin, and my sister used to send me Keating's powder to deal with the lice. But that was no good at all. Then one day, a member of the Pioneer Squad came into this latrine. He had been disinfecting the trench with a cylinder of white disinfectant powder. I was young and inexperienced, and didn't know what this powder was, but I asked him if he'd oblige me by giving me a little. But I didn't tell him what purpose I wanted it for. And he gave me a little in an envelope that I gave him. And after he'd left I emptied the contents of this envelope down the inside of the seam where the lice had gathered. But I soon realised that the powder I'd used had a destructive nature to it, and was burning the cotton of the seam of my trousers. And eventually it rotted the seam and the trousers fell apart. I subsequently found out that it was chloride of lime.

I went along to the medical officer because this stuff had burnt the inside of my legs and my legs were very raw. When I sweated, it had set the powder into a burning mass which was burning my legs and also the clothing. The medical officer gruffly said, 'What's your trouble?' so I said to him, 'I'm lousy, sir.' He said, 'Lousy? Hm . . . we're all lousy.' I said, 'Well, I've never been used to it, sir.' He said, 'Do you think I have?' I'll never forget that. And he said, 'What have you been doing?' So I told him, I briefly outlined what I'd done. And he said I'd rendered myself unfit for duty. But in no way I was going to be excused duty. So I had to just carry on as usual.

**Sergeant Charles Quinnell**
*9th Battalion, Royal Fusiliers*

For the midday meal, two or three chaps could amalgamate and one would open his tin of Fray Bentos bully beef [corned beef]. On top of the bully, there was always a quarter of an inch of fat. Now that fat was very precious because with it, you could chop up the bully beef, and fry it up in your mess tin lid. And you could smash up your biscuit with your bayonet, powder it, and put it in with the chopped bully. That was quite tasty.

Sometimes we were issued with raw potatoes. Now raw potatoes in the front line – to the uninitiated – were simply a waste of time, but when the chaps had been out there a few months they utilised everything they could lay their hands on. You could take a raw potato and if you cut it into very, very thin slices then you could fry that in your bacon fat in the morning. It was like sauté potatoes, and it was quite edible.

### Signaller Leonard Ounsworth
#### 124th Heavy Battery, Royal Garrison Artillery

We used to have Maconochies – a sixteen-ounce tin, which was supposed to have ten ounces of meat and four ounces of potato and two ounces of other vegetables in it. And it was a flat tin, you could heat it up on a fire – puncture a hole in it, you see, otherwise it would burst.

### Private Harold Hayward
#### 12th Battalion, Gloucestershire Regiment

We carried emergency rations that were not to be eaten until we were given instruction to eat them. The best thing I can tell you is that they were made up of hard dog biscuits. It had to be a good dog to bite them. When we were in action, and there was no orderly ration, I had recourse to these biscuits. I saw several fellows with broken teeth trying to bite them. I used to try and break them with my knife, and then just suck them down. Hardly any taste at all. But there must have been some nutrient in them.

### Rifleman Robert Renwick
#### 16th Battalion, King's Royal Rifle Corps

We used to go on ration parties when we were out of the line, on rest. It was almost worse than being in the trenches. You could be out in the open, sometimes under heavy fire. You'd carry the food in sandbags, and the water in unused petrol tins. You'd collect it from a dump, and you'd go up through the communication trenches. You'd take it up to the front line, and give it to the sergeant, or the officer, and they'd distribute it.

### Lieutenant Norman Dillon
#### 14th Battalion, Northumberland Fusiliers

There were constant carrying parties. We were carrying forward rolls of barbed wire, pickets for hanging it on, shovels, sandbags, wood, posts and wire for revetments and the sides of trenches, duckboards for wet places. Everything had to be carried up.

## Sergeant Charles Quinnell
### 9th Battalion, Royal Fusiliers

During the day, in the front line, there was always some digging to be done. You see, the sides of the trenches were always giving way especially in wet weather, and you would find that perhaps during the night the side of the trench had come in. Well, the trench had to be built up with sandbags filled with earth. There was always a repair job to be done; there was always a support trench needed repair.

And there was always a lot of sleep going on during the daytime. You see, you reversed the order of your usual living. Night-time was the period of activity. There was always something to do at night-time. There was the ration party, there was the water party, there was a wiring party, there were patrols. After a few weeks, a soldier could curl up, and he could be asleep in two minutes. If nobody came for you to do a job you simply got down to it and you were asleep, any time of the day.

At night-time, if there was any suspicion of activity, Very lights would go up. Each platoon sergeant had a Very light pistol and he also had his cartridges, and if the sentry reported any activity in front, the sergeant would send a Very light up. This pistol was like a brass starting pistol, and you'd cant it at what angle you think you want the light to drop, and plop! And that would go up in the air and light everything up.

## Second Lieutenant W. J. Brockman
### 15th Battalion, Lancashire Fusiliers

If you were in no-man's-land when a Very light went up, your instinct was to lie down – but that was wrong. You should stand absolutely still. There were all sorts of things you could be mistaken for in no-man's-land – wire and stumps of trees.

## Sergeant Charles Quinnell
### 9th Battalion, Royal Fusiliers

Wiring was always done in the dark and it was done by a party who had been trained. It sounds peculiar I know but there was a certain amount of waltzing to it. Barbed wire used to come on a wooden framework with a hole through the centre, and a pole used to be put through that framework, one man on either side. The man who did the actual wiring was always issued with a pair of very thick leather gloves because barbed wire can be very, very vicious.

aking wire up to the forward area.

A working party ready to dig.

**Private Harold Hayward**
*12th Battalion, Gloucestershire Regiment*
The first time I went over wiring, we were told to go quietly, not a word to one another. We were going to make a proper continuous line. I happened to step to one side, and I fell into an old French latrine. I thought to myself, 'I am not going to die like this!' They pushed their rifles down, and I caught hold of two of them, and they pulled me out. No one would come near me for the rest of the time in the line.

**Sergeant Charles Quinnell**
*9th Battalion, Royal Fusiliers*
Another duty at night was to man the listening posts. A shallow trench would be dug from the front line out into no-man's-land – perhaps a hundred yards in front, depending on what distance the two opposing lines of trenches were. The listening party would consist of a corporal and two men, and their job was to just lay in this listening post with their head above ground level, and just watch and listen. For example, if they heard any barbed wiring going on or a German patrol they would return to the line and report it and we'd open fire on wherever this activity was.

**Rifleman Robert Renwick**
*16th Battalion, King's Royal Rifle Corps*
The listening post was a very dreary do. I went out with an officer one night, and I had an idea that the lad on the listening post was asleep. Somehow, I got in front of the officer, in case he was. And when I got there, the lad was just dozing off. I woke him up. It would have been a serious crime if he'd been found asleep.

**Sergeant Charles Quinnell**
*9th Battalion, Royal Fusiliers*
And at night, there'd be trench raids. We knew these were a waste of time, we just hated them. But some general about thirty miles behind the line wanted to know who was in the trenches opposite, and he would send up a message 'Raid and get prisoners'. He ought to have had the job himself. And you'd have artillery preparation to destroy their wire, and perhaps a whole division of artillery would put down a barrage on the German wire to smash it down,

and then they would put what they called a 'box barrage' down. Twelve guns would fire on one point of the German trench line to seal off everything from there. But by doing that you're sending an open postcard to the Germans, aren't you, that you're coming over? Oh God, the men just hated it.

## Corporal Don Murray
### 8th Battalion, King's Own Yorkshire Light Infantry
We were supposed to go over with the sole intention of bringing a prisoner back. We had to black our faces up. As a matter of fact, we blacked ourselves up once for a raid – and it snowed like hell. On another raid, I had an officer called Morris in charge of me. Mr Morris was ever such a nice chap, but he spoke with a lisp. Instead of Morris, his name was 'Morrith'. He had a way of inspecting your rifles, and he'd say, 'There'th a thpeck of dutht down your barrel!' He was a regular figure of fun, and he was beside me, and a shot came, and went through the front of his cap, hit his cap badge and flew up. It didn't hurt him. He said, 'I'll never be killed now, Murray! Look at that!' And there was a hole from his cap badge, right through the top of his hat.

## Private Harry Hall
### 13th Battalion, York and Lancaster Regiment
If we could go out and pinch a couple of Germans, and bring them back, they were thrashed in the orderly room. I don't mean mentally thrashed, I mean physically thrashed. They would torture them, and they would tell them all they wanted, depending on the nature of the fellow, of course. Because some fellas spit it all out, and others try to hold it in. That was the object, getting to know who was in the line opposite us at that time, where they came from, and all that sort of thing.

## Sergeant Charles Quinnell
### 9th Battalion, Royal Fusiliers
We had a very, very keen officer by the name of Van Sommer. It was a Dutch name but he was English all right, a very, very brave man he was, and I used to hate going out on patrol with him, because he would walk straight across no-man's-land, straight up to the barbed wire, standing up all the time, and he would take a pair of snips with him and he'd take a sample, the Germans popping away at him, and bring back the sample, and he would walk away, and he expected you to do the same. I used to hate him.

A narrow escape.

## Second Lieutenant W. J. Brockman
### 15th Battalion, Lancashire Fusiliers

We had a very gallant fellow with us, a Jew of German extraction, name of Mandelberg. He was the sort of bloke who would go out into no-man's-land and explore. He went out one night, and as he came back through the wire, he was challenged by the sentry, who said, 'Who goes there?' 'Captain Mandelberg!' he replied. He'd gone too far along, over to another regiment – and the sentry shot him. Fortunately, he was only wounded, and the sentry was arrested. He was asked, 'What did you do that for? Shoot a British officer?' 'I thought he said *Hindenberg*,' he said, 'so I shot him.'

## Corporal George Ashurst
### 1st Battalion, Lancashire Fusiliers

I went out one night with three men, on a patrol to find out if Jerry was doing anything. We went over the top, and under our wire – we were sliding along on our bellies, with bombs ready to throw, and I had a revolver. If there had been any Germans out there, it would have been a case of who got their bomb in first. Then, Jerry opened up with a machine gun. It was a fixed gun, so you had a chance. He used to skim his bullets along the top of the trench – a foot above the top. If you could lie below that foot, you were safe – even if it was only just missing you. The three men with me had never been out before at night, and, in between these machine-gun spurts, I said: 'Lie flat! Let the bullets go over you! Keep flat down!'

## Private Harold Startin
### 1st Battalion, Leicestershire Regiment

Trench raids is why 'trench clubs' came into being. When I came home on leave, my dad was a bit on the religious side, and he said it weren't right that human beings should use cudgels on other human beings. I am sorry to say the one that is on display in the Imperial War Museum has actually been used. That was my one.

## Corporal Henry Mabbott
### 2nd Battalion, Cameron Highlanders

I joined a party that was going out at night, staying out all the next day and not coming back until the next night. That was a ghastly experience. We were not able to move during the day. We were in a shell-hole, where we partly covered ourselves with camouflage, and we were listening – trying to find out exactly what was happening. When we were coming back in, they put up Very lights, and they found us, and opened up on us. Those that didn't get hit straight away got into shell-holes, and in due course we decided that we'd take a chance on getting in. I made a run for it. I was getting through the barbed wire when my right foot went dead. When I got into the trench, I discovered that a bullet had gone right through without touching any bone, tendon, or anything.

**Sergeant Charles Quinnell**
*9th Battalion, Royal Fusiliers*
As you looked over your trench through your periscope, all you could see was the devastated land of no-man's-land, and the German barbed wire, and you never saw a sign of life. It was one of the most desolate sights in the world. And yet you knew, very well, that within shouting range there were hundreds and hundreds of men.

**Corporal George Ashurst**
*1st Battalion, Lancashire Fusiliers*
There was always sniping. Every minute of the day and night there was sniping. We suffered a lot of casualties from it. There were no precautions we could take – just to be careful.

**Lieutenant James Pratt**
*1/4th Battalion Gordon Highlanders*
We were trained in how to cope with German snipers. One way was by putting a turnip on the parapet of your trench and waiting for the sniper to hit it. He would have a go at it and make a hole. Then you put another turnip up at another point and the sniper would have another go. Then you looked through the bullet holes and that gave you a close approximation of his position.

**Lieutenant William Taylor**
*13th Battalion, Royal Fusiliers*
We always had snipers on duty, and when walking along the line, I would occasionally take the sniper's position and see what he was looking for. I can

remember having a shot myself, once or twice, at what I thought was the enemy. They were a fair way away, and it was only very occasionally one caught sight of them.

## Private Ralph Miller
### 1/8th Battalion, Royal Warwickshire Regiment

When you were sniping, you set yourself a site, you saved yourself a little space, you got a good view of something and you let go. Aiming at anything that bloody moved. Sometimes, you'd strain to look at a tree trunk, and you'd see it move, and the more you stared, the more it moved, and you had to be very careful. If you let go at something like that, there might be one of their snipers, having a go at you.

## Sergeant Wilfred Hunt
### 9th Battalion, Devonshire Regiment

Often in the trenches, instead of a rifle, I would carry a cudgel – a stick with a piece of lead at the end – and I walked up and down. The men were spaced out, all along the trenches, and I wanted to make sure that they were doing their jobs all right.

## Lieutenant William Taylor
### 13th Battalion, Royal Fusiliers

The officers had to enforce a certain amount of discipline. Particularly with regards to keeping rifles clean, and the men keeping themselves clean. We inspected the men's feet, because we got very wet, and unless a man changed his socks, and kept his feet moderately dry, you got trench foot, and became a casualty.

## Corporal Harry Fellows
### 12th Battalion, Northumberland Fusiliers

The officers were mainly public schoolboys. They came through the officers' training in the public schools, and they were given commissions. They weren't taught to think. Only to lead.

## Lieutenant William Taylor
### 13th Battalion, Royal Fusiliers

The association between officers and men was so much closer in the line than on the parade ground at home. The discipline wasn't as strict, and one was so much closer to one's men, that one got to know them better. The friendship was different to what it was at home. My men were friendly with me. I knew every man's name, and I got to know more and more about them. I would talk to them in a casual way.

## Lieutenant Norman Collins
### 6th Battalion, Seaforth Highlanders

I had a lance corporal, called Meekle, and we were extremely close. We often used to go out together in no-man's-land, and I would have a chat with him, and he told me a lot about himself. He was a small man, and he stammered, and you wouldn't think he'd 'say boo to a goose', but his men worshipped him. When a shell dropped near, and the fragments whistled through the air, Meekle would say, 'You want to watch out, boys! There's death in those pieces!' It was his sense of humour. Well, Meekle and I used to do two hours' patrolling, and then four hours on a wire bed in a dugout, before going back out to do another two hours' patrol. When we came back to the dugout, to get into the wire bed, the dugouts were lit by candles, and there were rats' holes in the wall all around them. We'd blow out the candle, and quickly we'd have to put our blankets over our faces, because immediately the candle was out, the rats darted out of the holes to eat the candles.

## Second Lieutenant W. J. Brockman
### 15th Battalion, Lancashire Fusiliers

These men's lives were in your hands, and they relied on you. Their education was pretty low. My chaps were Lancashire labourers, and the class distinction was much greater then, than it is now, and they *preferred* to be led by what they described as the 'officer classes'. When you got used to them, they were marvellous chaps.

## Second Lieutenant Tom Adlam VC
### 7th Battalion, Bedfordshire Regiment

I had a very happy platoon. Perhaps that's because I'm a good mixer. And, always, if anyone could do something better than me, I let them do it. Some officers would think they had to do better than their men. But if I found a man who could do something better than me I'd say, 'Well, you do that.' And I think they liked it.

## Private Reginald Glenn
### 12th Battalion, York and Lancaster Regiment

Our officer – Bardsley – was one of us. He'd come up from the ranks, and he slept with us and lived with us.

## Corporal Jim Crow
### 110th Brigade, Royal Field Artillery

I got on wonderfully well with the bulk of the officers. But some of them didn't know as much about ranging a gun as I did, and I used to advise them. While we were covering the Australians, I took an officer called Melly up to the front line before dawn, and just as we got up there, they were standing down after being on duty all night. When we got to the sentry, he pulled us up and asked us for the password. The password was 'Tacker'. I gave it, and he said, 'Pass, friend!' The officer came up, and the sentry asked him, and he burst out laughing. I managed to get him off and we went into the line, and we were stood alongside some infantrymen who were cleaning their rifles, and the officer says to one of them, 'My good man! What would you do if the Germans came over now?' 'Give them a bloody rough time!' said the Australian.

A bit later on, we observed the Germans carrying munitions to a strong-point. We watched them for a bit, and then one of the infantrymen said, 'Why the hell don't you get a gun on them?' 'Oh yes,' said Melly. 'Good idea! What gun's on duty, Crow?' "A' subsection, sir.' 'Give them actioning then! Give them five degrees right!' 'What range, sir?' 'Three thousand yards!' I was supposed to pass this down the line. 'Excuse me sir,' I said, 'you'd be wrong.' 'Why?' 'The guns are two thousand yards behind us, sir,' I said. 'You give that deflection, and you'll be firing on the New Zealanders!' He took a bit of persuading, but in the end I persuaded him. He observed the first shell, and then he gave another ridiculous range. By the time he'd wasted three or four shells, the Germans knew what we were doing, and they promptly packed up. But there weren't many officers as incompetent as that. Just the odd one or two.

**Sergeant Wilfred Hunt**
*9th Battalion, Devonshire Regiment*
The quality of officers was shocking. *Shocking.* The one that we got, at first, collapsed when we got to where the guns were opening up. He just collapsed, and we never saw him any more. He ought to be in a tomb. He was a mummy's darling.

**Second Lieutenant W. J. Brockman**
*15th Battalion, Lancashire Fusiliers*
We had to eliminate those officers that we called 'yellowbellies'. They were more bother than they were worth. The 'windy' ones. Many of the officers were posted back to England, and were able to say, 'Oh, I've been in France,' when in fact they'd been there for about a week, and they got lovely jobs at home – because those of us at the front said that we didn't want them. There was another way of getting rid of them. If anybody was asked to supply the name of an officer for a course, you gave the name of one you didn't want. So, after a bit, you knew you could rely on the people you'd got. But, of course, the rate of casualties amongst the officers was absolutely fantastic. There was a time when they reckoned the life expectancy of a subaltern was about three weeks.

**Second Lieutenant Tom Adlam VC**
*7th Battalion, Bedfordshire Regiment*
The men a little up the scale in the officer line could be a little *trench shy*. One was a bit nervy, and he came round when things were going wrong, to haul us over the coals. He was looking over the trench, and I put my hand on his shoulder and said, 'Not there, sir, there's a sniper often shoots there.' After I'd done it about four times he was eating out of my hand.

**Lieutenant Phillip Howe**
*10th Battalion, West Yorkshire Regiment*
Our divisional general was Major General Pilcher who was a bit of a character, rather a bloodthirsty man. I remember on one occasion when we were in the trenches, he came round, and there was barbed wire in front of our line with a large red rag stuck on the barbed wire, and he said, "Why don't you go fetch it in, to show how brave you are?' I said, 'That would be damn silly. They

put it up there to attract someone out, and if you fall for it, you get shot.' He said, 'Yes. I know. My son got killed doing that.'

## Sergeant Frederick Goodman
### 1st London Field Ambulance, Royal Army Medical Corps

We had clergymen, representing the Church of England, the Catholics, or whatever, and we would have many men who were badly wounded, in an awful state. The clergymen would come along and administer the last rites, and that was fine, but there were times when some of these clergy fellows did not have their feet on the ground. By that I mean that they should know that a man who is passing out doesn't want religion pushed at him too hard. He's not in a fit state to give it careful consideration. So the man would sometimes tell the padre to go away – not with the best of language – and it was pretty awful.

## Second Lieutenant Tom Adlam VC
### 7th Battalion, Bedfordshire Regiment

I remember what one of the men said about our padre: 'He's a grand chap. He don't ask if you're a Roman Catholic, Church of England, or a Hottentot. He just takes you and buries you.'

## Corporal Don Murray
### 8th Battalion, King's Own Yorkshire Light Infantry

We had a sergeant. Sergeant Bates. A terrible man. He used to take his shirt off, and run his teeth up the seams to kill the lice. With his teeth! A dreadful man. He always used to say what he'd do if he got hold of the Germans. He would have done, too – he'd have torn them limb from limb.

He was a great big hulking man. In civil life, he'd done nothing but wheel steel in a barrow to a melting forge and tip it in. And he was ignorant. He couldn't remember anybody's name. There was one fellow called Courtenay, and he used to call him 'Twopenny'. That was the nearest he could get. He could remember me for one reason: like a fool, I'd made some tea in the middle of the night, and I'd offered him some. 'What's your name?' he asked. 'Murray.' 'Right,' he said, 'I'll remember that.' And he bloody did remember it. Every time he wanted someone for a fatigue party – 'Murray!' I was the only one he could think of. I was working like the devil. I said to him that I was going to complain: 'I'm going to see the officer!' 'What for?' he said. 'I'm getting no sleep!' I said. 'It'll be all right,' he said, 'I'll make out a rusty duster.' 'What's that?' I said. 'All the sergeants have them!' he said. I thought a bit. He meant a duty roster.

### Lieutenant Phillip Howe
#### 10th Battalion, West Yorkshire Regiment

I met a lot of peculiar characters. I had one soldier, a very old soldier, who had been in the Egyptian war. Whatever was going on, he was always perfectly shaved every morning, he always had his buttons cleaned and shiny, but unfortunately, whenever he had the opportunity, he got himself completely unconscious through drink. He spent all his time out of action suffering field punishment number one, because he was always drunk. But in the front line – he was magnificent.

### Second Lieutenant W. J. Brockman
#### 15th Battalion, Lancashire Fusiliers

I was in charge of a fellow called Private Mason, and if he could do anything wrong, he would. Once when we were going over duckboards, up to the line, a message came up from the back, 'Mason's dropped his rifle in the water.' He was one of those awkward people – you couldn't help but feel sorry for the chap. But the amazing thing about Mason was that as soon as the war was over – they couldn't demobilise everybody at once – they started educating some of the troops. Officers had to recommend people, and by way of a joke, I put Mason's name down. The next time I saw him, he was a sergeant, and he was teaching others. At last, he'd found the thing he could do.

### Private Philip Cullen
#### 4th Battalion, Oxfordshire and Buckinghamshire Light Infantry

We'd had sixty recruits from Devon. They were older men, and this was no war for an old man. We were going back, and being shelled to hell, and this forty-five-year-old man slipped on a footbridge, and fell into a ruddy trench, and it took eight of us half of an hour to get him out. We were being shelled all the while, and I wanted to get away. I lost my temper. I was only a private, but I was in charge, and I truly told him what I felt. I was sorry for it afterwards, but it was the only time I lost my temper.

## Second Lieutenant Tom Adlam VC
### 7th Battalion, Bedfordshire Regiment

My company commander I always looked upon as the bravest men I ever saw – except that he never knew what fear was. He'd go anywhere as long as he had a cigarette in his hand. And all the men thought worlds of him, so did the officers, because he was such a great chap. He went right through the war, came back on leave, went back again, right through the war, the whole lot of it. And then after the war, went mountain climbing and got killed. Extraordinary thing.

## Corporal Bill Partridge
### 7th Battalion, Middlesex Regiment

Captain Gillett was such a splendid company commander. They called us 'Lucky B' – not meaning lucky bastards, but meaning lucky B Company, because we had the least casualties of any company in the batallion. We put it all down to his leadership – whether it was going out doing night raids, going out in front doing the wire, or just dealing with ordinary trench shelling, mortars and *minenwerfers* – he was uncanny in his leadership. Not only that, but he was with us all the time. Never asked us to do anything he wouldn't do himself. He became Lord Mayor of London after the war.

## Sergeant Charles Quinnell
### 9th Battalion, Royal Fusiliers

Captain Cazalet was a very gallant officer; a splendid man in himself in addition to being a very, very efficient man. He had a way with him. He would never bark an order at you; he would give an order in a conversational way. 'I would like you to do so-and-so,' and by God you did it, too. You gave everything you had.

## Corporal Henry Mabbott
### 2nd Battalion, Cameron Highlanders

Anybody would do anything for anybody else in the trenches. It was a wonderful bond. In fact, one of my platoon sergeants offered to become my best man, but unfortunately he developed trouble with his wound, and he wasn't able to do it.

**Private Philip Cullen**
*4th Battalion, Oxfordshire and Buckinghamshire Light Infantry*

On my twenty-first birthday, I was sent out from the trenches with a fictitious message that was supposed to be from company headquarters to battalion headquarters. I was sent down, and as I arrived at battalion headquarters I was met by Jimmy Bishop, the sergeant major. 'Hello!' he said. 'What do you want?' 'I've got a message for you from Captain Greenwall,' I said. 'Give it to me. And go in there!' he said. 'I've got to go back, sir!' 'You're going in there!' he said. I was in there for ten minutes, when a tumbler of neat rum came in. I was drunk for twenty-four hours.

**Corporal Harry Fellows**
*12th Battalion, Northumberland Fusiliers*

One night we'd all got down, but for some reason I couldn't sleep. I crawled out, trying not to wake up the other three lads, and walked away and lit a cigarette. Then the Germans sent over a shell that hit the bivouac. Two of the lads were killed, and my particular friend – Dick Turnbull – had both his legs shattered. That was the saddest moment of my time in the army.

**Private Philip Cullen**
*4th Battalion, Oxfordshire and Buckinghamshire Light Infantry*

I lost some good friends. All the same, I wasn't affected. The fact of your pal falling – you had to leave him and carry on. Once, I was on duty with a man called Harold Doubleday, when a whizz-bang came over. Harold was hit in the shoulder by the nosecap, when I was standing beside him. I called for stretcher-bearers and left it at that. That was all that could be done.

**Corporal Jim Crow**
*110th Brigade, Royal Field Artillery*

I found out that my brother was nearby with the Royal Welsh Fusiliers, and I went to the captain and asked if I could go and see him. We weren't too busy just then, and he said yes, and he told me to take the bicycle. I found my brother. I hadn't seen him for seven years, and I had a few hours with him, before I went back. He wanted me to transfer into his regiment, but I wasn't prepared to do that. And seven days later, he was killed. He was in a salient, and our artillery opened a barrage up and hit him. We were told that

The burial of a major.

he'd been killed in action, but members of his regiment told me how he was killed.

### Private Tom Bracey
*9th Battalion, Royal Fusiliers*

My pal Tom Smith came up to me, and said, "'Ere, my young brother's out here! He ain't eighteen yet! I'm going to see the colonel about this!' Tom had bumped into his brother, and said to him, 'What the devil have you come out here for?' and his brother had said, 'I didn't know it was going to be like this!'

### Lieutenant William Taylor
*13th Battalion, Royal Fusiliers*

An officer censored the men's letters. To see that there was no mention of where we were, and that there was no defeatist talk. One didn't read it through word for word. One glanced through.

### Major Murray Hill
*5th Battalion, Royal Fusiliers*

One man wrote a letter saying to his wife: 'I hope this letter finds you as it leaves me. I've got a bit of shrapnel in my bottom.'

### Private Ralph Miller
*1/8th Battalion, Royal Warwickshire Regiment*

I bought four silk postcards to send home, and I sent one straightaway, but it was censored and destroyed. They were worried that the ship they were on would be torpedoed, and they'd give information away to the Germans. The other three, I just wrote on them 'OK, Ralph'.

### Second Lieutenant Tom Adlam VC
*7th Battalion, Bedfordshire Regiment*

We used to get our letters at the front. I was unfortunate because I read that my dear mother had died. They applied for me to come home on leave. I went to see the adjutant. 'Well, if you go back,' he said, 'by the time you get there the funeral will be over. I advise you to stay here. You can't do any good going home.' So I stayed. And if I had gone back, I shouldn't have won the Victoria Cross . . .

An Anzac soldier writes home.

Men of the 25th Infantry Brigade gather to welcome the King.

**Private Tom Bracey**
*9th Battalion, Royal Fusiliers*

I was mending my trousers one day. There I was, sewing them, when an orderly came along and said that Lieutenant Van Someran wanted to see me. I said that I'd be along as soon as I'd mended my trousers. So I went along, and the lieutenant told me to make myself as clean and tidy as I could, because eight of us were to 'go back'. He didn't say what it was all about. So I had to go behind the lines with these seven others and we slept the night, and in the morning we had to brush our boots and we were taken to a farm.

And then King George showed up – to inspect the division. So the King arrived in a car, got out, walked steadily through the ranks, spoke to one or two people, and within five minutes he was gone. We had to put our hats on our bayonets, and wave them around, and then we had to go back to rejoin our battalion. We didn't think much of all this. You ought to have heard the language . . .

# Verdun

*Many men had their feet frozen: some of them had to cut them off.*


J ust as the Allies were making plans for an offensive that would bring the war to an end, so too were the Germans. On February 21, 1916, Germany launched an attack on Verdun, a strongly fortified city, 150 miles south-east of the Somme. Verdun was carefully chosen as an objective by General Falkenhayn, the Chief of the German General Staff, for its symbolic significance to the French, which was out of all proportion to its strategic importance. Verdun had repeatedly offered determined resistance to German attacks down the centuries, most recently during the Franco–Prussian war of 1870. Falkenhayn expected – and hoped – that the French would defend this symbol of national pride to the very last man, giving rise to a long, bloody struggle, that would 'bleed the French Army white'. France, believed Falkenhayn, would eventually be compelled to agree to a peace on German terms, which in turn would force Britain out of the war.

In the event, the French behaved much as Falkenhayn predicted. They defended Verdun furiously, and within a month had suffered almost a hundred thousand casualties; within four months, half a million. The fight for Verdun had a number of far-reaching effects on the intended attack on the Somme; firstly, it gave the attack extra importance as a means of relieving the intense pressure on Verdun. Secondly, it meant that far greater responsibility for the Somme attack would now fall on the British. Thirdly, it ensured that the attack would have to be swiftly mounted, before Verdun fell, which in turn meant that Haig's hopes of a decisive breakthrough on the Somme might have to be sacrificed in favour of a more hastily prepared – and potentially far bloodier – attritional struggle.

**Henri Lacorne**
*French Artillery Observer*

We arrived near to Verdun on February 16. It was snowing and very cold. We knew that something was going to happen because the Germans were directing fire on almost every French battery they had discovered, but it was very light fire – in order not to call our attention to what was going to happen. We naturally thought that we were going to enter into a very big event. Trenches were being made at the back of our first defences, that showed that we were preparing for the future.

On February 21 we were around Douaumont, in the very close vicinity of this fort, and the bombardment began at twilight and, for seventy-two hours, we had a bombardment which did not cease except for a few minutes in the early hours of every morning. The noise was absolutely tremendous. Shells fell all over the place, and there was hardly a part of the ground where a shell had not fallen. You could see – especially at night – the light of the German guns and the light of the shell exploding. The noise was more terrific when a shell, instead of exploding on the ground, exploded in a tree. It made a tremendous roar: you could see clouds of black smoke coming from the explosions and various colours from blue to red to yellow to orange. It looked like fireworks – but not very well-regulated fireworks. Naturally.

My duty was to direct the fire of my battery on the German trenches, twenty-five metres from the one in which I was. Around me, everybody was very nervous. The shells which came right into the middle of the French trenches, and killed many people, did not appease our fear. We were afraid – but we had to do our duty and everybody did it.

I was connected to my battery with a telephone and I gave that battery every order to make the fire as effective as possible. We had a very small observation post in that trench, and one day I found the captain who was doing the work which I was about to do, killed by a bullet in the forehead, looking through the hole of the observation post. No need to say, it's an experience which gave me some fright. The privates and the officers during this battle were absolutely working as one man; everybody was doing what he could. Everybody thought it was necessary to do what they were ordered to do, no matter of how difficult or how terrible it was during that tremendous roar.

When the German fire ceased, the Germans jumped out of their trenches and tried to get into ours. There were terrible fights inside the trenches, because our soldiers were trying to hold the assault. It was a very sad thing to see all these soldiers, German and French mixed together, sometimes fighting with bayonets.

During the rare moments of rest, the soldiers were not lonesome. They had still a very good spirit, teasing each other, and keeping busy as much as they could, in their private mood. For instance, they were very much interested in the copper belts of guns, which they used to make rings – using small files – for their sweethearts or their wives or their sisters.

When the wind was in our favour, we could smell ether from the German soldiers, which they drank in order to make the assault more effective. On our side we were given brandy to pep us up.

## Private Georges Pilliet
### *Private, French Army*

At the end of April, we were astonished to see that the Germans had put sign boards on their trenches, writing in French that 'You are going to Verdun and good luck to you'. The battle had started in February, and we knew what was going on. We left our trenches and we were taken by train to a place a certain distance from Verdun and we had to walk by night – a very difficult long and hard walk. We arrived at Verdun and remained south of the city in barracks. We were there for a day. We were told not to move and not to show ourselves. When the night came, we went to the front. I had to go into a tunnel on the railway line from Verdun to Meaux. In this tunnel lived about a thousand men, who had been there for months. It was filthy, smelly; we had the impression we could cut the air with a knife. From there we went to the Fort of Tavannes. My job was to run from the Fort of Tavannes to the Fort of Vaux which was about two miles, running from shell-hole to shell-hole. What was most surprising was the landscape. There was not an inch of earth that had not been turned over and over. Some troops were digging trenches, to enable us to get from one place to another. As quick as they could work, the trenches were filled again by bombs and shells.

The Germans attacked heavily every day and every night. We had to live on our reserve foods – biscuits, chocolate, corned beef, but sometimes soup and coffee would arrive, if the men who had gone to fetch them were not killed on the way. The most terrible thing was thirst. As a runner from Tavannes to Vaux, I had to bring water and orders, and come back with the wounded on my shoulders – or on stretchers if we were lucky enough to have two of us together. What we were eager to know is how long we would stay. We knew that we would be relieved from Verdun when the casualties would become a certain percentage of the troops.

Every morning when a runner could come to our lines, he was asked what are the casualties today. It's rather cold to think that we hoped that the casualties would be heavy, so that we could leave this hell. It was hell. It was really hell. When we left Verdun, the remains of my troop were gathered, and we had to walk from Verdun to Bar-le-Duc along the Voie Sacrée, which was a stream of mud, on which we walked with many difficulties, because there was many holes and bumps and lorries going up and down. We had to walk along, and we were very weary, thirsty, hungry but all the same we could walk miles and miles because we were escaping from that hell – and very happy to escape.

All the same, during those ten days of walking, we had no sleep, no rest at all. We just went on without much thinking. Arriving at the middle of Voie Sacrée, we were told that General Petain was there. His habit was to stand on a little perch, at the top of a few steps, to salute the men that were coming back from Verdun. We felt so powered that the general would come and salute the men who took his orders.

## G. Fenetrier
### 70th Infantry Regiment, French Army

I was an officer, driving lorries, carrying soldiers. So I had to run the Voie Sacrée, going to Verdun. It was the only road going to Verdun which it was possible to run over. Day and night, without any stopping, there were lorries going and coming back with soldiers, barbed wire, bombs, food – all things necessary for the armies, and coming back with men, wounded, tired, or changing.

Every ten metres, there was an old soldier throwing some stones in the holes of the road. The holes were made by the lorries and also by the bombs which were thrown day and night by the Germans. They knew without Voie Sacrée, we had lost Verdun. But we won Verdun because we kept Voie Sacrée. Every day, the lorries were running, one behind the other, with men, tired, half sleepy. Sometimes there was a car or lorry that was damaged; it was immediately pulled out of the road, immediately. The road ought to be kept safe. That was the rule and the order.

## Stephen K. Westmann
### German Army Medical Corps

Early in 1916, the Battle for Verdun started. I was a medical officer with the artillery formation firing at the French force at Verdun. Douaumont had been taken, and up there we had our observation posts looking far into the enemy countryside. One day I got a telephone message that a man up on an observation post complained of heavy pain in his stomach, and vomiting. It was an abdominal emergency, and I had to go up. There were two communication trenches going up and down, and the French artillery knew exactly where these trenches were, and they fired without pause. I had to go up, but before I got up, somebody told me that I had to take a gas mask with me. I never saw a gas mask before, but we knew that the French artillery fired gas shells on to the German positions. Up I went with my gas mask – consisting of a piece of gauze with a bit of cotton wool soaked *in a certain fluid* – and up I went, to the top of Douaumont.

In Douaumont, we had two observation posts looking through slits in the very strong concrete bunkers, right down into the enemy territory, and there was my man with an acute appendicitis. We carried him down to the floor itself, and down, down, down we went. Many yards underground, protected by reinforced concrete, the French had established a little operating theatre, where there were constantly two German surgeons on duty. One of them was by chance from Berlin, my native town. He operated on this man, and now came another question: how to get him down into the German lines.

I wandered through the casements, and there I found one casement bricked up, and on it somebody had written, 'Here lie one 1052 German soldiers.' I asked what that meant. I was told that one thousand and fifty-two German soldiers – a whole battalion – had been in that casement, where they had stored barrels of fuel for the flame-throwers. Somebody had been very careless and the whole thing blew up and nobody was left. They couldn't even get at them, so they bricked up the casement and wrote this notice about the dead soldiers.

So now the question arose, how to bring the casualties, and this just-operated man, down to our positions. We had the experience with the British, that whenever they had a wounded man in their forward lines, they went along with the Red Cross flag and we did not fire at them. The German guns were silent until the Red Cross flag had disappeared. The British didn't fire at us, either. Artillery fire ceased completely and infantry fire stopped. So we got the idea to do the same trick with the French. We formed a kind of convoy, in front of it a man with the Red Cross flag, in the middle another man with the Red Cross flag, and in the rear a third man with the Red Cross flag, but unfortunately the result was exactly the contrary. The French artillery opened up. It was intense fire and several of the stretcher-bearers were wounded and killed, so we had to give up this attempt. We had to bring the men down at night. There must be a little difference between the English word 'gentleman' and the French word 'cavalier'.

## Ernest S. Karganoff
### French Officer

One day, we were ordered to pack and start a march of sixty-six miles to join the battle at Verdun. We could hear the bombardment from the very first day. We used to walk twenty miles a day. We joined Verdun in May 1916 after the big rush, but still the position was in very bad conditions. We had a long way to walk to reach our trenches which were in very bad condition. They had been bombarded, they had been razed out, many soldiers had not yet been buried. We were suffering of mud everywhere and the food supply came irregularly, because we had to ask volunteers to go far behind the line under the bombardment to get our food: bread, wine, soup and sometimes some meat.

I don't know whether it's due to the sense of humour of the quartermaster's service, but one evening we had for supper salt herrings. Needless to say, in Verdun, the water was rather scarce, and we had wine but it doesn't replace the water when you are very thirsty. The water we had to find by ourselves. We had to try to find a spring or get water out of a bomb hole. For a while, we were taking water from a small spring. One day, looking for a missing comrade, I went to the spring. The body of my comrade was in the spring. We carried on drinking the water all right. Nothing happened.

We had bombardment every day, sometimes the whole day, sometimes the whole night. Our shelters were very poor; we couldn't expect to escape with that kind of shelter, we just had to creep in the mud to find a bomb hole not full of rain water, and stay there to keep our guns clean if possible. And we had rats to keep us company.

One day, we were supposed to be relieved by another regiment but – and it happened very often with the army orders and counter orders – we remained eight days in the snow. Many men had their feet frozen: some of them had to cut them off. Our losses were pretty high, especially in officers. The quarters behind the line where we used to take our rest was very poor. The straw was sometime moist or rotten, and the welcome was not very warm because the people had been seeing so many soldiers from both sides. We were so filthy, that we put all our clothes, guns and helmets in the river just to wash them. That was the only way, so once we were clean we started on leave.

War being a tough game, soldiers needed some compensations, and during the war we had the compensation of so-called 'Mariannes de guerre'. We got into touch with these women through advertising in a weekly illustrated newspaper called La Vie Parisienne. We received many very friendly letters from these ladies, sometimes with pictures of them. Some were even married. They sent us packages, they usually asked us what we were in need of, tinned food, chocolate, home-knitted woollen socks. One of my 'Mariannes' was quite particular. She sent me flowers, perfume, cigars. I don't know what the perfume was for. When I was on leave I used to visit my 'Mariannes'. We used to go to the theatre, or to restaurants or to movies. We had as good a time as we possibly could have during the war. At the time, I was in correspondence with seven of them. As my leave was ten days, I had time to meet all of them. I continued to write to three of them until the end of the war – and I nearly married one. But I changed my mind.

# Cometh the Hour

*We were told by our officer that we were to take part in the attack, and the men were excited. Everybody thought it would be a walkover.*

In late May, Haig was visited by Joffre, who informed him that the French Army would be 'ruined' by the German attacks on Verdun unless the assault on the Somme could be mounted by July 1. Haig would have preferred to hold off until mid-August, but his protests fell on deaf ears. He was forced to accept that the needs of the French were paramount, and the date of the attack was set for June 29. Haig still believed that the infantry could achieve a breakthrough, to be exploited by the cavalry, which would lead to the total defeat of the German Army. Yet by June 16, he was declaring – in an order to Sir Henry Rawlinson, Commander of the Fourth Army – that the aim of the offensive was now to relieve the pressure on the French at Verdun. Talk of a breakthrough was set aside.

In the meantime, preparations were taking place at a furious pace. Huge numbers of troops needed to be trained in assault tactics before being ferried to the front. Artillery and ammunition had to be brought forward. The majority of the guns were eighteen-pounders and 4.5-inch howitzers, but heavy guns, howitzers and trench mortars were also distributed regularly along the front. To cope with all this movement, road and rail links had be built, improved and maintained. Thousands of miles of telephone lines had to be dug into the ground, deep enough to guarantee their safety from shellfire. Work began on tunnels stretching underneath the German lines, in which explosive charges were laid, to be detonated prior to the attack. Casualty clearing stations had to be built, vast quantities of water and rations had to be made available, and all of these preparations had to be concealed from the enemy.

The artillery barrage in advance of the attack began on June 24. More than a million and a half shells were fired on to enemy positions, but as the attack grew closer, bad weather pushed zero hour back to 0730 hours on July 1.

**Private Frank Lindlay**
*14th Battalion, York and Lancaster Regiment*
In June 1916, we were rushed to France for a big attack, to liberate the French at Verdun. They were getting a real doing, and we had to make a diversion.

**Corporal Don Murray**
*8th Battalion, King's Own Yorkshire Light Infantry*
They took us from the line, back about ten kilometres, right away from the fighting. There, they had the whole country flagged out, a precise replica of the German lines with little flags. We started practising, ready for the big attack that was to come. And there was all sorts of speculation about the date, no one knew it exactly – in case we were taken prisoner.

**Captain Philip Neame VC**
*Headquarters, 168th Infantry Brigade*
The troops [of 56th Division] did training out of the line before the first of July and this involved marking out the skeletons of the German trenches we were going to attack, and they were rehearsed in forming up and in advancing in attack formation, to attack the German trenches, so that each unit knew intimately where and how it was going to carry out the attack. They were moving in small columns of a few men separated at intervals – that is to say three or four men in a little column, and then a few yards away another little column, and a few yards away another little column. In 1914 and 1915 they had advanced in shoulder-to-shoulder line. As the result of the casualties which occurred from the enemy machine-gun fire, these different formations were taken up to avoid the great casualties.

### Private William Holbrook
#### 4th Battalion, Royal Fusiliers

They had taken photographs of the German trenches on the Somme that we had to take, and we were taken to the coast near Calais, and we dug the trenches exactly as they were in the photographs, and practised attacking them for ten days. There was barbed wire in front of them.

### Private Tom Bracey
#### 9th Battalion, Royal Fusiliers

We had a mock-up battlefield. The trouble was that we were all concentrating on one point. All these men attacking one trench. But when we came to the actual attack, you couldn't do that. There was barbed wire and artillery fire, and it wasn't like the practices.

### Lieutenant Norman Dillon
#### 14th Battalion, Northumberland Fusiliers (attached to 178th Tunnelling Company, Royal Engineers)

I was attached to a tunnelling company, digging mines for the Somme offensive. What I did with them was to *listen*. That meant sitting down in the bowels of the earth, in front of the village of Fricourt. You had to listen to what the Germans were doing. You had to outsmart them. You could easily hear people tapping away long distance through the chalk. If they were making an explosive chamber to put the charge in, you could hear a much more hollow sound and then, following that, you would hear the sinister sliding of bags of explosive into the chamber, and following that, you got out . . . if you could . . . otherwise there would have been no following that . . .

There was someone listening twenty-four hours a day. It was vital to know what the Germans were doing. If you didn't, you lost track of the whole operation. It wasn't very pleasant work. Tunnelling companies lost a great number of people with a very high casualty rate. But one was young, and took it all in one's stride. And at least you were under cover, and out of the range of shellfire.

When I was on relief duty, the Germans blew a small mine, which killed an officer and two men. That was one of the accepted risks. It was all right in the mine shafts. There was a primitive form of ventilation from the surface – a man blowing a bellows down a long pipe leading under the chalk. There was very little support needed, so we didn't need lots of props holding the roof up. The tunnels were about three feet high by two feet wide.

The unit was commanded by a relation of the Duke of Wellington, a very nice chap called Wellesley, who was killed in a stupid way while souvenir hunting, when he tried to pull a rifle grenade to pieces and it blew up in his face. The men of the company were miners. They did the digging. No troops came in to help. The earth had to be carried out in sandbags, because any noise of a truck trundling would give away the situation at once. They brought out all the spoil themselves. Morale was very high amongst the tunnelling company, strangely enough. One of the strangest things was that we were supplied with very nice little $2^1/4$ horsepower twin-engined Douglas motorbikes. Why they were supplied to a tunnelling company, I have not the least idea. I can only assume that the authorities considered the tunnelling companies certain death to belong to, so their morale might improve if they had a motorbike with which to get out of the line and have a drink. I certainly considered it pretty risky. You were bound to feel that death was around the corner.

**Sergeant Charles Quinnell**
*9th Battalion, Royal Fusiliers*
The miners were a rough lot but, by God, they were brave men. They used to mooch into the trench. They had a rifle but they didn't know how to fire it; they weren't supposed to, they were just miners, you see. You could always tell a miner, he never bothered to clean his buttons. He was a miner, he wasn't none of these posh soldiers. We had a sergeant who was a very regimental type of man. His first day in the trenches, two of these miners slummocked along into the front line, walking along with their heads down. They took no notice of us, and we took no notice of them. Anyway, this sergeant didn't know who they were and he yelled out, 'Halt!' – and they didn't attempt to halt, and he gave the order 'Halt!' again – they didn't, so he brought up his rifle – bang, he shot the first man through the head and the bullet went through both of their heads. He killed them stone dead.

**Corporal Don Murray**
*8th Battalion, King's Own Yorkshire Light Infantry*
Before the battle there was a constant procession of guns, guns, guns going up.

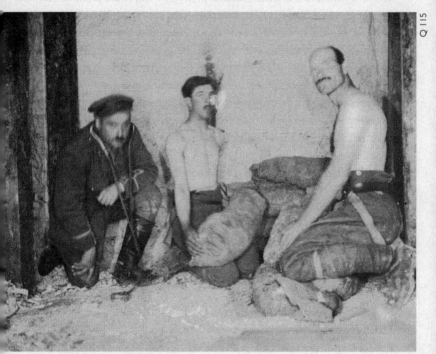

Miners laying a charge in a mine chamber.

The big guns used to lie miles back, but they were bringing them right up into the front. Right up.

## Second Lieutenant Stewart Cleeve
### 36th Siege Battery, Royal Garrison Artillery

We were the first battery to arrive with guns any bigger than 6-inch, and caused a great deal of attention by the higher authorities because of the sheer weight of ammunition which these 8-inch howitzers could produce. But they were improvised howitzers, because they were old 6-inch Mark Is, cut in half and the front half was thrown away. They were monstrous things, and extremely heavy, but the machinery of the guns was very simple and that's why they did so extremely well, and they didn't give nearly as much trouble as some of the more complicated guns that came to appear later on.

We moved to a splendid position near Beaumetz. The guns were dug into an enormously deep bank about ten feet deep by the side of a field. The digging we had to get into that gun position was simply gigantic. We camouflaged it extremely well by putting wire netting over it, threaded with real grass. We had an awful job to manoeuvre the guns into it. We had to manhandle these enormous monsters – they weighed several tons. When they were in position, they were very well concealed – so much so that a French farmer with his cow walked straight into the net, and both fell in. We had the most appalling job getting this beastly cow out of the gun position. The man came out all right … but the cow … However, it was enormous fun. It was one of those delightful moments when you all burst out laughing.

## Signaller Leonard Ounsworth
### 124th Heavy Battery, Royal Garrison Artillery

For our four 60-pounder guns, we accumulated 5,000 rounds of ammunition in holes and pits. We dug some pits, but we'd strewn them out within a radius of a hundred yards behind the battery, so as not to risk too much being hit, in case the enemy started shelling round there. And by the end of the week of bombardment, we'd used up all that ammunition – plus what had been brought up, as well.

It was brought up in wagons to the nearest point on the road, and then we had to carry it from there by hand after dark, to whatever pits we were putting it into. We carried it by slinging two shells together with a stick, and slinging

An 8-inch Mark V howitzer in a camouflaged emplacement.

them over the shoulder. They were very hard on your shoulder, a 60-pounder shell, so we used to put a folded sandbag under our braces, like a shoulder pad, otherwise your shoulder was very sore by the end of the spell.

### Bombardier Harold Lewis
### *240th Brigade, Royal Field Artillery*

On the 18-pounder gun, the officer was Number One and he would shout at the rest of us. The best gun layer, the Number Three, was an NCO. He opened the sights. Number Two was the range drum. Numbers Four and Five were the loaders. Five had to work the 'corrector bar', a brass affair like a slide rule. I was Number Four, and I had to be pretty active, because if we were keeping up a rate of fire, I would have to dispose of the hot charge case as it came out. If the cases were just thrown on the ground, people would fall over them. I would have the next round ready as the breech opened, catch the brass charge case as it came out, throw it aside and load. We could achieve twenty rounds in a minute, but not continuously all day long. The gun had to be laid for each individual round, because the recoil could interfere with the accuracy.

### Corporal Don Murray
### *8th Battalion, King's Own Yorkshire Light Infantry*

We were working like beavers. We were carrying trench mortars that weighed fifty-six pounds each, one on each end of a sandbag, slung over our shoulders, taking them up the communication trench into the front line. Stacks and stacks of them.

### Gunner Norman Tennant
### *1/11th West Riding Howitzer Battery, Royal Field Artillery*

Most of our ammunition was shrapnel shells. A shrapnel shell was a shell with a small charge at the bottom and the body of the shell was filled with small balls; dozens of little pellets. The fuse on a shrapnel shell could be set to explode a given number of seconds after it left the gun. The case of the shell itself got very much thinner towards the top – so when the explosive charge at the bottom went off, it threw all the pellets forward, rather like the shot out of a shotgun. The idea was to set the fuse so that the whole thing exploded short of the advancing infantry. So that all these pellets would spread out and cause death and destruction.

An 18-pounder gun team in action.

## Captain Philip Neame VC
### Headquarters, 168th Infantry Brigade

All the German trenches were defended with a thick belt of barbed wire in front of them, and in the early attacks in the war this barbed wire had to be cut either by hand or by what were known as Bangalore torpedoes [twenty-foot long steel pipes filled with explosives, placed in position by hand]. Well, then it was discovered that shrapnel shells – set to burst very low – would blow lanes through this barbed wire. So artillery fire became the recognised way of cutting the wire. They would cut a series of lanes through the barbed wire through which the infantry could get.

## Henry Holdstock
### 6 Squadron, Royal Naval Air Service

We were ordered through to take up a spotting position for a whole week before the battle started. We lay in a little valley there – a slight proclivity in the chalk, and observed quite successfully for some time. On the eve of the battle, the night before they were to go over at dawn the next morning, the combined armaments were crashing all together. The whole earth trembled. The line that was holding down the balloon was shaking. You could feel the vibrations coming up through the earth, through your limbs, through your body. You were all of a tremor, just by artillery fire only. Not so much from the crashing of the shells, as the gunfire from the rear, all concentrating in one wild blast of gunfire. It was shattering. The whole ground trembled, and you felt sorry for anyone within half a mile of wherever they were piling it. It must have been terrible for them.

## Lieutenant Cecil Lewis
### 3 Squadron, Royal Flying Corps

Flying through the bombardment was terrifying. We were flying down to about one thousand feet. And when you went right over the lines, you were midway between our guns firing and where their shells were falling, and during that period the intensity of the bombardment was such that it was really like a sort of great, broad swathe of dirty-looking cotton wool laid over the ground. So close were the shell bursts, and so continuous, that it wasn't just a puff here and a puff there, it was a continuous band. And when you looked at the other side, particularly when the light was failing, the whole of the ground

British artillery bombarding German trenches at Beaumont Hamel.

A German trench hit by artillery fire.

was just like a veil of sequins that were flashing and flashing and flashing. And each sequin was a gun.

The artillery had orders – we were told – not to fire when an aeroplane was in their sights. They cut it pretty fine. Because one used to fly along the front on those patrols, and your aeroplane was flung up by a shell which had just gone underneath and missed you by two or three feet. Or flung down by a shell that had gone over the top. And this was continuous, so the machine was continually bucketing and jumping as if it was in a gale. But in fact it was shells. You didn't see them: they were going much too fast. But this was really terrifying.

### Corporal George Ashurst
### 1st Battalion, Lancashire Fusiliers

It'll never be seen or felt again. I walked along our front line, looking at the German lines, and I could see the bursts of the shells, all over, big ones in the distance. We could see the dirt from the sandbags, dancing up and down, and when you turned around, you would see flashes all along our skyline. Hundreds of them. You couldn't see the guns – just the flashes. And the noise was like a hundred trains over the top of your head, all at once. I thought the bombardment would be a success. I thought it would shift Jerry. He couldn't stand up to something like this! Well, he didn't have to! He had dugouts thirty feet deep!

### Stephen K. Westmann
### German Army Medical Corps

For seven days and nights we were under incessant bombardment. Day and night. The shells, heavy and light ones, came upon us. Our dugouts crumbled. They fell upon us and we had to dig ourselves and our comrades out. Sometimes we found them suffocated, sometimes smashed to pulp. Soldiers in the bunkers became hysterical. They wanted to run out, and fights developed to keep them in the comparative safety of our deep bunkers. Even the rats became hysterical. They came into our flimsy shelters to seek refuge from this terrific artillery fire.

Q 1208

Looking towards Thiepval in the early morning.

**Private Pat Kennedy**
*18th Battalion, Manchester Regiment*

We were told by our officer that we were to take part in the attack, and the men were excited. Everybody thought it would be a walkover. The bombardment was so heavy, and the men were in excellent spirits. They were all volunteers, and they were looking to beating the Germans, and finishing the war quickly. No one believed there could be a defeat. Everyone was eager, and anxious to go forward.

**Private W. J. Senescall**
*11th Battalion, Suffolk Regiment*

A couple of days before the attack, we were waiting to go up. We were in a field, with a hedge between us and the next people, and all of a sudden a rifle shot went off. We didn't take much notice. We thought someone was cleaning his rifle, and let one off, but then somebody said, 'Someone's shot himself in the knee!' We didn't trouble to go through and look, but a few minutes later, through the gate, came this chap being carried on a stretcher, with two men marching each side of him with bayonets fixed. It confirmed that he'd shot himself through the knee. I've often wondered what happened to him.

**Corporal George Ashurst**
*1st Battalion, Lancashire Fusiliers*

We were issued with the new steel helmets before the battle. I didn't like them. They were damned heavy and uncomfortable things to put on your head. They only just fitted and fellows thought they'd very soon rub them bald. I thought the same. I wore it. I had to. But you got quite used to them in a short time.

**Lieutenant Norman Dillon**
*14th Battalion, Northumberland Fusiliers*

I was standing in a reserve trench, when a man came up to me with a peculiar-looking helmet. It turned out to be one of the new steel ones. 'What's that?' I asked, and I put it on – as one does with a new hat. At that very moment, a shell burst overhead and knocked the helmet off, putting a great dent in it, but leaving me unharmed. I was very grateful for that helmet – even if it was a very uncomfortable thing to wear and, at first, a very strange thing to look at.

They looked like straw boaters made in steel, and they were very uncomfortable because they didn't sit on your brow like a straw hat does; they pressed your hair down on your scalp and made you want to scratch the whole time. There were plenty of reasons to scratch in the trenches, without having to add to them.

### Private Tom Easton
### 21st Battalion, Northumberland Fusiliers

During the build-up to July 1, a carrying party was caught in shellfire whilst carrying poison gas. One of the gas cylinders was fractured, and before they could do anything, seventeen of these men were gassed, and eventually died. My battalion had to go out into Albert cemetery, and dig the graves for these men. It was a very heavy job, because it was chalk subsoil, and when you've got three foot of soil off, the rest is solid chalk. But we got the graves down to the depth required, and then the bodies were brought, and the priest did his work and we laid the bodies down. And I looked across and I saw one of my men, sitting crying. I went across. 'What's the matter?' He said, 'I can't do it, with his face there, looking up at me!' So I said, 'Turn around. I'll cover his face up, and you can get on with the job.' 'Thank you very much,' he said, 'from the bottom of my heart.'

### Corporal Harry Fellows
### 12th Battalion, Northumberland Fusiliers

One night, just before July 1, there was supposed to be a raid, and we were all standing to, in the trench, but nothing happened. At stand down, at daylight, the lance corporal who was in charge said he wanted to go to the latrines, so off he went. I was looking though a periscope, over the top, when I heard somebody behind me and I thought the corporal had come back. I turned round – and I saw a German. He had a white bib on his front and back, and a Maltese cross in luminous paint. He had two stick bombs on each side of his belt, a dagger and a revolver, and the only thing he said was, 'Cigarette!' I gave him a cigarette, and I never thought of disarming him. He took the bombs out of his belt, put them on the fire-step, sat down and I sat beside him, and both of us sat there smoking. Some of the other chaps came into the trench, and said, 'Who's this?' He couldn't speak English, we couldn't speak German, and all we understood was that he pointed to himself and said, '*La guerre kaput!*' meaning the war was finished for him. He showed us a photo of his wife and two kiddies. He gave me his revolver, he gave two of the other lads a bomb each and another lad got his revolver. Shortly afterwards the sergeant-major ran up with his revolver; the word had gone round that a German had captured us, and we were being held hostage in the trench! Then our captain arrived, and he took the German away, and we had to hand over our souvenirs.

Afterwards, our battalion intelligence officer told me that this German had joined a specially trained unit for raiding trenches. They used to lay tapes out across no-man's-land before they made a raid, but on this occasion the tape had been moved, and his raiding party had come to the wrong part of the wire. He'd found a zigzag in our wire, he'd got into the trench and he'd stood at the end of a communication trench for an hour, waiting for daylight, and he never saw a soul. And then he came up behind me. He'd said that the Germans knew there was going to be an attack on June 30.

### Private Albert Day
#### 1/4th Battalion, Gloucestershire Regiment
We knew something terrible was going to happen; the Germans knew it as well. My two cousins sorted me out. We were out of the line, and we had an hour or two together. One cousin was a tough young chap, a strong, healthy kid, but his brother Fred was a bit more weak. We spent most of the evening together, and had a few drinks. When they were leaving to go back to their battalions, Fred shook my hand and said, 'You will never see me again, Bert.' 'You mustn't talk like that, Fred,' I said. 'I feel it!' he said.

### Corporal George Ashurst
#### 1st Battalion, Lancashire Fusiliers
Our battalion was formed into a three-sided square outside our village – and up came the general. He was on horseback, with one or two lagging behind him, and he started to make a speech; he said that we were going to make this attack. And he knew that we would do our duty, as we always had done before. He said that there'd be no Germans left to combat us when we got over there. The barrage and the shelling would be so terrific, the guns would blaze day and night for a whole week. He said that if you placed all the guns side by side, wheel to wheel, they'd stretch from the English Channel to the

The 1st Battalion, Lancashire Fusiliers being addressed by General de Lisle on June 29. One of these men is Corporal George Ashurst.

Alps. He made it sound like it was going to be a walkover. You can imagine what all the lads were saying round about. They were cursing during the speech: 'Shut up, yer bastard!' Our officer would turn round and whisper, 'Shut up!' But it didn't make no difference. The men all kept swearing and cursing: 'I wish the bloody horse would kick him to death!'

**Private Donald Cameron**
*12th Battalion, York and Lancaster Regiment*
On June 30, the Corps Commander, General Hunter-Weston, made a speech, saying we were superior to the Germans in arms, artillery and everything else. He said that by the time our artillery had finished bombarding their trench and we went over, we'd be more or less on a picnic. What a lot of bullshit he talked. After that, the regimental band played, 'When You Come to an End of a Perfect Day'. As Larry Grayson says, 'What a gay day!'

**Corporal H. Tansley**
*9th Battalion, York and Lancaster Regiment*
On the last day of June, we marched up. We knew that a lot of us would be casualties on the morrow, and it was interesting to see the different response from different soldiers. I remember one man who walked off on his own, communicating with himself. He seemed moody and I tried to cheer him up. Others tried to put on a form of jollification. When the march started towards the line, it was all happy: singing 'A Long Way to Tipperary', biscuit tins being hammered, all to keep up the spirits.

**Lieutenant Norman Dillon**
*14th Battalion, Northumberland Fusiliers (attached to 178th Tunnelling Company Royal Engineers)*
The mines were blown on the morning of July 1, and I was within half a mile when they went up. It was tremendous. The craters were eighty yards across. I believe the shock was heard in London.

**Lieutenant Cecil Lewis**
*3 Squadron, Royal Flying Corps*
When the zero hour was to come, we were flying over La Boisselle salient, and suddenly the whole earth heaved, and up from the ground came what looked

like two enormous cypress trees. It was the silhouettes of great, dark cone-shaped lifts of earth, up to three, four, five thousand feet. And we watched this, and then a moment later we struck the repercussion wave of the blast and it flung us right the way backwards, over on one side.

**Corporal Don Murray**
*8th Battalion, King's Own Yorkshire Light Infantry*
New drafts had come out from England, young boys who'd never been in action, and they made us up to our full strength. And we were all in dugouts, ready to go over.

**Major Alfred Irwin**
*8th Battalion, East Surrey Regiment*
I was young and optimistic. I didn't think much about the future. I took it for granted that the wire would be cut, and that we would massacre the Boche in their front line.

The explosion of the mine at Hawthorn Redoubt on the morning of July 1.

# July 1, 1916

> *I heard the Germans calling from their trenches,*
> *'Come on Tommy! We are waiting for you!'*

On the first morning of the Battle of the Somme, British troops prepared to attack along a fourteen-mile stretch of line. Almost half a million soldiers of Sir Henry Rawlinson's Fourth Army were ready to carry out the main attacks, whilst men of Sir Edmund Allenby's Third Army prepared to carry out diversionary attacks, and Sir Hubert Gough's Reserve Army stood ready to capitalise on a breakthrough.

At 0700 hours, the British artillery bombardment reached a staggering crescendo. Over the next hour, almost a quarter of a million shells were fired across the entire fourteen-mile front, whilst seventeen massive mines were detonated under German positions. The largest mine, near La Boisselle, shot earth four thousand feet into the air, leaving a crater – which became known as the Lochnagar Crater – almost a hundred feet deep, and 450 feet across. At half-past seven – *zero hour* – British troops went over the top along the entire front.

### Lieutenant Ulick Burke
#### 2nd Battalion, Devonshire Regiment
Immediately the daylight came, the men had their rum ration. The quartermaster was always good on those occasions. And then I gave the men my last orders. They had ladders – two bits of wood nailed together with three or four cross-pieces – to help them to climb out of the trench. And five minutes

before the time of going over . . . this was the worst time for the troops. That's when their feelings might break.

**Private Albert Day**
*1/4th Battalion, Gloucestershire Regiment*
They gave us rum; I suppose that made it a little bit better. The fact that the others were there kept you going – but I had a terrible feeling; I thought I was going to have an accident in my pants.

**Private Basil Farrer**
*3rd Battalion, Green Howards*
We had got the ladders ready, and next to me was a sergeant, who had the Distinguished Conduct Medal, and he was rubbing a piece of earth, a piece of clay, between his feet.

**Lieutenant Ulick Burke**
*2nd Battalion, Devonshire Regiment*
I shouted down the left and right of my sector, 'Five minutes to go!' Then four minutes, then three minutes, two minutes, half a minute, then, 'Ten seconds . . . get ready . . . Over!'

**Private Reg Coldridge**
*2nd Battalion, Devonshire Regiment*
When I went over, I didn't really think of anything. I just had to go. That was all.

**Stephen K. Westmann**
*German Army Medical Corps*
For seven days and seven nights our German soldiers had had nothing to eat, nothing to drink, but constant fire, shell after shell bursting upon us. And then the British Army went over the top. Our gunners crawled out of their bunkers, redded eyes, sunken eyes, dirty, full of blood. And they opened terrific fire . . .

A German machine gun perched on a parapet.

A patrol crawling towards German trenches on the morning of July 1.

## GOMMECOURT TO BEAUMONT HAMEL

In the most northerly sector of the front, two divisions of the British Third Army attacked the Gommecourt salient. This was a diversionary assault, intended to distract German artillery and infantry from the main thrust of the attack further south, where the Fourth Army was attacking the German lines between the villages of Serre and Montebaun.

The 18th Battalion, Durham Light Infantry, the 16th Battalion, West Yorkshire Regiment (The Bradford Pals) and the 15th Battalion, West Yorkshire Regiment (The Leeds Pals) suffered heavy losses whilst attacking Serre village. The 12th Battalion, York and Lancaster Regiment (the Sheffield Pals) and the 11th Battalion, East Lancashire Regiment (the Accrington Pals) were also ripped to shreds in the attack. A few men of the Accrington Pals managed to enter the village, but were forced to retreat. The 14th Battalion, York and Lancaster Regiment attempted unsuccessfully to reinforce the attack. Further south, the 1/8th Battalion, Royal Warwickshire Regiment entered the Heidenkopf Crater and the German supporting trenches, but these were abandoned the following day. Overall, in this sector, no ground was taken.

**Private James Snaylham**
*11th Battalion, East Lancashire Regiment*
I went over the top at 0730 and my next-door pal was killed straight away. I kept going and going, being the youngest, and daftest I suppose. I got as far as the Jerry wire, before a shell exploded and a lump went through my leg. I laid there until seven o'clock in the evening. I crawled back into every shell-hole I came to, and there were lads wounded, shouting, 'Send somebody! There are wounded here!' and eventually I got back to our trench.

**Private Herbert Hall**
*12th Battalion, York and Lancaster Regiment*
I went over carrying a full kit, blanket in the pack, a rifle, helmet, a full-size navvy's pick across my shoulders, the pack on my back, two hundred rounds of ammunition and twenty Mills bombs. I could have been a mule, you know, not a human being! We had to jump out of the trenches with that, and not

only did I carry my own twenty bombs, but I collected two bags of twenty each from one fellow that was wounded, and another that had come down with shell shock. So I went in with sixty bombs. I was a moving arsenal! A bit of shrapnel would have shot me into the clouds!

I didn't get across; I got about forty yards over the top. There was nobody with me. All the others had dropped down or were wounded, so I dropped into a shell-hole. About mid-afternoon, I saw one or two people crawling in, so I went with them. I couldn't fight the German army alone, could I? They didn't intend me to, did they? Some made it to the German wire, and they made all sorts of cries of pain and suffering.

### Private Donald Cameron
### 12th Battalion, York and Lancaster Regiment

The first wave went over at 0720. They lay down about a hundred yards in front of our own barbed wire. Then the second wave went over, and lay down about thirty yards behind them. During this time, there was high explosives, shrapnel, everything you can imagine, coming over. Terrific hurtling death. It was soul destroying, but I wasn't frightened: I was impatient, I wanted to get moving.

The night before, they'd laid tapes, showing us the way to the cuts in the German wire. But when we went over, these tapes were missing, so we headed off in what we thought was the right direction. We'd been told that we had to walk at arm's length from each other, and that's how we started. But not for long. When we saw people dropping like ninepins on either side, we bent double, and in the end we started crawling. After a while, three of us, and Sergeant Gallimore, got down into a shell-hole. It must have been about eight o'clock. The firing went on, and we kept peeping up, looking over the top to check, and the bloody Germans were sniping our wounded. They were even firing at the dead. They couldn't see us in our shell-hole. I must have prayed a dozen times. I used to go to church when I was a lad, but I prayed more in that shell-hole than I ever prayed in church.

### Corporal A. Wood
### 16th Battalion, West Yorkshire Regiment

The Pals were the finest soldiers that you've ever seen. And we were all friends. About ten minutes before we climbed out of the trench, we were issued with a very strong dixie of rum, out of a stone bottle. We were told that the wire had been cut in front of our front line, that there'd be no difficulty at all for us to get through and that there wouldn't be a German within miles. We went up the ladder, on top of the parapet, and immediately anyone appeared, the blast of the machine guns knocked them back into the trench. There were Germans sat on the parapet of their trench with machine guns, mowing us down. In fact, I don't think half a dozen of our people got beyond our front line, never mind to the German front line.

### Private Frank Raine
#### 18th Battalion, Durham Light Infantry

Oh, my God! The ground in front – it was just like heavy rain; that was machine-gun bullets. Up above, there were these great big 5.9-inch shrapnel shells going off. Broomhead and I went over the top together. We walked along a bit. A terrific bang and a great black cloud of smoke above us. I felt a knock on my hip which I didn't take much notice of. I turned round, and Broomhead had gone. I walked on and I could not see a soul of any description – either in front of or behind me. I presume they got themselves tucked into shell-holes. I thought, 'Well, I'm not going on there by myself,' and I turned round and came back.

### Private Reginald Glenn
#### 12th Battalion, York and Lancaster Regiment

We didn't know about the attack until the day before. We went into the line that night, and we relieved the regiment that was in. By now, everybody knew we were going in to attack, and we all had our big overcoats, and our haversacks with rations in. I had my rifle, and a telephone, and a mile of wire as well. Other people were carrying wire cutters and digging equipment. Actually, I wasn't meant to go over, but one man, a university student, got shell shock, and he dropped out on the way into the line. So I was detailed to take his place. I was supposed to reach the German lines, and go through there into Serre village.

The signal to attack was a whistle. The officers were the first to jump up – and they only had revolvers. We had a creeping barrage that was supposed to be creeping forward as we moved forward. The first line went, and then they all lay down. I thought they must have had different orders to us – we'd been told to walk. But the reason they lay down was because they'd been shot. They were mown down like corn. Then we went forward – and the same thing happened. I didn't know what was happening around me. There were gaps in our wire, where it had been cut, that were marked by white tape on the ground. We were told to walk and to carry the rifle at high port, but I was just trying to find my way through the shell-holes. I didn't get as far as the British wire. There was so much pandemonium. I lay down, but soon we all got orders to get back to our trenches.

**Private Frank Lindlay**
*14th Battalion, York and Lancaster Regiment*
At the start, we were lined up ready to go over, at the whistle, at half seven. A huge mine went off to the right. It went off too soon, and it gave the Germans a chance to come up out of their deep dugouts and concentrate on us. I think they were very surprised to see us walking. In our orders, we had to walk across. We had been led to believe by 'higher-ups' that the big bombardment, over the days and nights, had obliterated the enemy. But we knew it hadn't because their positions were so strong. Their dugouts were way down under the parapets of the trenches, and they couldn't be reached by artillery fire. All they did was to wait down there until our barrage lifted, and then they came up to have some target practice at us. We were held up by huge coils of barbed wire, and in the odd gap that we made for, we were greeted by their heavy machine guns. There was no question that we could get through to them. Whole lines of our lads were mown down one after the other, and we were shifting from shell-hole to shell-hole, trying to pick one or two Germans off their front line.

**Private Arthur Pearson**
*15th Battalion, West Yorkshire Regiment*
At zero hour, everybody climbed out of the trenches. Two platoons formed the first wave. Every man climbed out of the trench at the officers' whistles, and not a man hesitated. I was lucky; I was at a part of the trench where the parapet had been battered down, and when I ran out of the trench, I was under the hail of bullets that were whizzing over my head. Most of our fellows were killed, kneeling on the parapet. There was nobody coming forward with me – only one man – and the reserves had been shelled in our lines and blown to smithereens.

**Private Ralph Miller**
*1/8th Battalion, Royal Warwickshire Regiment*

We got to the point that we thought the quicker the bloody whistles go, the sooner we go over the top, the better. We always said to one another, 'Well, it's a two-to-one chance. We either get bowled over, or we get wounded and go home. It's one of the two.' We got so browned off with the waiting. To the extent that you didn't care what happened. In fact, I was pleased to go over – I wanted a Blighty wound. You can just imagine, there were hundreds of fellows, shouting and swearing, going over with fixed bayonets. We had no chance of getting across no-man's-land, there was so much barbed wire. Of my football club from back home, we all went over together, and ten out of twelve of us were killed.

**Private Stanley Bewshire**
*11th Battalion, East Lancashire Regiment*

When we got into the German front-line trench, there was nobody there, they had gone. There were only dead men lying about. I moved forward. I hadn't gone very far before I got a whack on the head. I didn't know what had hit me. I went down. How long I lay there I didn't know, but it must have been in the afternoon when I had came round. Whoever did it had left me, taken my gun and gone. When I came round, all was quiet.

I got up, moved back into no-man's-land, and I'd got about fifty yards across, under fire, when I found a machine gun. I picked up this gun and jumped down into a shell-hole. I gave the gun a go, to see if it was in order, and I saw that right in front of me were the German communication trenches. I lay in the shell-hole for about half an hour and then some Germans came out – about ten or fifteen of them. I was right in front of them. After two or three bursts, they turned back – what was left of them. I thought now was a good chance for me to move.

So I picked up the gun and went about fifty yards. On my way, bullets were flying all over me. I had a marvellous escape. One bullet went through my haversack, breaking all my day's ration. It went through my water bottle and all my water started spilling out. Then, shrapnel hit my sack and started hitting my equipment, and it broke off.

**Private Herbert Hall**
*12th Battalion, York and Lancaster Regiment*

I heard the Germans calling from their trenches, 'Come on Tommy! We are waiting for you!' It was weird. In perfect English. I killed a few, of course, and I took a prisoner. He walked into us in no-man's-land. I brought him back and walked him to the back lines, passing the whole lot of the British Army lying in stretchers, dead bodies, and all the rest of it. I don't know what happened to him afterwards. I think somebody might have shot him.

And afterwards, a general came to see us. I know his name and I won't mention it. He said, 'Did any of you people see anything meritorious?' There wasn't a single sound. There was only about seventy of us, and that included the first line reinforcements. Not a sound. We thought it was a very unnecessary question. And, of course, to insult us, they awarded the medals to the colonel's runner and the senior stretcher-bearer.

**Sergeant A. S. Durrant**
*18th Battalion, Durham Light Infantry*

I reached the German trenches, but I was wounded, and I saw the entrance to a dugout. So I dragged myself along to the steps of the dugout, and I thought, 'Let's see if I can get in there...' I dragged myself to the steps of the dugout, and I managed – somehow – to get myself into a half-sitting, half-lying position, on the steps leading down to the dugout. Suddenly, the mouth of the dugout fell in. A high-explosive shell must have burst very nearby, and I was thrown into a doubled-up position. I didn't seem to be hurt any further, but the entrance down to the dugout was blocked so I dragged myself out and rested in the open. This went on until the evening, and I gradually dragged myself in the right direction, to the British lines, and eventually I crawled to safety. And, on arriving at what I thought was safety, I saw an old college friend of mine, nicknamed 'Whiskers'. I shouted, 'Whiskers!' He came along. 'Hello! What are you doing here?' He was in the Royal Army Military Corps, and he took charge of me, put me on to a stretcher and conveyed me to a medical shelter.

**Private Donald Cameron**
*12th Battalion, York and Lancaster Regiment*

At midday, the sun was hot and I fell asleep. You've got to remember that we'd been up all night, and we'd been on working parties for a fortnight before that, digging trenches, filling sandbags. We were dead tired. When it was dark, we found our way back to our own trenches, where there was a roll-call. Out of the eight hundred that went over, only a hundred answered. The rest were either wounded or killed. At the time, our parents used to send out food parcels, wrapped in cloth. So there were parcels for eight hundred men waiting for us, to be shared amongst a hundred.

**Private Frank Lindlay**
*14th Battalion, York and Lancaster Regiment*
As we were making for the gaps between the shell-holes, we were covered by their fire. They opened up with whizz-bangs, and one hit us. I was wounded by a piece of shell through my right thigh. I managed to drag myself down to a dressing station behind the lines. On the way down, I could see our reserve trenches were full of dead and wounded. The Germans had lifted their barrage as we'd gone over, and all our reserve troops were decimated at the back. Everything was quiet as I went past. When I got to the dressing station, they gave me a shot for tetanus, wrapped me up and bunged me in an ambulance that went to Étaples, where they operated. They yanked the piece of shell – and my trousers – out of my leg, and I was dispatched back to Blighty.

**Private Arthur Pearson**
*15th Battalion, West Yorkshire Regiment*
The sergeant decided that as the attack was finished, we'd go back and try and get into our own line. We climbed out of a shell-hole and made a dash, and my rifle got caught on the wire. It stopped there. I didn't have time to get it free, and we got back in the line. I noticed one of our chaps, Jim, laying in the trench with a severed leg, and a block of timber across it which was acting as a tourniquet, stopping the bleeding. I ran down the trench, looking for stretcher-bearers, and I bumped into an officer with half-a-dozen men. He stopped me, and wanted to know where I was going. I said, 'I'm going for help! There's Jim, there, with his leg off!' 'Never mind him!' said the officer. 'Fall in with my men!' So I picked a rifle up, wiped it and fell in. But when I got my first chance, I lost him. Well, Jim was found and carried out, and sent to Blighty, and he made it through!

**Private Ralph Miller**
*1/8th Battalion, Warwickshire Regiment*

There were so many falling. I was hit by a shell blast. I didn't know a thing from that moment on until I was back in Birmingham. I don't know who picked me up and saved me. I was hit by shrapnel in my hand, my arm and I lost two fingers on my right hand. When I came round at the University Hospital in Birmingham, I was told that my parents had been to see me. I was in a nice comfortable bed – but it was the shock of my life: 'Where am I? What am I doing here?' I asked the military orderly. 'You're in Brum,' he said, and I shook his hand.

**Private Stanley Bewshire**
*11th Battalion, East Lancashire Regiment*

I came to Serre, and there was Colonel Rickman and Lieutenant McAlpine. They said, 'Have you just come over, my lad?' I said, 'Yes.' The colonel said, 'Was that you firing over there? Are they Germans?' I said, 'Yes sir, they were just coming down that communication trench, and I felt they were going to counter-attack.' He said, 'You did very well. We've been watching you. Take his name and number, McAlpine!' The colonel then told me to move down the line. Later on, when I was in a Canadian hospital, a sergeant from the battalion came to see me. He said, 'It's come up on battalion orders – you've got the Military Medal.'

**Private Reginald Glenn**
*12th Battalion, York and Lancaster Regiment*

I fell back, but the British line was smashed up by artillery fire, and we fell back to the support line. Only twenty of us got back to the support line. And then, at noon, we received a message from divisional headquarters, telling us that we had to do it again. *Twenty of us* had to make another attack on the German lines. We were shocked, like sheep who didn't know what was going on. That order was countermanded – we couldn't have gone, there weren't enough of us. And we had no idea what was happening anywhere else. There was no communication.

That night we went out, and if we heard anybody crying or moaning, we helped them back into our lines. The stretcher-bearers were working, but they couldn't cope on their own. There was no firing from the Germans, and we did a lot of that, all night.

**Private James Snaylham**
*11th Battalion, East Lancashire Regiment*
As I crawled into the communication trench, a sniper fired and it whizzed past my face. It was a miracle. Anyway I crawled on and on until I come to a field dressing station, where I was told, 'I don't know what to do with you! Look at all this lot wounded!' He said, 'I will take you on to the main road, and probably an ambulance will come along and pick you up.' Well, eventually an ambulance did come along and it was full, but they took me in and it took me to a big chateau. There was a tremendous drama there – it was full of wounded. So they carried me in and they operated on me – one man holding my arms and another holding my legs, while they pulled the shrapnel out.

**Corporal A. Wood**
*16th Battalion, West Yorkshire Regiment*
I got a field dressing on my wound, and then I made my way – as best as I could – back to the railhead, which was a miniature railway. I lay there for two or three days without anyone coming near me, because the train that was supposed to take us to the hospital had broken down. Eventually, it did come and we got down to the Canadian General Hospital in Boulogne. We all got nicely tucked up in bed, and then the Zeppelins came over and bombed the hospital out of existence. After that we were all shipped back to Blighty. Half the soldiers wouldn't have got back home if it hadn't been for the Zeppelins; they'd have been patched up, and sent back up the line.

**Sergeant A. S. Durrant**
*18th Battalion, Durham Light Infantry*
It took me over a week to reach England, and when we arrived at Bristol station we were laid out on the platform and the good Bristol folk came and gave us cigarettes, tobacco and sweets. I was conveyed to Southmead Hospital in Bristol and dumped on to a nice clean bed in exactly the same state as I'd been in France, all covered with mud and crammed full of lice. A nurse came to take off my clothes, and I was heartily sorry for her, having to drag those clothes off me and make me reasonably clean. For two or three days after, the odd louse kept finding its way into the bedclothes.

## Beaumont Hamel to Thiepval

Further south, the 1st Newfoundland Regiment was the only Dominion regiment advancing on the first morning of the battle. Out of 810 Newfoundlanders who attacked the village of Beaumont Hamel, only sixty-eight men – and no officers – escaped serious injury. A hundred bombers of the 1st Battalion, Lancashire Fusiliers advanced to a sunken road in no-man's-land, but were forced to retreat. Men of the 36th (Ulster) Division attacked and captured Schwaben Redoubt, and made further advances into German territory, but fell back under 'friendly' British artillery fire.

**Corporal George Ashurst**
*1st Battalion, Lancashire Fusiliers*

Before the attack, you couldn't move in the trenches, they were so packed with men. They were grumbling and grousing; some were trying to be brave, and joking. There were all sorts. It went quiet, and then it was time to go. When I stepped on top of our trench, there was a corporal lying there, hit by a whizz-bang, and all his shoulder was gone. Blown away. And he looked up at me, and he said, 'Go on! Get the bastards!' I said, 'OK,' and buggered off as fast as I could. There were bullets everywhere; there was gunsmoke; you could hear a bullet hitting someone, and you'd hear him groan and go down. I was running fast, zigzagging. All I was thinking, was, 'I've got to get forward!' Keeping my head down. I was expecting to feel a bullet any second.

I came to the sunken road, 150 yards from our trench, and I dived into it. You couldn't see the German trenches from it. There were others in there, including the colonel, and he said, 'Every fit man, over the top again! Come with me!' He went over the top, and out, and I followed him; whether a lot of others did, I don't know, but I ran on and I realised that there was nobody with me. I was by myself. I got a bit frightened and I dropped into a shell-hole. I lay down and I looked back towards our front line. I was looking at our wounded, and I saw one or two of them getting up and trying to get back, and then dropping. They were being shot *again*, as they tried to move.

As I was lying there, I had a drink out of my water bottle. I knew that Fritz couldn't touch me – unless he threw a bomb. On the left, I could see that the Royal Fusiliers were running back to their trenches. I thought Jerry was counter-attacking, and I thought, 'What about me? If Jerry comes *here*, I'm for it!' So I made my mind up to move – bloody quick. I got up and dashed down the slope, and dived down into the sunken road once more. I was safe again and I found a few other men in there. We started to make a bit of a barrier against the slope.

Later on in the day, a message came across, saying, 'One officer, one NCO, twenty-five men ONLY to man the sunken road.' There was only the one officer in there, and I was a corporal, and we put a few men at either end of the road and some others in the middle of the road. Everything quietened down and we stayed there all night. The stretcher-bearers were very busy that night, though, and the wounded were cleared by the morning.

As dawn came, I was against the barrier and I heard voices coming from the other side. I stood up to have a look and I saw three Jerries a hundred yards away, stood in a ditch. I shouted, 'Jerries!' and I fired at the middle one. He disappeared. I don't know if I hit him, but we never saw them again. The officer came down to see what the trouble was – and I told him. He said, 'Right, lads, dig in now! Jerry's going to bloody well let us have it!' And he was right. Jerry started on us with *minenwerfers*. We could see them coming, and one dropped right on the body of men in the middle of the road, killing three of them, wounding the others. He dropped one on us – but it was a dud. Six yards past us – we were expecting it to blow us up – but it never went up. He dropped several more, but we had no more casualties.

As soon as it was dark, another messenger came, with word to evacuate the sunken road. So we ran back to our lines as fast as we could. We ended up back in the front line. And there were only a few men there. I didn't see any officers. Eventually, an officer came and picked us up, and we followed him down the communication trench, and he told us to bed down for the night. That night, the officer gave me an order to go back out into no-man's-land, to collect what rifles and identity discs I could, but I never did it. I'd had enough of no-man's-land. And I never saw the officer again.

### Second Lieutenant W. J. Brockman
### 15th Battalion, Lancashire Fusiliers

One fellow asked me to shoot him. He was half in and half out of a shell-hole, hopelessly wounded. But I didn't do it. I put his rifle on the ground and put his tin hat on top of it, hoping that somebody would find him.

A wounded man is brought in along the sunken road at Beaumont Hamel on July 1.

A wounded man of the 1st Battalion, Lancashire Fusiliers is tended in the trenches.

**Private Harold Startin**
*1st Battalion, Leicestershire Regiment*

We had to bury the Newfoundlanders at Beaumont Hamel. If they were lying face downwards it wasn't too bad but if they were lying with their face up, and the sun had been shining on them, the faces were smothered in flies and blue-bottles and it was enough to make you sick. There were no graves dug for them – they were put into shallows. You might get three, four, five or six into the crater and then you shovel down earth with a spade, and cover the bodies up. There were no crosses put there. We had no wood, we had no nails, we had no hammer. So they were just covered up and left.

Yes – death had no horrors then. Oh death, where is thy sting?

## THIEPVAL TO MAMETZ

South of the Schwaben Redoubt, the German-held villages of Thiepval, Ovillers, La Boisselle and Fricourt all resisted the British advance. The 8th Battalion, King's Own Yorkshire Light Infantry, starting from just outside Authuille Wood, managed to reach the third line of German trenches, but was beaten back. The 9th Battalion, York and Lancaster Regiment, following in support, was cut apart by machine-gun fire from Thiepval Spur; 423 men of the battalion were killed.

The 21st Battalion, Northumberland Fusiliers advanced to the north of the Lochnagar Crater – created by the explosion of the La Boisselle mine – and moved towards the village of La Boisselle, but was not able to hold its position.

The 10th Battalion, Lincolnshire Regiment, and the 11th Battalion, Suffolk Regiment, advanced alongside the crater, but were unable to make significant progress towards the German lines.

To the south, the 10th Battalion, West Yorkshire Regiment initially took six hundred yards of German front-line trench. However, its new position, on a down slope two hundred yards from Fricourt village, exposed the battalion to unrelenting machine-gun fire, and within two hours more than half of the battalion was dead.

## Lieutenant A. Dickinson
### 10th Battalion, Lincolnshire Regiment

At seven-thirty that morning, the ground rumbled, the trenches trembled, the earth rose up in the air and the explosion of the mine blackened out the sun.

## Corporal Don Murray
### 8th Battalion, King's Own Yorkshire Light Infantry

The previous night, at about 12pm, each dugout had a gallon bottle of rum put into the dugout. Nearly every man was drunk. *Blind drunk.* I thought to myself, this looks to me like a sacrifice. I never touched any. I determined to keep my head. Just as well I did.

At half past seven, Mr Morris – the officer with the lisp – pulled out his revolver, blew his whistle, and said, 'Over!' As he said it, a bullet hit him straight between the eyes and killed him. I went over with all the other boys. The barbed wire that was supposed to have been demolished had only been cut in places. Just a gap here, a gap there, and everyone made for the gaps in order to get through. There were supposed to be no Germans at all in the front line – but they were down in the ground in their concrete shelters. They just fired at the breeches in the wire and mowed us down. It seemed to me, eventually, I was the only man left. I couldn't see anybody at all. All I could see were men lying dead, men screaming, men on the barbed wire with their bowels hanging down, shrieking, and I thought, 'What can I do?' I was alone in a hell of fire and smoke and stink.

## Corporal Wally Evans
### 8th Battalion, King's Own Yorkshire Light Infantry

When we got into the German trenches, they changed hands several times. We advanced into the third line, got beaten back to the second, then beaten back to the first. We then found that we were being enfiladed by machine-gun fire, and bombed out with German bombs. There was no leadership and no orders, and I ran back into no-man's-land.

We went into action with twenty-five officers and 659 other ranks. At the end of the day, only 110 other ranks answered the roll-call. There were enormous losses. At night the battalion was withdrawn. What surprised us was the false information we'd been given that they were going to offer no resistance, and there'd only be dead Germans in the trenches opposite us. Also, we felt that we'd been let down by our senior officers, three of whom left the battalion just before the battle. The commanding officer in charge had been made a brigadier-general, one major had gone to the back to be the town major and another had been told to report sick. So we were commanded by a captain. This aroused the men's feelings that they'd been left in the lurch at a very critical moment, and the very first test of our exploits as a new army.

**Private H. D. Jackson**
*75th Field Ambulance, Royal Army Medical Corps*
No one can describe what the Battle of the Somme was really like unless they were there. It was one continuous stream of wounded and dead and dying. You had to forget all sentiment. It was a case of getting on with the job. We went in action on the Somme the midnight before the action started. We took over a dressing station called Black Horse Bridge, at Authuille Wood. The field ambulance we were taking over from were taking rather a long time getting out, and we were all crouched down outside, waiting to get in, while shells were bursting around us. We used to put stretchers on wheels (we could run them down the road *if there was a road* at any time). Bits of shrapnel were sparking on these wheels, and we were wondering if we were going to live to get into this dressing station. Anyway we eventually got in.

When the ration party came up with supplies, it was two mules and a sergeant on horseback. A shell came over and burst right in the middle of them, killing them. The mules' heads and the horse's head were smashed clean off like a razor. All our dressing station outside was distempered with blood. We had four days and four nights there, and it was one continual stream of wounded. Our dugout was almost like a tunnel dug in the bank, and we used to have acetylene lights. Blasts from nearby shells would put these lights out, and the fumes from the light would be terrible, and we'd light it again.

I was assisting the doctor, holding the tray and instruments and torch for him. With the fumes and that, I started feeling faint, and he looked at me and said, 'Are you all right, Jackson?' I said, 'I am feeling a bit queer, sir.' He said, 'Go to the door, get some fresh air,' and he called another man to take over. That happened two or three times, but we had to keep going. This doctor was Captain Beatty, who became a Harley Street specialist after the war. He

Men of 34th Division advancing on La Boisselle.

was really marvellous; I don't know how he stuck it. He seemed to just carry on, as if he was in the theatre. He looked like a skeleton himself, thin and white.

I always remember one chap who was shell-shocked very bad. It took four or five of us to get him into the ambulance and hold him down. He thought we were taking him back into the trenches again, instead of taking him to hospital. And I remember one wounded man, who gave me a letter he had written. 'See this goes,' he said, 'it's to my wife, bless her heart!' So I said, 'Right! I will see that it goes!' A bit later, I went into a dugout to sleep. It was where they put the dead before they were picked up. I laid down on this improvised bunk, made out of wire netting, and I happened to see an arm on a stretcher, poking out from a blanket. I pulled the blanket over, and it was the chap who'd given me the letter. When things happened like that it really brought it home to you. Life seemed so cheap.

## Corporal H. Tansley
### 9th Battalion, York and Lancaster Regiment

We went through the lanes cut in the wire. After a while, I looked around for the line, and it seemed to have disappeared; they were lying around on the ground. There was severe machine-gun fire coming from Pozières, half-left. For a soldier who's been in battle, machine-gun fire is not so terrible a thing. It's a whistling sound. It didn't have such a shattering effect as the heavy explosive. As long as you dodged it you were out of it. But my mate, who was with me, went down, shot through the legs. In some cases, if it was a slight wound, some of the Tommies were quite pleased, because it meant they would be out of the war for a bit. I attended to my mate, and he had some qualms of conscience, because he wasn't facing the enemy when he went down. I didn't notice it myself, but he was an old regular soldier and it troubled him so much. I put a field dressing on him, and then he was hit again, through the mouth, and it killed him.

I didn't know when my moment would come. I expected it at any moment. The best thing I could do was to lie low and keep quiet. Another wave of troops came over, and as they were passing, the enemy fire hotted up. They went farther on to meet the same fate. When the fire died down a bit, I looked around for a shell-hole and found one, but it was chock-a-block full of dead, wounded, unwounded perhaps, and I couldn't get in it, so I had to stay on the surface. One man was trying to worm his way back to the front-line trench on his hands. He said, 'Give us a hand!' Soon after he said that, a big shell dropped close by. And he got up and ran like a shot.

## Captain Alan Hanbury-Sparrow
### 2nd Battalion, Royal Berkshire Regiment

I was given a place with my signallers about four hundred yards behind our front line on a bank where you could see very clearly on a fine day. The troops advanced out of the trenches, but by this time, although the sky was clear, the shells had thrown so much smoke, rubble, and a reddish dust was over everything. There was a mist, too, and hardly anything was visible.

One saw these figures disappear into the mist, and as they did so, so did the first shots ring out from the other side. I thought our men had got into the German trench – and so did the men that were with me. I reported as such to the division. I said, 'I'm going forward, I can't really see what's happened.' I got a message to stay where I was, so I stayed. Presently, as the barrage went forward, so the air cleared and I could see what was happening.

In the distance, I saw the barrage bounding on towards Pozières, the third German line. In no-man's-land were heaps of dead, with Germans almost standing up in their trenches, well over the top – firing and sniping at those who had taken refuge in the shell-holes. On the right, there were signs of fighting, and I saw Very and signal lights go up in the trenches.

Then I waited, and another brigade was ordered to resume the attack. Providentially for that brigade, the order was cancelled when greater realisation came in as to what had really happened. It was the most enormous disaster.

## Lieutenant A. Dickinson
### 10th Battalion, Lincolnshire Regiment

The air was full of bullets. Men began to fall all around us. It was tragic. When these men were hit, they just fell flat on their faces. One bullet went between my fingers; it just clipped the edge of each. When we came to want something to eat, when you got your haversack off your back, you found that the bullets had gone through your Maconochie ration, or tin of bully beef. Some very near misses.

When we arrived at the mine crater, our orders were to man the lip. Of course, the Germans played their machine guns on the lip, and one after the other, men were hit in the head, and rolled down into the bottom of the crater, which tapered down to a point. It was still hot as an oven down there.

## Lieutenant Cecil Lewis
### 3 Squadron, Royal Flying Corps

We flew right down to three thousand feet to see what was happening. Of course, we had this very well worked-out technique which was that we had a klaxon horn on the undercarriage and I had the button and I used to press out a letter, and that letter was to tell the infantry that we wanted to know where they were. And when they heard us hawking at them from above, they had red Bengal flares in their pockets, just like the little things one lights on the fifth of November. And the idea was that as soon as they heard us make our noises above, they would put a match to their flares, and all along the lines, wherever there was a chap, there'd be a flare. And we'd note these flares down on the maps and Bob's your uncle. But, of course, it was one thing to practise it, another thing to really do it when they were under fire. Particularly when things began to go a bit badly. Then, of course, they jolly well wouldn't light anything, and small blame to them, because it drew the fire of the enemy on to them at once. So we went down on that particular morning, looking for flares all around La Boisselle, and down to Fricourt, and I think we got two flares on the whole front. And of course we were bitterly disappointed, because this was our part to help the infantry – and we weren't able to do it.

## Private Tom Easton
### 21st Battalion, Northumberland Fusiliers

We reached the German trench and we spread out, and there were few Germans in that trench, except the dead or wounded. We had many wounded of our own, and bombers were instructed to proceed up the communication trench, towards the village of La Boisselle. We spread out, and prepared to defend the trench from the other side, against attack. We found a German dugout, and it was immediately decided to make that the headquarters for the battalion. At that time, we only had one officer left, who became adjutant. I remember going into this dugout. It was about twelve steps down, and must have been twelve feet long and six feet wide, and it was safe from the ordinary 18-pounders, which was the calibre of shell that was used on front-line trenches. It was much more elaborate than the British trenches.

The entrance to a deep German dugout.

The interior of a German dugout.

## Lieutenant Phillip Howe
### 10th Battalion, West Yorkshire Regiment

The trenches we had to get out of were deep, and it was necessary to climb up ladders. Naturally this made us a bit slow, so the people who came behind suffered many more casualties than those who got over first. I put down my survival to the fact that I was first over the top, and got almost as far as the German trenches, before anything happened.

I met a German officer whose idea was to attack us as we crossed no-man's-land and he was armed with a whole array of stick bombs which he proceeded to throw at me and I replied by trying to shoot my revolver. I missed every time and he missed with his stick bombs as well. After this had gone on for a few seconds – it seemed like hours – somebody kindly shot this German officer and I made my way on to the place I was told to go to originally, which was a map reference, a hundred yards behind the German front line.

I made my way to this little trench which I had seen by aerial photographs. I had started off with more or less the whole battalion, but I found myself in this trench with about twenty men. I had been shot through the hand, and we quickly discovered that we were surrounded on all four sides. So I got all the men down a dugout which had very steep sides, and twenty steps leading down from the trench at the top to the dugout below. Just then, another officer came along, who had been shot through the leg and wasn't particularly mobile.

I sat halfway up the dugout steps. I was not able to shoot because I was shot through the hand, but the other officer, who was only shot through the leg, was able to shoot, so he lay at the top of the steps looking down the trench both ways, shooting the Germans as they came around the corners. The men down below loaded the rifle, handed it up to me and I handed it up to him.

It seemed a very long time before anything happened but just as our ammunition was running out, some English troops came down the trench from our left and they said, 'Oh, what are you doing here?' We tried to explain, but they said that there was no Germans within miles. I told them that the Germans were just around the corner, but they wouldn't believe me, and they turned the corner, and I heard a crash of bombs. Me and my men ran the other way. What happened to the other people, I don't know. We went back to our own lines. The rest of the battalion who had followed me over the top at the beginning were all casualties. The few men I had got left was all that was left of the entire battalion.

**Corporal Harry Fellows**
*1/4th Battalion, Northumberland Fusiliers*
On July 1, my brigade was allocated a section of the trench about six hundred yards north of Fricourt. We were up all night, and the most tremendous barrage I'd ever heard went on until nearly half past seven. A few minutes before that, the ground shook, and the crater at La Boisselle went up. For several minutes after, the debris from this was rattling on our steel helmets. At about nine o'clock, a stream of prisoners came down the communication trench. I'll never forget the look of terror in their eyes. They'd been under bombardment for a solid week, and some of them had their arms up and looked like they would need a surgical operation to get them down. Nothing more happened until about noon, and then we had the order to move forward. We got into the front line, and then we learnt what had happened. The Green Howards had been very reluctant to leave their trench, until an officer climbed on top of the parapet and urged the men over. Part of his citation reads, 'As he lay mortally wounded in the bottom of the trench, he continued to urge on his men.'

**Lieutenant Norman Dillon**
*14th Battalion, Northumberland Fusiliers*
We were pioneers and we had to follow behind the leading troops at some distance, the idea being that we had to help to consolidate the newly won positions. The troops that went before us would pull out their trenching tools and make a scratchy line; that's where we came in. The idea was that we would follow on and enlarge those little scratches in the ground into proper trenches. It was all terribly badly managed. Any digging could have been done by the troops on the spot. Another thing we did was to turn around the old German line. It just meant putting barbed wire on the opposite side and cutting a fire-step on the other side of the trench. Of course, it had its disadvantages, because the deep dugouts faced the wrong way, which meant that any shell coming over might easily have popped down the stairs and exploded underneath.

**Corporal H. Tansley**
*9th Battalion, York and Lancaster Regiment*
Just before three in the afternoon, I managed to crawl into a hole. I'd stayed

the flow of the blood in my groin. I knew how to apply pressure to stay the blood. There were casualties everywhere. More than the Royal Army Medical Corps could cope with. I must have lost consciousness for part of the time, then revived a bit, and asked them to get me away. 'Oh, yes, we'll come to you!' they said. It was really a godsend that they did pick me up, and bring me out. So many never got away. My battalion suffered casualties up to eighty per cent. The colonel was found a day later – shot to pieces – hanging on the German wire. His adjutant was by him.

**Corporal Don Murray**
*8th Battalion, King's Own Yorkshire Light Infantry*
I began to creep back towards the line, through mud and shell-holes, and down into the trench, and still there was nobody there. Gradually, we congregated in ones and twos, and we mustered forty-three. We started off 1,060. We trained for twelve months, and it took twenty minutes to destroy us. We went back to the quartermaster's stores, and we passed the Sherwood Foresters, who were to attack after us, and take Mouquet Farm, which we were supposed to have taken. We got back to the stores. There were cookers there with stew in, everything ready for us. The quartermaster was an acting captain, and he said, 'Is the battalion on the march back?' A lance corporal was in charge, and he said, 'They're here . . .'

**Private Tom Easton**
*21st Battalion, Northumberland Fusiliers*
Roll-call was taken next morning, outside Brigade Headquarters, and out of 890 men, we could only muster a company – less than two hundred. We only had one officer left standing. We were collected by a captain, who had not been in the battle, and after feeding we were marched off into billets. Captain McClusky was the only surviving officer that came back with our battalion, and he was made the adjutant. I was pleased to see that my brother was also present at the roll-call.

**Private W. J. Senescall**
*11th Battalion, Suffolk Regiment*
We had no roll-call, after we got back, because there was only about twenty-five left out of eight hundred. There was nothing to count. All the packs were

left in a great stack, with personal and army things in. We spent about a week, taking all these to pieces and sorting the army stuff from the civilian stuff, and putting the civilian stuff into parcels and sending it off to relations in England.

## MAMETZ TO MONTAUBAN

East of Fricourt, lay Mametz, a heavily fortified village. XV Corps managed to force the Germans from Mametz, although at a price: 159 men of the 9th Battalion, Devonshire Regiment were killed by a single machine gun, mounted in the base of a religious shrine in Fricourt Wood.

The far end of the British advance was on the village of Montauban. The 7th Battalion, Bedfordshire Regiment attacked to the west of Montauban, and broke through the German trench lines. The battalion overran the strongly defended Pommiers Redoubt, and then moved north to occupy White Trench.

The 8th Battalion, East Surrey Regiment pushed forward to the west of Montauban, reaching the west end of Train Alley. The 16th and 17th Battalions, Manchester Regiment entered Montauban village at five minutes past ten in the morning, to find it deserted and in ruins. The only visible occupant was a fox. The 17th Battalion moved on to Triangle Point, north of Montauban, where it consolidated its position.

The 17th Battalion, King's Liverpool Regiment – the right-hand British battalion on the Somme – moved forward against little German resistance. Joining with the French, who were advancing in parallel, the battalion captured Glatz Redoubt. As though demonstrating the strength of the entente, the commanding officer of the 17th Battalion, Lieutenant Colonel Fairfax, had marched over the top arm in arm with Commandant le Petit, the neighbouring French battalion commander.

Sergeant James Payne
*16th Battalion, Manchester Regiment*
The attack was about to start. I had a boy with me; he'd been out of school for six weeks. I said, 'What are you doing here?' He said, 'I've been sent out from England. I've arrived today.' I said, 'Hang on to me!' It was just stupid. The

boy couldn't hold a butty knife, never mind a bayonet. He was killed. Shot down next to me.

We were attacking the very last German trench. We were all knocked out. Their machine guns were waiting for us. We didn't get through. None of us. There was a big shell-hole full of dead and dying and blinded. Tall men got it through the jaw, shorter men through the eyes. I was five foot ten and shot through the cheek. I was walking along, and a bullet blew all my teeth out. I fell forward and spat all my teeth out. I collapsed and, hours later, I came round. My left eye was closed. I couldn't talk. I could breath, that was all. I got my field dressing out and wound it round my face and left eye. I could see through my right eye and I saw one of my corporals who'd been shot through the foot. I took his boot off, bandaged it up, put his boot on again and he used his rifle as a crutch and together we went back. There was nobody around. Just the dead.

We saw a man. A shell had come over and hit him and knocked off his left arm and his left leg. His left eye was hanging on his cheek, and he was calling out, 'Annie!' I shot him. I had to. Put him out of his misery. It hurt me. It hurt me.

## Major Alfred Irwin
### 8th Battalion, East Surrey Regiment

I was commander of my battalion on the first day of the Somme – and it was a great difficulty to know what to do. One's instinct was to go over with the chaps, to see what was going on. On the other, we had been warned, again and again, that officers' lives must not be thrown away in doing something that they oughtn't. As a matter of fact, we had been told that commanding officers of battalions should lead from behind, and that when the attack had lost its impetus, *then* was the moment to go forward.

So when the impetus died down, in the mid-morning, I felt that was the moment I could be of some use, and I went over the parapet by myself, and stood out in the open, saying, 'Come on! Come on!' And they all came on quite smoothly. They didn't know what to do after they'd taken their first objective. I think I acted properly, but I really don't know. We reached the third German reserve line, to the left of Montauban. There were so few of us that there was very little we could do that night. But I posted the men as well as I could, and we were not attacked. We were heavily shelled – but not attacked. We got away with it, and the next day we were relieved. We'd come down from about eight hundred to under two hundred. It seemed to me a dreadful waste of life.

Captain Neville was commanding B Company, one of our assaulting companies. A few days before the battle, he came to me with a suggestion. He said that he and his men were all equally ignorant of what their conduct would be when they got into action. They had four hundred yards to go, covered by machine-gun fire, so he thought that it would be helpful if he could furnish each platoon with a football, and allow them to kick it forward and follow it. I sanctioned that, so long as he and his officers *really* kept command of the units, and didn't allow it to develop into a rush after the ball. If a man came across the football, he could kick it forward, but he mustn't chase after it. I think it did help them enormously. It took their minds off it. But they suffered terribly. Neville, his second captain, and his company sergeant major were all killed.

I recommended Captain Gimsun, of the Royal Army Medical Corps, for a Victoria Cross. It was his plain duty that he did, but he was completely unperturbed by the very heavy machine-gun fire, and he and his stretcher-bearers were at it the whole morning, bringing in chaps who were lying out in the open. I was so impressed by his calmness. He was taking no notice of the battle – he was just getting on with his job. I thought this was enough for a VC. General Maxey, who was commanding our division, came up the next day and found me writing up Gimsun's recommendation, and he told me that it wasn't sufficiently journalistic, and rewrote it for me, and I think that's why Jimmy didn't get it.

### Private Jack Cousins
#### 7th Battalion, Bedfordshire Regiment

It was a question of get stuck in, and kill or be killed. It wasn't a question of wandering around the countryside looking for mushrooms. We had to get going. We were told, 'Don't advance on your own! Go together at the same pace! If machine-gun fire takes place, drop down flat to the ground!' And our platoon officer said, 'You'll find the barbed wire in front of the German trench blown away.' Blown away? Nothing of the sort! It was as solid as anything. That was the whole trouble! We were disillusioned that it wasn't blown, and the Germans were firing at us from all angles. A lot of men were caught on the wire, and they were sitting ducks.

We got into the front-line German trench and my instructions were to follow the communication trench back to the German lines. Well, I had my Lewis gun, my head down below the trench, my gun crew following behind with spare ammunition. Suddenly I could hear voices in front: I knew that they were German. I stopped at the bend, and suddenly I saw, coming around the bend, Germans in single file. When they spotted me, they started to unsling their rifles, but I didn't give them a chance, and I drove my finger on the Lewis gun trigger, and with a burst from the gun, three or four of them dropped dead. The others threw down their rifles and came with their hands up. I signalled for them to get up and walk back to our people as prisoners.

My number two was carrying a revolver, and there was nothing accurate about the thing, but he started to take potshots at some of these Germans. I told him to shut up and be quiet. Then we came into a Jerry dugout. Their dugouts were very effective – they used to tunnel down yards and yards. I got hold of a Mills bomb, pulled the pin and threw it down the dugout. There was a bit of a bang after four seconds, then I heard somebody moaning. I took a chance. I went down into the dugout, and there was this Jerry laid with a great hole in his chest, blood pouring everywhere, pointing to his mouth. I knew what he wanted. He wanted a drink. I gave him my water bottle. The water went in his mouth, and came out of his holes. He was gone in a few seconds. It really upset me, I felt morally responsible for his death. It could have happened to me.

**Private Albert Hurst**
*17th Battalion, Manchester Regiment*
We were in the second wave to go over. When the first wave went, we could hear excessive rifle and machine-gun fire. We couldn't see what was happening, and there was a very short interval between their attack and ours. We were carrying our full pack, and rifle, but we all had some extra load. I was carrying two extra bandoliers of rifle ammunition, two Mills bombs, a water bucket full of Lewis gun ammunition, and a full-sized pickaxe. It all slowed me down, and made me less manoeuvrable. It would have been impossible to run. It was an effort just to walk at a normal pace. On the back of our packs, we had a yellow cloth to distinguish us as Manchesters, and a bright metal plate to reflect the light, so that the aeroplanes could see how far we'd advanced.

The attack started when the officer looked at his watch, and said, 'Now!'

There were a lot of ladders to get us over the top, and it was a struggle to get up with all the gear. By this time, the previous wave had occupied the German front line, but we still came under a lot of rifle and machine-gun fire as we went over. It must have been coming from the German second line, over the top of our first wave who – I later found out – had captured the first line of the German trenches. The whole battalion moved forward in block formation – ten men keeping close together in files of five. It was daft, it made us very vulnerable, but I didn't have an impression of people falling around me. The British wire had been cut for us, and we had no problem getting through. Then we endeavoured to recognise the points that we were making for.

The fire got heavier as we went across no-man's-land. I could hear the bullets whistling in the air. There was no cover. I was exposed, I was frightened, and I got a bullet through my water bottle. We *were* suffering casualties, but I didn't know it at the time. Of our platoon, perhaps about a dozen out of fifty men were casualties. When I got to the German front line, it was so blown up that I couldn't see very much, but there were six dead Germans lying in front of the trench. The 2nd Royal Scots Fusiliers had captured it and were holding it, but we carried on past them, and there were no British troops ahead of us now. We went on to the village of Montauban, which seemed to be flattened. The only thing left intact was a figure of Christ on the Cross, at the corner of the Péronne Road. We didn't see any Germans in Montauban and we took up a position on the right hand side, facing Bernafay Wood.

By this time, we were too exhausted from carrying so much gear to start digging trenches. We lay down where we were and made use of the ground as we found it, on the outer edge of an orchard. There was no noticeable firing from the German side, and we were there for three days, expecting a big counter-attack which never came. We were a sort of auxiliary reserve for the machine gun; we ourselves weren't on the gun, but we were suppliers of the ammunition. The machine-gun team was in advance of us, and there were two bombers, lying doggo, covering them. And we couldn't see any Germans, or any defences, ahead of us in Bernafay Wood. It looked open.

**Private Pat Kennedy**
*18th Battalion, Manchester Regiment*

As we progressed towards the German trenches, gaps appeared in our lines. But the men still went forward. I could see the French troops advancing on our right. It was a splendid sight to see them with their coloured uniforms and long bayonets. They advanced in short, sharp rushes, and they seemed to make good progress. Their artillery was giving them plenty of support, and as they vanished into the distance, I thought, 'They're doing very well! Very well indeed!'

After taking the village of Montauban, we advanced about four hundred yards, and dug in. The officer near us said, 'We've taken a position, but can we hold it?' The Germans made three counter-attacks. We beat every one off, except the last one. They got in, we drove them out, but no reinforcements came up and we had orders to stay where we were.

During one counter-attack, I couldn't get my ammunition out of my pouches quick enough. So this old sergeant with the South African War ribbon said to me, 'Eh lad, put your clips on the top of the parapet. It's easier!' That was a good tip – because I had to load very quick and fire. The Germans were coming with fixed bayonets. The old sergeant said, 'By God, if we get any in here, we'll have to go and meet them with the bayonet!' I had a round in my breech, to shoot in case I missed with the bayonet. They got very near on top of us – a few feet away – and they were coming full pelt, yelling at the top of their voices. It was a nasty feeling. But they were beaten off.

**Private A. A. Bell**
*17th Battalion, Manchester Regiment*

I thought, 'This is going to be easy!' Behind us was a battery. They were slinging it over, and the noise was terrible. 'They know what they're doing!' I thought. The whistle was the signal to go. We had our places allocated. I was a bomber, and I was to attack Triangle Point, beyond Montauban. Several of the bombers from the platoon had been detailed to go there, and we carried ten bombs and we were to receive two bombs each from other members of the platoon. Before I got to Triangle Point, I learned that Sergeant Jackson had been hit, and as I was looking for the place – on my own – I came across a number of Germans with their hands up. I could hardly believe it. I shouted to them, '*Par la! Par la!*' and they went *par la*. That was lucky for me.

Then, I saw some retreating Germans with a gun, and I lay down and had a pop at them. I didn't see that I hit any of them. After that, I found Triangle Point and one or two of my platoon were there; not many of them. And there were other people besides. We settled down to improve the defensive position. There was a young lance corporal in charge, and eventually we settled down for the night. At the end of the evening, I had a good drink of coffee out of a dead German's water bottle. It had been a very hot day, and a very hot business altogether, and I was terribly thirsty. This caused me a good deal of trouble; the coffee upset my stomach. As we moved towards the village of Montauban, there were still some German machine-gunners firing away, but when we got close to the village they put up a white flag. Some of our men were detailed to clear out the dugouts, and I expect they *cleared them out*.

## Sergeant Ernest Bryan
### 17th Battalion, King's Liverpool Regiment

We were behind a creeping barrage, that means to say a barrage chucked down twenty yards in front of you, and then it's supposed to go on to the German front line for a minute only, and then lift, and that was our chance to charge and get in. But it was nothing like that. We never saw any lift, and we couldn't tell if shells were our own, or the Germans'.

We went about twenty-five yards, and got through what was left of our wire, stumbling through the front line. It was only then I realised what a terrible weight we were carrying. I was carrying a loaded Lewis gun, weighing just under thirty pounds. When we got towards their front line, up pops their machine gun, and chained to this gun was a German. The first thing I did was sling my Lewis gun under my arm and press the trigger. The German gunner went down; whether he was hit or not I didn't know and I didn't care, he was down. I sprayed right along the top, to keep the Germans' heads down. That gave us a chance of getting in.

When we got into the German front line, the fun started. We were getting enfilade fire from right and left. From rifle, and machine-gun fire, and also from artillery. My immediate concern was to get my Lewis gun on to the trench. We stayed an hour there, until all the objectives were gained – not only by our battalion, but also by the French on our right. Then we moved forward. Our colonel picked out a piece of land, and we dug in a hundred yards ahead. And we were carrying such a hell of a weight that we were exhausted, but that's no excuse! You were still carrying a trenching tool, and a spade was stuck on your back. You pull that down, and start digging a new trench. We knew why; we knew very well that all the Germans would start shelling their old trenches. They had their range all right, but not the range of the new trenches that we were digging.

### Henry Holdstock
#### 6 Squadron, Royal Naval Air Service

There was great excitement. We had the news that some German prisoners were coming in, so we ran to the chalk-covered road that ran to the base and, sure enough, there was a young infantry officer there, walking with a German officer, and about seventy to 120 German prisoners walking behind them, very dejected, with pale yellow faces and German pill-box hats. I remember the expressions on their faces when they saw us. They could see we were navy, and we could see them pointing at us, and saying to themselves that not only were they fighting against the British Army, but they were fighting against the navy as well. They were all pointing to us with great excitement as they walked down, out of the war for ever. Which I thought was very nice. And the two officers were walking side by side, quite at peace. Two hours before, they'd been trying to kill each other, and now they're walking off almost hand in hand, with their little brood behind them, going back to captivity and safety. For me, it was very affecting to watch.

### Sergeant James Payne
#### 16th Battalion, Manchester Regiment

We walked on and came to a trench with some German prisoners in it and one of them was a doctor. I asked this doctor to bind the corporal's foot up and he wouldn't. I told him to do it or I'd shoot him. He spoke English and he said, 'Blame your own government!' I said, 'You won't bind his foot up?' He said, 'No!' So I shot him. We had to walk fifteen miles until we found a railhead where I found an ambulance. There were some German prisoners on stretchers there. I tipped them off, put the corporal on and put him in the ambulance and saw him off. I walked on until I found another ambulance and I was taken off.

German prisoners captured on July 1, behind a wire 'cage'.

**Private Albert Hurst**
*17th Battalion, Manchester Regiment*

We had achieved our objectives, and, as far as we were concerned, all the attacking battalions must have been similarly successful. As it began to go dusk, we came under heavy artillery fire. One or two of the men were killed, and one man of our platoon had his leg blown off. Our biggest problem was shortage of water. I had none at all myself, because I'd had a bullet through my bottle. That night, the bombardment was heavy. Eighteen-pounders and whizz-bangs were firing at us. The Germans seemed to have our range, and I don't remember sleeping at all that night – or for the next three days. We were bombarded for three days, until we were finally relieved by another battalion, and by the end I was desperate. I was eating grass to try and get rid of my thirst.

**Sergeant Ernest Bryan**
*17th Battalion, King's Liverpool Regiment*

We were relieved on July 3. When we got back we were taken to Bray, and our brigadier thought it a good idea that warrant officers and senior NCOs should say what should have been done differently during the action. I saw the Lewis gunners and our officers looking at me. They knew how bitterly I'd felt at the terrific weight we'd been carrying. I asked the brigadier if it was possible for his brigade major to put our equipment on. He said, 'Certainly!' I got two Lewis gunners, privates, my boys, to put on everything: bombs in their pockets, sandbags, spade, kit, rations, extra ammunition round the neck, all full. I said, 'How do you feel?' The brigade major said, 'It's a hell of a weight.' I said, 'You haven't started! You forgot the rifle, you've got to put that up, and where are you going to carry it? Slung over your shoulders? You can't, because you've got to have it in your hand, ready. There's a farm field at the back here, just been ploughed. Try walking a hundred yards and see how you feel – and that's a playground compared with what we had to go over.' The brigadier said, 'You feel very much about it.' I said, 'Wouldn't you? Wouldn't anybody?'

**Private Pat Kennedy**
*18th Battalion, Manchester Regiment*

We didn't know that the day was a disaster. We didn't know that the only success was where our division and the 18th Division gained their objectives. We thought the war would soon be over, and that our men were flushed with success.

It was long afterwards that we found out that the battle had been a disaster, except for us. We only heard about the shocking losses and the great numbers of wounded, from the Royal Army Medical Corps men. July 1 was a walkover for us, compared with the battle that followed. After we took Montauban, I though that we would get reinforcements and exploit our success. But nothing happened.

## Major Alfred Irwin
### 8th Battalion, East Surrey Regiment

As we were taken out of the line, the Canadians had a Highland brigade in support of us. They were so impressed with the success of the few chaps of ours that were left, that they sent their pipers to play us out of the line. We have a connection with Glasgow, and our regimental march was familiar to the pipers, and they played that. It was a great compliment – but they were big, hefty chaps, and my little Londoners couldn't keep up at all. And they couldn't get the long step necessary for the swing of the kilt. So, although they played us out, it was rather an irregular march.

After that, drafts came in, and it was no longer the 8th East Surreys in spirit. All my best chaps had gone. We buried eight young officers in one grave, before we left. It was a terrible massacre. The attack should have been called off, until the wire was cut. They ought to have known through their intelligence the condition of the wire, before we ever got to July 1.

The success of these advances in the Montauban sector – at the cost of 1,740 lives – is often overlooked, or considered irrelevant, when placed alongside the sense of suffering and waste evoked by the first day of the Battle of the Somme. Yet, had a stronger reserve been in place, it is possible that the British army could have taken advantage of these advances, and broken through on the Montauban front. And it is certainly arguable that – even without a breakthrough – the day served its intended purpose; the Germans had been placed under great strain, and could no longer exert overbearing pressure on the French at Verdun.

The fact remains, however, that on a single day, 19,240 British and Dominion soldiers had been killed, and at least 35,493 wounded. In human terms, July 1, 1916 was nothing less than a disaster.

**Lieutenant Ulick Burke**
*2nd Battalion, Devonshire Regiment*
There was frustration. We'd lost so many people, and taken so little ground. And men began to wonder, 'Why?' There was no feeling of giving up; they were just wondering 'why?' And when you came out into the billets, you saw these endless lines of walking wounded, and ambulances, and we wondered how long we could exist.

**Corporal George Ashurst**
*1st Battalion, Lancashire Fusiliers*
Our battalion had five hundred casualties, and I'd lost most of my friends. These were my platoon lads, they'd been boozing with us in the villages. But it was no use bothering. We knew they'd gone.

**Corporal Harry Fellows**
*12th Battalion, Northumberland Fusiliers*
When I came out of the line, having lost a lot of men, I'm sorry to say that I didn't feel any sadness. The only thing I thought about was that there were less mouths to feed, and I should get all those men's rations for a fortnight before the rations were cut down. That's all I can tell you honestly.

**Corporal Bill Partridge**
*7th Battalion, Middlesex Regiment*
Well, if I said the morale was high I'd be telling a lie. As a matter of fact, I think the thoughts of most of us, after the maiden attack, was that we wanted either a Blighty one or ones that were a top storey. We didn't want to be mutilated – that was our main thought. That, and smoking a cigarette, and wondering if it was going to be the last one.

**Second Lieutenant W. J. Brockman**
*15th Battalion, Lancashire Fusiliers*
What was so wrong about it was that even though it was a complete failure, it was reported as being a success in the newspapers. And what was worse, was that they still persisted, knowing perfectly well that they were getting nowhere. It went on, and on, and on, and on.

A roll call of the 1st Battalion, Lancashire Fusiliers after the first day of the Battle of the Somme.

Wounded British soldiers.

**Private Basil Farrer**
*3rd Battalion, Green Howards*
We used to say – if it's got your name and address on it, then it will find you. So what's the use of worrying?

# Out of the Trenches

*People in England had no idea whatsoever what was happening in France.*

Great War infantrymen did not spend the entire war in the front line, or even in the trenches. There was a system of continuous rotation in place that ensured that men were consistently moving between front-line trenches, the reserve trenches and billets behind the lines.

### Reverend Leonard Martin Andrews
*Chaplain, attached to Royal Fusiliers*

I arrived in France on one of the coldest nights you can imagine at this little *estaminet* place. It was the coldest place I'd experienced for years and when I got into bed, the sheets felt like sheets of ice. I was woken up in the morning by a charming chaplain standing by my side, who said, 'I'm very sorry to butt in like this but I've been sent to tell you that a man is to be shot at dawn tomorrow and the Divisional Commander wants you to break the news to him, stay with him all night, and after he's been shot, to bury him.' I was silent for a few moments, then I said, 'There are a million men in France. Why choose me when I've just got here?' He said, 'I'm very sorry but somebody's got to do it.'

So I went to see the officer in charge of courts martial and I said that I'd take on this job so long as I'd be allowed to be a prisoner's friend at the next court martial. He said, 'I can't agree with you more. I'm a barrister in private life and I'm doing my utmost to get these poor devils off!' So I went to see this fellow in his cell at seven o'clock at night. The firing party had just arrived – they would be sleeping there. And this regular soldier stood to attention when

I arrived. He said, 'I know what you've come for, sir. You've come to tell me that I'm going to be shot.' So I said, 'Yes, I'm afraid I have. I'd like to know if you want me to write any letters or do anything.' We talked. The minutes seemed like hours and I thought the night would never go but he seemed very awake. He told me, 'I've deserted five times and if I went back again I'd only desert again. I can't face it again so I don't mind dying.'

We were watching every minute on my watch and it was getting nearer and nearer to dawn. I said to him, 'Would you like something to eat?' 'Yes, sir,' he said. A six-footed corporal in charge of the guard came in and I told him that the prisoner wanted some tea and toast. 'We've got some ready sir, in case he wanted it.' A few minutes later, he returned with a big mug of tea and the biggest plate of thick burnt toast covered in butter. It made me almost ill to look at it but, to my utter surprise, this poor dear started devouring it. Fortunately, the doctor had given me two pills to make him sleep better and I managed to get these pills into his tea and he gradually went off to sleep.

About an hour later, I heard activity outside. Dawn was breaking and the firing party was up. I went out and introduced myself to them and said how sorry I felt. 'Oh, we're all right, sir!' one of them said. 'We shall have our backs to him until the moment we shoot.' They were all crack shots and old soldiers and they didn't seem to mind very much.

The prisoner was brought into position and the firing squad was ready to fire, and just at the critical moment the prisoner put up his hand. The sergeant in charge rushed to him and he said, 'I'd like to shake hands with the padre.' It was the longest walk of my life. I walked from the firing squad to this poor creature about to be shot. I shook him by the hand and promised that I'd write home to his mother and I walked back. Then it was all over. Afterwards we had the burial and as the sergeant threw the last piece of earth on the grave, he said, 'You know, sir, at the retreat from Mons, he was one of the bravest men in the regiment!' 'It's a bit late saying that now,' I said, 'why didn't you say that at the court martial?' 'I never had the chance, sir,' said the sergeant. 'Neither had that poor devil!' I replied and with that I went off.

## Private Philip Cullen
### 4th Battalion, Oxfordshire and Buckinghamshire Light Infantry

When we went out of the line, we'd no sooner got into billets, when we heard, 'Firing party wanted.' Everybody scuttled like a rat. Somebody had been found guilty of cowardice, and it meant a firing party up against a wall, and nobody wanted to do it.

## Captain Maberly Esler
### 9th Battalion, Border Regiment

When we were having our rest out of the line, the colonel sent for me and said, 'I have a very unpleasant duty for you to perform, which I won't like any more than you do.' One of our own men had absented himself from the front line on two occasions when battle had started and, when it was over, came back and made some excuse that he'd mislaid his way. Well, of course, I realised that this was a very serious offence; the first time I sentenced him, myself, to some severe sentence, but it happened again, and I realised he must be sent up to army headquarters for a court martial.

They court-martialled him, and sentenced him to death by firing squad, and the unpleasant task the colonel set me was to attend the shooting and to pin on his heart a piece of coloured flannel, so that it'd give the marksmen something to fire at.

So the following morning he was to be shot at dawn, and I lay awake thinking of it all night, and I thought, 'Well, I'll try to help out this fellow a bit.' So I took him a cupful of brandy and presented it to him, and I said, 'Drink this, and you won't know very much about it.' He said, 'What is it?' I said, 'It's brandy,' and he said, 'I've never drunk spirits in my life, there's no point in starting now.'

That, to me, was a sort of courage. Two men came in and led him out of the hut, where he'd been guarded all night. As he left the hut, his legs gave way, then one could see the fear entering his heart. Rather than being marched to the firing spot, he was dragged along. When he got there, he had his hands tied behind his back, he was put up against a wall, his eyes were bandaged and the firing squad were given an order to fire.

The firing squad consisted of eight men, only two of whom had their rifles loaded. The other six carried blank ammunition – so that they wouldn't actually know who had fired the fatal shot. I wondered at the time, 'What on earth will happen if they miss him, and don't kill him completely?' I was very anxious about this, but when they fired he fell to the ground, writhing about – as all people do. Even if they've been killed, they have this reflex action of writhing about, which goes on for some minutes.

I don't know whether he was dead or not, but at that moment the sergeant in charge stepped forward, put a revolver to his head, and blew his brains out. That was the *coup de grâce* which – I learnt afterwards – was always carried out in these cases.

I was a medical man, but I think this punishment was absolutely essential. It was setting a bad example to the men. They would begin to feel that you only had to walk off during a battle, and then come back afterwards, and you escaped any penalty of death or mutilation. You would be leaving your comrades in the lurch. I dare say in the Second World War, they were looked on as shell-shock cases, instead of just being what they were – cowards. It was a necessary punishment.

### Lieutenant Norman Collins
#### 6th Battalion, Seaforth Highlanders

When we were behind the lines, there was a court martial trying a number of people. One of them was an officer in a Highland regiment, and I was his 'officer's friend'. He told me a lot about himself. He was awaiting court martial because he had taken too much rum when he was going over the top, and he was incapable of carrying out his duties properly. He was a charming man, and I felt very sorry for him. I knew that the least punishment he could get would be to be reduced to the ranks, and sent back to his regiment as a private. Well, in the event, before his court martial could take place, this officer shot himself dead.

There was another officer charged with a lesser offence, who was reduced to the ranks. I can remember the battalion being paraded, and this officer stood out in the middle while his badges of rank were cut off, and he was marched away to rejoin the regiment as a private. I heard afterwards from somebody who knew him that he made a very good second start. He could never become an officer again, but he rose to the rank of sergeant major, which was a tremendous achievement.

And I can remember one other case from the courts martial. A private was sentenced to be executed, and he was a man of about thirty-five, with a family of seven children. And I can remember the judging officers, all spick and span, mounted, carrying fly whisks. They came from another world.

## Private William Holmes
### 12th Battalion, London Regiment

We'd been told that the next day our battalion would be taken up to a place five miles away, where our whole brigade would make a practice attack. They'd chosen a part of the country as similar as possible to the contours of the place where the actual attack was going to be. So after marching us five miles, we found the other three battalions lined up. Everybody in our battalion was put into two ranks, and the order came, 'Pile arms!' That meant every four men would get hold of their rifles and stand them up with their butts on the ground, leaning them against the other rifles. And then the rifles would stand there by themselves, until they were taken up again. So we did that.

Then, my sergeant came to me and said, 'Bill, I want you to go round to all the chaps, give them these dummy cartridges, and tell them to put four in the magazine and one up the spout.' There were no bullets, but when the rifle was fired, it would make a noise, so that when the attack was on it would sound as though everyone was shooting. It took me quite a time. There were so many men I had to hand these things to, and when I got back to my own place I picked up my rifle, and just as I was putting the last one into my magazine, I heard the sergeant shout, 'Drop to your knees! Ready to attack!' It so frightened me that I put the last cartridge up the spout and . . . unfortunately for me . . . I pulled the trigger. Well, of course, the explosion that it made, it made such a noise, that everybody was looking. And the brigadier who'd been inspecting the troops came galloping up to us, and shouted, 'Put that man under close arrest!'

So the sergeant ordered my two mates, who were on either side of me, to fix their bayonets, take away my rifle and march me three hundred yards to where the cooks were. The sergeant of the cooks had to take charge of me. I was sent to my officer commanding, who said, 'I've been ordered by the brigadier to charge you for the most serious thing that you could ever have done! If you had let your rifle off, in a real attack, it would have told the Germans where we were, and it would have given the whole game away! The whole point of a sudden attack would have been falsified! I am to give you the Number One Punishment! Tomorrow morning, you're to be spreadeagled on to the wheel of one of the big guns, and you're to be tied on to it for two hours, every day for seven days!'

I'm told that my officer, and my sergeant, went and spoke up in my defence, and tried to get the punishment annulled, but the CO said that he was doing it on the brigadier's instructions. And I considered what I'd done, and that if it had been the real attack, I'd have prejudiced the whole thing, and that when they said that I'd be tied to the wheel of a gun, I knew that I fully deserved it.

So, the next day, I was taken by the sergeant to the military police headquarters. In their yard, they had this very large old gun. The sergeant told me what was going to happen, and he tied one of my legs to a slant, with wire, and then the other leg, and both hands. It was a terrible feeling. My body wasn't used to being in that position, and to this day I can still feel the sensation. When they released me after two hours, the sergeant said, 'Bill, we feel that you've had quite enough. I'll fill in the form saying that you've done it for seven days, but you needn't come any more.' I could hardly believe it was true!

**Private Philip Cullen**
*4th Battalion, Oxfordshire and Buckinghamshire Light Infantry*
I saw the Aussies come along and cut a man free from the gun wheel, because they wouldn't put up with it.

**Corporal Hawtin Mundy**
*1st Battalion, Oxfordshire and Buckinghamshire Light Infantry*
Early on in the war, it was the strict discipline of the old days. Many men were court-martialled and faced the firing squad, simply because their nerves went. It was nothing more. It happened often. If they were shelling heavily while the men were standing to in the trench, and someone dived back and lay in the dugout, he would be shot for it. If someone was caught asleep on his post, he would be shot. If someone was found wandering at a distance behind the lines, he would be shot. The parents of those chaps had a lovely letter saying that their sons died whilst fighting for their country. But things started to change in 1915. All the ambulance trains were altered quickly to have padded cells in them. I know that's right, because I altered them after the war. The chaps that had breakdowns – they couldn't help it – were sent home, and sent to asylums, and cured.

### Rifleman Robert Renwick
*16th Battalion, King's Royal Rifle Corps*

Shell shock was a horrible thing. I saw quite a bit of it. People would lose control of themselves and start shaking. They would sometimes try to climb out of the trench, and they had to be held down. They didn't know what they were doing.

### Second Lieutenant W. J. Brockman
*15th Battalion, Lancashire Fusiliers*

You've got to bear in mind that some people can't take it. I had a sergeant who was as brave as anybody could be, and he cracked one day. He couldn't go on, and he cried like a baby. He could have been court-martialled – so I quickly sent him down the line. Nothing more was said about it. He had his breaking point. Most people had. There were some incredible people who I think *liked* it. People with no fear at all, and they're an absolute menace to everybody else. There was a chap who commanded a battalion in our brigade, who was the bravest of the brave. He was wounded nineteen times, and got himself killed in the end. He got a Victoria Cross first.

### Private Fred Dixon
*10th Battalion, Royal West Surrey Regiment*

Bravery is shown when a man is fearful but continues to carry out his obligations. But bravery, to my mind, should never be confused with rashness. I remember when a signaller wanted a nose cap so he went searching for one. Of course, he was seen by the German observation post, and a shell came over and killed him. That wasn't bravery. It was sheer foolhardiness.

### Rifleman Robert Renwick
*16th Battalion, King's Royal Rifle Corps*

I remember in one attack, a big strong Welshman twice tried to turn back. I said to him, 'Taffy, for goodness sake, pull yourself together! You've got a sporting chance, going forward, but if you go down the line unwounded, you know what to expect!' He was all right after that, and it was never mentioned again.

**Lieutenant Norman Collins**
*6th Battalion, Seaforth Highlanders*

I was frightened. In my opinion, nobody could be in the trenches, could be under shellfire, without being frightened. I can't imagine it. Mind you, people didn't show it. If you were shaking a bit, or your teeth were chattering, you made every excuse. You pretended it was the cold, or something else. I remember one occasion when my teeth started to chatter, because we were under heavy bombardment, and I was in a hole in the side of a trench. The sergeant was trying to make a cup of tea in a billy can, heated on a tallow candle, and my teeth started chattering. I apologised to him. I said, 'It's so cold, isn't it?' I knew perfectly well, the reason my teeth were chattering was because I didn't like the shells dropping closer and closer. He said, 'Yes, it is cold, sir!' And eventually, I stopped. I pulled myself together. But I don't mind admitting that I was never the stuff that heroes are made of.

**Private Fred Dixon**
*10th Battalion, Royal West Surrey Regiment*

Fear becomes cowardice when one withdraws oneself from one's moral obligations. It can be accounted for. I wouldn't like to assess cowardice in anybody, because it's affected by poor health, lack of sleep, physical wretchedness and one's emotional and mental equipment. I remember once, I had a bad toothache. I went to the medical officer and asked him if he could have me sent to the casualty clearing station to have it out. He wouldn't do it. That day, we were given some sweet beer. None of our chaps would drink this stuff but I used to have the whole bucket down the side of my bed at night-time and, when my tooth plagued me, I'd drink it down. I had no rest. When I went up the line, I was as jittery as a chicken.

**Corporal Hawtin Mundy**
*1st Battalion, Oxfordshire and Buckinghamshire Light Infantry*

Once you left England as a young man, once you'd stepped into the front-line trenches and had a bashing with shellfire, you weren't human again after that. You turned from a human being into a machine, and you didn't know what you were doing half the time, or you wouldn't have done it. I've seen chaps – many times – who did things that they should have got a Victoria Cross for, and I've seen the same chaps later on, worried, crying, depressed. Had they been seen on either occasion they'd have either had a medal or a court martial.

### Private Philip Cullen
#### 4th Battalion, Oxfordshire and Buckinghamshire Light Infantry
One night, my left-hand man got a dose of the funks. I had to threaten him, or he wouldn't have gone forward. He was a six-footer. I didn't report him, because I'd had it myself.

### Corporal Jim Crow
#### 110th Brigade, Royal Field Artillery
I wanted a man called Taylor to go across to Ovillers, to repair a wire. But he funked it. He wouldn't go. I cursed him to all eternity, and I picked the telephone up . . . and in the end, he went off to do it. I didn't report him. When he came back, he said, 'You know, Corporal, you gave me such a talking to, I would have walked into a shell after that.'

### Second Lieutenant W. J. Brockman
#### 15th Battalion, Lancashire Fusiliers
You got into a state of mind in the end, when you rather hoped something would hit you.

### Corporal H. Tansley
#### 9th Battalion, York and Lancaster Regiment
There was a wood behind our position – Authuille Wood, nicknamed Blighty Wood. In this wood was a light railway, for carrying supplies. Alongside the railway was a hessian camouflage, and this was pitted with machine-gun holes, about a foot from the floor. And it was said that troops would go and stand there to get a Blighty one. It was well known that if you gave yourself a Blighty one previous to a big show, it was straight across the water to England, whereas at a quiet time, you went down to a base hospital and back up the line again.

### Sergeant Frederick Goodman
#### 1st London Field Ambulance, Royal Army Medical Corps
We did have *bad types* who wounded themselves. I say bad types, but let's face it – we're not all the same. People had nerves, some more than others, we're

not all built the same, and someone might have felt the only way he could get out of it was to use a little pop gun on his foot. We had to consider any foot injury very carefully. We'd examine it, cross-question him as to how it happened – we took a lot of convincing – and we'd often discover that it was self-inflicted. That meant a rough time for him. He'd have a lot to answer for. He could be shot as a deserter.

### Private Albert Hurst
### 17th Battalion, Manchester Regiment

One of my friends shot himself through the hand while we were waiting to go over the top. He said, 'I'm not going over!' He asked where the clean sandbags were, put one over the rifle, and shot himself. I was astounded. He was a very brave man – the last man I'd ever expect to do that. We all saw him do it, but no one reported him, and he took himself off to the dressing station.

### Corporal Jim Crow
### 110th Brigade, Royal Field Artillery

I got to know half a dozen Irish soldiers. One day, I was told they'd all got Blighty ones through the fleshy parts of their legs. They'd all been out on patrol, and they'd gone down, one, by one, by one. It transpired that they'd been in the line, and they'd come out, got some beer and, for punishment, they'd been sent straight back into the line again. So they drew lots as to who would be shot first – and when they went out on patrol, they all shot each other. And they got away with it. And what the hell! It was only natural in a way. We kept quiet about it.

### Private Victor Polhill
### 1/5th Battalion, London Regiment

Two of our chaps were on duty, and I was supposed to go on duty at six o'clock, but before then, one of these chaps came back with a hole in his boot and said that shrapnel had hit him between his toes. I'm quite sure that he did it himself. He had a German revolver and ammunition, and I'm quite convinced he did it. He must have felt it was time he cleared off. Anyway, I was told that I should take his place, and I did, and at six o'clock another man took my place. And as he was coming out of the dugout, a stray shell came over and killed him. I thought that was terrible. This chap had shot his own foot, and I should have been replacing him, but instead it was someone else, a man who'd only been with us for a couple of weeks.

## Corporal Jim Crow
### 110th Brigade, Royal Field Artillery
One thing that was done quite a lot was breaking a shell or a bullet open, and chewing the cordite. That would give you a high temperature. People used to get away with it, but if you took too much of it …

## Private Victor Polhill
### 1/5th Battalion, London Regiment
Some of the worst gas cases were cases where gas shells came over: they were in the road, and people picked them up and sniffed them.

## Private Basil Farrer
### 3rd Battalion, Green Howards
When you had been on the Somme, you'd very soon had enough of the heroics. You would go into battle, and you would be going up, the battle would be some hundred yards in front, and the wounded would be coming back. Fellows would be coming back covered in blood, their arms in a sling, and you'd envy them. *You lucky buggers!* Real envy. It wasn't the fear of death. It was a nasty death you'd fear. If it came clean, it was clean out. If it was a Blighty – that was lovely!

## Corporal H. Tansley
### 9th Battalion, York and Lancaster Regiment
An old sergeant with three chevrons on his sleeve – which meant that he'd served twelve years – said, 'I just hope I get a Blighty one as soon as I get on top of the parapet.' And he got his wish. He went over just in front of me, and he got one through the knee. He was down right away.

## Private Albert Day
### 1/4th Battalion, Gloucestershire Regiment
This is a fact. We wanted to get wounded. That was your only hope in the first three or four weeks of the Somme. If you didn't get wounded – you'd get killed.

The joy of a Blighty wound.

**Corporal George Ashurst**
*1st Battalion, Lancashire Fusiliers*

The sensation of being hit by a bullet all depended on where you were hit. I was hit through the left thigh – and I could be shot there, right now, in the same way, and it wouldn't hurt me much. It came right through the thigh. There was just a little white spot where it went in, and a spot where it came out. But my pal had the bones in his leg smashed to smithereens – and if that happened, I would be screaming out with pain.

**Lieutenant James Pratt**
*1/4th Battalion, Gordon Highlanders*

I was shot in the arm and I had rolled around on the ground to get away so my arm had got very dirty; particularly in that ground which was heavily cultivated and full of all sorts of bacilli. The first thing that happened was that I found that I'd got gas gangrene inside. The doctors made a lot of incisions and apparently that wasn't enough because they came to me and said, 'I'm afraid we've got to take your arm off.' I said, 'Well, you're the doctor.' He said, 'You're taking it very calmly!' I said, 'Well, what else can I do?' But when I came to, I still had my arm. They'd come to the conclusion that I'd lost so much blood that if they took off my arm, I'd probably die. So they started a new sort of technique of cutting right down into the arm which was the size of a normal leg and they filled it with tubes which they irrigated with disinfectant fluid every three to four hours. That apparently did the trick, except that I was in delirium for about a week. Completely off my head.

**Corporal George Ashurst**
*1st Battalion, Lancashire Fusiliers*

One night, we went up, and we had to dig a cable trench, well in reserve. Four hundred yards from Jerry. We had to dig this trench before daylight. It was marked out for us by tape. I didn't do any digging: I was supervising the men, and they were doing fine. They came to some water, so they took their shoes and socks off, and put their shoes back on while they dug the remainder. One of them was a lance corporal – I was a corporal – and he said he wasn't digging in the water. I said, 'You blooming have to!' 'I'm not!' he said. He was always a bit jealous of me. He was a regular, while I was only a special reservist, but I had the higher rank. I said, 'Get in! Get it done! We have to be away at daylight!' 'I don't care a bugger!' he said, 'I'm not taking my shoes off! Who do you think you are?' He thumped me, and I thumped him. The lads were watching as we were scrapping, and then Jerry started firing his machine gun. Me and him never heard it, but the lads were shouting, 'Get under! Get under!' It was too late. He dropped into the trench, shouting, and I dropped in after him. The stretcher-bearers were called, because he'd got it in the leg. Then I realised *my* leg was going a bit dead, so I said to the fellow next to me, 'I think I've been hit, too! Feel this!' And he felt the blood, and said, 'You've got it too, corporal!' So they took the pair of us down to the dressing station, but while the doctor was attending to mine the gas alarm went, and we had half an hour with those damn masks on our faces. The doctor said to me, 'You're all right, corporal. It's missed the bone, and missed your main artery by an eighth of an inch.' 'Is it a Blighty, sir?' I asked. 'Yes,' he said, 'I think so. I'll give you a fiver for it!' I said, 'You can't have it for five bloody thousand, sir!'

Then the doctor said, 'You've done far better than your pal over there. He's smashed his bones to smithereens.' I called over to him, and he shouted back, 'Oh, it's all right!' 'Aye,' I thought, 'but you're a leg short when we get back.'

## Sergeant Charles Quinnell
### 9th Battalion, Royal Fusiliers

I was taken to a big marquee about a mile behind the line, and there I was given the various shots of anti-tetanus, and by this time I was utterly exhausted and I went to sleep. And when I woke up I was being lifted into a motor vehicle, taken down to the railhead and from there a train journey down to Étaples, which was forty or fifty miles away.

They tried to save my leg. I had seven days with my foot in a bath of hot water, and I was taken into the operating theatre where tubes were put in to drain it, but by this time it was turning septic, the leg was swelling up like a football.

So they amputated the leg – but they made such a hasty job of it that they left bits of dead bone in the stump, and it was the best part of a twelve-month before they found these. Well, you just imagine a surgeon doing twelve amputations a day. The man was tired, tired, tired. He had a butcher's apron on, a waterproof apron, and you were just another case; he didn't even look at you to see who you were.

## Corporal Henry Mabbott
### 2nd Battalion, Cameron Highlanders

I can remember a blinding white light. I got up to run, but I went down. Something happened to my right leg. I got up again to run, and once again I went down. I felt for my leg, and halfway down my calf there was nothing. It was bleeding very badly, and I cut the string of my gas mask, put it round my thigh and tied it as tight as I could. I put the knife I was using back into its sheath, and put the sheath in and turned it until the blood had stopped flowing, and I hung on to it. All was well, until somebody found me and carried me to a stretcher. There was an awful amount of shelling going on, and he took an awful long time to get me down to a dressing station. The doctor in the dressing station put a needle into my wrist, and I know no more until I woke up in hospital. I was given what was known as the 'guillotine operation'. Nothing more was done.

Then they discovered that I had gangrene. I was taken to another hospital where they opened up my spine and pumped something in. I was visited by a Salvation Army major who wrote to my parents, saying that I'd lost my right leg, but that I was one of the most cheerful people in the ward. A couple of days afterwards, a Salvation Army lassie came along, and she wrote home that I'd lost my left leg. I learnt many months afterwards that they were of the opinion that I'd lost both.

I was brought home to a private hospital in Grosvenor Square. A Harley Street man, who was giving his services absolutely free, told me that he would have me up into the operating theatre the next morning. I asked him what he was going to do and he explained everything to me. He said he would saw through the bone, seal it, and he would connect the nerves and the ligaments, as though he was putting an electric cable together.

They put me to sleep, and I woke up in my bed. Each morning, it had to be dressed, and there was a huge tube inside, which had to be brought out, sterilised and put back again. The pain was getting far too much, and as the tube was taken out one morning, I said to the nurse, 'That's not going back!' She said, 'It is!' I said, 'It's not!' She went to get matron, who said it must be done. So I took everything out of my locker, and managed to get the locker up, and said that the first person that attempted to put that tube back would get the locker full force. They waited until the doctor arrived, and he agreed that the tube shouldn't go back.

In due course, I was taught to use crutches, and the very first thing I did was to go to Selfridges, with two others. The lift attendants were young women, and that morning one of them had very short trousers on, and I smacked her leg as I entered the lift. She objected to it – and I was turned out of Selfridges. They never had my custom again.

## Private Basil Farrer
### 3rd Battalion, Green Howards

I was walking along the top of my trench when I got a bullet right through the lower left arm. I got down into the trench, and I was quite near a dugout where there was an artilleryman who bandaged me up. I went back to my regimental aid post, and I was sent further back. Walking along, I heard somebody yell out, swearing at me. It was almost dawn, and the artillery were opening out for attack – and I was walking bang right in front of them. I would have been blown to pieces, without this fellow yelling out to me. From the front, I was sent on a train back to hospital in Rouen. I must have got dirt in the wound, because by the time I was in Rouen my arm had swollen and I had gangrene. They had to slash quite a lot of it off. It is only small now, but it was a terrific gash. I remember coming round and a medical officer saying, 'I have given you a Blighty.' I was walking wounded when I went in, and they carried me out on a stretcher.

I was taken up to Le Havre, and then across the Channel. Orderlies came around, asking us what part of England we would like to be sent to. They liked to send the wounded as near to their homes as they could, so they could be visited by their relatives. The result of that, when we arrived at Southampton, I was put on an ambulance train and taken off at Warrington, because my mother lived on the outskirts of Manchester. I remember as soon as I got there, I had to have my wound re-dressed. The nurse came up to me and she saw my face, and she said, 'Are you frightened?' I was nineteen. I was only a kid. 'What are you frightened of?' she said. 'Are you going to hurt me?' I said. 'I won't hurt you,' she said. I asked that because in the tented hospital in Rouen, every time the nurse dressed my wound in Rouen, she used to pull it. Oh! It was agony! She was callous. So when I got to Warrington, the nurse saw I was a bit scared. But she dressed my wound, and I never felt it. She was a proper qualified nurse. I was in that hospital for two or three weeks.

I was so pleased to have a Blighty wound. After that, I was moved to St

Helens and they were nuns there, with just one qualified civilian nurse, and I was there until the end of December. I was discharged, and I had Christmas at home. Then I reported to the depot at Richmond, with the Yorks. It was the first week of January, and I hadn't properly healed. I had no use of the fingers or thumb. I couldn't bend them – the bullet had gone through the nerve. I was on early morning parade with my rifle and everything, and I passed out like a log. I just fainted. The result was I was excused parades.

Then I was posted to West Hartlepool, and from there drafts were formed to be sent back to France. But I appeared before a medical board – and I was recommended for discharge, with a pension of sixty per cent. I didn't have use of my hand, and the general feeling was that no one who had been in France for any length of time wanted to go back. Oh no! But while I was waiting for my discharge, some order must have been passed that men who could still be used must not be discharged. They must be retained and put in departmental corps. I wasn't consulted at all, and I was transferred to the Army Pay Corps at St Helens.

I was in St Helens for a few days, and then sent down to Nottingham, where they were opening a pay office to deal with the accounts of the Labour Corps. I was going to be a clerk, in the lowest category. I was billeted out on civilians, and I had only been in the house for five minutes, when the landlady – if you'd like to call her that – said, 'There's a soldier at the door, and he wants to speak to you.' It was a Canadian soldier – and I didn't know him. He said, 'I saw you arrive just now, and I want to ask you a favour.' I said, 'What favour?' He said, 'I'm on special leave from the front, and I'm getting married tomorrow, and returning the next day. I know nobody in town. Will you be my best man?' I said, 'I don't know you.' He said, 'It doesn't matter.' I said, 'I don't know what to do.' He said, 'It doesn't matter. Just pass me the ring.' So the next day, at a church nearby, I was best man at this soldier's wedding. Afterwards, we went and had a drink at one of the houses. Never heard or saw him again.

## Lieutenant Norman Collins
### 6th Battalion, Seaforth Highlanders

We were drawn out of the line for a rest. We were sent near Auchonvillers, and we had a clean up, and we got back into our officers' togs. We recovered very well. We had musical evenings, with the pipes playing; we had boxing matches. I was upset, though, because I was detailed to go back up the line with a working party. We had to go to a dump, where we had to pick up barbed wire and posts and take them up a communication trench, and get out after dark, and mend the wire in front of the line. I thought this was most unfair, having just come out of action, but there you were, this sort of thing happened.

So, we got as far as the dump, and we picked up the material and entered the communication trench. I had my squad of about a dozen men with me, and I heard the shriek of a shell and it sounded different. I knew a lot about the shrieks of shells by this time. It was getting louder and louder, and I thought it had my name on it. It landed just behind us, and it killed, or badly wounded, the whole of the squad. I was blown down, but I was the least injured, and I got a piece of the shell in my thigh. We were all taken into a first-aid post, and a doctor examined everybody. He kept saying, 'Dead, dead, dead, take them out!' He didn't want to bother with those. The dead were grey. As soon as they died, they went a grey colour. The doctor did the best he could with the wounded, put them on stretchers and got them on to ambulances. I was able to walk because I hadn't broken any bones, and I walked with the wounded to the ambulance, got in and we went down the road.

As we drove along, we passed the artillery, the field guns, and then the heavy guns, and after a while the noise of the guns died away, and we knew that we were out of the danger zone. We went into a tented hospital, and that night we slept in white sheets. After that, we were sent back to England and I landed up in the Brighton workhouse, which had been converted into a hospital. I was glad to be there.

## Lieutenant Ulick Burke
### 2nd Battalion, Devonshire Regiment

A lot of men died between being wounded and getting to a casualty clearing station, or a base hospital, because there was no blood plasma in those days. And also your journey – especially if you were on a stretcher – was very precarious. A fellow would step on what he thought was a piece of the road – but it was a hole – and down he'd go, and over would go the stretcher, and you'd be hurled into the road. And there was so much mud and dirt that could get into the wound, that gangrene was the worst enemy.

## Captain Maberly Esler
### 9th Battalion, Border Regiment

As the battalion medical officer, I had a sergeant and a corporal and I had three stretcher-bearers allotted to each company, and there were four companies in the battalion, so that gave me twelve stretcher-bearers to call on, in an emergency. I had a first-aid post in a dugout just behind the trenches, which could hold twenty or thirty wounded men. The stretcher-bearers went out and found people who were lying out, and couldn't get in themselves, and brought them to the first-aid post where we did all the dressing we could do.

The function in the front line was to pick people up immediately they were wounded and put on a first-aid dressing, or give them morphia. All we could really do was to cover the wound, keep it from getting infected and stop haemorrhaging by compression on the main vessel. If an arm or leg was shot and bleeding profusely, you had to stop the whole thing by putting a tourniquet on, but you couldn't keep a tourniquet on for longer than an hour without stopping the blood supply and losing the leg altogether, so it was very necessary to call a field ambulance quickly, who could ligature the vessels. In those cases, they had to be on the ambulance in five or ten minutes.

The field ambulance could come up at any time of day or night. We would get in touch with them by field telephone and tell them we had these cases. The field ambulance could perform minor operations, then, as quickly as possible, they'd move them back to the casualty clearing station, which could do major operations and would sort them out. They decided if they were fit to go home, or fit to go back to their fighting units, or else they passed them back to a base hospital.

## Private Basil Farrer
### 3rd Battalion, Green Howards

In the morning, it was 'stand to', and then after that, as stretcher-bearers, we would be in the front line in our dugout, and we would be available on call if there was a casualty. We would pass the day playing cards, writing letters or reading – if you had anything to read. There was always something to talk about. You'd wander up and down the trenches looking for someone to talk to. Those that had nothing to do very often lay down in a dugout. If you had a dugout. Because we knew we may be on duty at night-time.

If there was a casualty, word passed down the line 'stretcher-bearer, stretcher-bearer', then, of course, we would go along the line and attend to the man. We'd see if he's wounded and if we could apply his dressing. Then we'd put him on a stretcher and take him down to the aid post. You would try not to hurt him – and the thing was to get him out. It's surprising what men could put up with. I have seen – during battle – men who have been crawling on their knees with half a foot off. And in an attack, you looked after your own wounded. As you passed, there might be a man calling for you; you looked on his shoulder and saw if he was one of your regiment. If not, you left the fellow. It wasn't an instruction as far as I can recollect, but it was a natural thing. You had plenty of your own.

### Corporal Wilfred Woods
### 1/4th Battalion, Suffolk Regiment

On the Somme, a lot of men were never picked up at all. There was a sergeant with his shin all ripped open, and he had been there about a week; it was all green gangrene, and full of maggots as big as that. He was alive and could talk to you. I said, 'I will do what I can to get you out!' We went back and left him there, and at night we heard, 'Stretcher-bearer! Stretcher-bearer!' and then, 'Bang, Bang.' The Germans were throwing hand bombs at him, you see.

### Sergeant Frederick Goodman
### 1st London Field Ambulance, Royal Army Medical Corps

When I first got to France, the very first time I saw real casualties, they were a German captain and one of our sergeant majors. They'd met each other over the top, they'd fired simultaneously and shot each other. I had to pick them up. We got them into the dressing station – and I fainted. It was the first time I saw blood in the 'real sense'. After that, I had to pull myself together, and as time went on I became quite callous. But we saw so much, and we had to get used to some very awful things.

Being a stretcher-bearer was a very arduous job. We had to carry stretchers for a hundred yards, up to our knees in mud, and there would be other men to take the man back to the advanced dressing station. And then, further back, there would be a main dressing station, and finally a casualty clearing station. There were times when we had so many casualties coming in at one time that we didn't always have adequate staff to deal with them. We did the best we could with them. We would do a first field dressing – rip up their tunic, and

Stretcher-bearers bringing in a casualty.

An advanced dressing station at Fricourt.

whack on the dressing – but if it was more serious than that, we'd put them on a stretcher. We did the best we could.

I had a great friend at school, who was rather partial to my sister. He was a very discerning young chap! They got on very well together. Well, he went off to join Princess Louise's, the 13th London, and one day I was called to give some assistance, and one man had some shrapnel, so I ripped up his tunic and applied the necessary. And as I was doing this, he looked up and he said, 'Good Lord! It's you, Fred! Well, I'm damned!' It was the very same chap.

On one occasion, we had a small truce. We had so many dead over the top – and so did the Germans – that we called a truce. An hour or two would be allowed, to go over the top and bury the dead. This was carried out, and eventually someone started firing again and that was the end of that. And we had a message from headquarters, saying that they knew what had happened and they didn't approve of it. We were fraternising with the enemy – and that must not be! And I can understand it too! We didn't want to fraternise with them! But we had to attend to our chaps. There were so many dead. The memory of it is awful. Dreadful. You have no idea.

### Lieutenant Phillip Howe
#### 10th Battalion, West Yorkshire Regiment
There were so many casualties on the Somme that they wanted to get rid of them to England, to keep the hospitals in France empty as far as possible to deal with the really serious cases. Myself being only walking wounded, they shoved me onboard a boat, which was over-laden with wounded, and hundreds of German prisoners too. It was a very slow crossing from Le Havre to Southampton.

### Private Harold Hayward
#### 12th Battalion, Gloucestershire Regiment
I got sent home to Blighty, and went to Lincoln General Hospital. I was very well treated, except for one thing. In this ward, there was a lady from one of the county families, who used to come once a week, and she was rather nosey. She wanted to know everything. At first I told her that I was wounded, but she said she couldn't see any bandages. Well, they were under the bedclothes. I pointed down there, hoping that would be sufficient. The next week she came back, and again she said, 'Where were you injured?' I knew what

Q 4094

A casualty clearing station near Vaux.

she meant, but I said, 'Guillemont.' 'No,' she said, 'where on your body are you wounded?' I was a bit fed up by now, and I said, 'Madam, if you had been wounded where I have been wounded, you wouldn't have been wounded at all.'

That was the last time she visited. Some of the men on that ward guffawed quite loudly – and she stormed out of the ward, and never came back.

### Private William Holmes
#### 12th Battalion, London Regiment

In hospital, in England, I was given what these drug addicts take now. Heroin. I was in such agony that I couldn't get to sleep, and the nurse asked if I'd like a cup of tea – and no sooner had I drunk it, than she put the heroin into my thumb. And the whole scene changed. My eyes were opened. I could see flowers about twenty-five feet high, lovely fountains. I felt *so* well.

### Signaller Leonard Ounsworth
#### 124th Heavy Battery, Royal Garrison Artillery

When I was out of hospital, I was sent before a Standing Medical Board in England. There were two or three officers there and you filed past them. They were examining about a hundred men in an hour. You went before them and they said, 'What's the matter with you?' and I said, 'Gunshot wounds in the arm, in the neck and the jaw and the back,' and they said I was all right; I said I couldn't open my jaws properly yet, so he then said to me, 'Well, go down to Market Square in Ripon this evening – do you know it?' I said, 'No, sir, I only arrived last night, in a snowstorm, in the dark.' 'So go down there,' he said, 'find the prettiest girl you can, take her down a dark passage and get her to tickle you under the chin. You'll soon open your jaw then.' That's the advice he gave me, 'Next one!', and I was bloody disgusted.

### Private Harold Hayward
#### 12th Battalion, Gloucestershire Regiment

I had to report to Horfield Barracks, not two miles from my parents' home. I was being 'rehabilitated' and that really broke my patriotism. We were drilled up and down the square by these fellows who got at us. To think these people, who'd been in England, were doing this to us, who'd been out in the trenches, and they treated us as though we were less than the dust. I lost a lot of my patriotism then.

**Major Alfred Irwin**
*8th Battalion, East Surrey Regiment*
People in England had no idea whatsoever what was happening in France. I was sitting in a restaurant in London, with my wife. We'd been married a very short time. My wound was recovering, and I was still on medical leave. A girl came in, with white feathers, and I was in civvies. There was nothing to show that I'd taken any part in the war, and she presented me with a white feather. My wife was *so* furious.

**Corporal H. Tansley**
*9th Battalion, York and Lancaster Regiment*
There were strikes going on in England at the time, because people were losing their pint of beer, or not getting this-and-that. They used to ask, why didn't we press the war and get on with it? Well, that showed a proper ignorance of the feelings of the soldiers at the front. We had pressures behind us that people at home could hardly dream of.

**Second Lieutenant Edmund Blunden**
*11th Battalion, Royal Sussex Regiment*
On leave [in 1917] I was asked to stay with some dear relations. They were very kind but they asked me how things were going. They pointed out the scale of the British victory. I had to confess that I didn't think that the victory amounted to very much since we hadn't got anywhere – and wouldn't. I gave an account of Passchendaele. This, I found, was a horrible offence against the natural order. My relative said, 'I fancy that this is quite enough, young man! You're fighting for the Germans! You'd better make up your mind where you'll be staying tomorrow night!' So I left the house under those conditions. That was a bit of a puzzle. It showed me that I hadn't been thinking enough of the people at home. Neither, for that matter, had they been thinking of us very much.

**Sergeant Charles Quinnell**
*9th Battalion, Royal Fusiliers*
The first night I came home to England on leave I got into my old bed and do you think I could sleep? No. Sleep wouldn't come. It was the first bed I'd laid in since I joined the army. And when my mother brought my cup of tea up in

the morning she found me fast asleep on the floor. I got so used to sleeping hard that I couldn't sleep on a soft bed.

## Bombardier James Naylor
### 30th Brigade, Royal Field Artillery

On my first leave in England, there were two army nurses walking along, talking to each other, and so you know, I hadn't heard an English woman talking for fourteen months and I was so impressed and interested. I just walked behind them and listened to them talking. I don't know what they thought of me. I've never forgotten it.

## Sergeant Charles Quinnell
### 9th Battalion, Royal Fusiliers

Life in France was a life apart from anything that you'd done in civilian life. You'd become a gipsy, you'd learned to look after yourself: whereas in your civilian life your mother did all the chores, now you had learned to do everything for yourself. You'd learned how to cook for yourself, make do, darn your own socks, sew on your own buttons and all things like that. You could speak to your comrades and they understood – but the civilians, it was just a waste of time.

## Private Horace Ham
### 16th Battalion, Middlesex Regiment

When I was convalescing after July 1, I was home at my home in Bournemouth, and my father wanted to see the film *The Battle of the Somme*, so we went to the Electric Theatre and we saw it. I saw the mine go up again – I had actually seen it go up! I saw our division being inspected by the general on the day before the battle. I didn't recognise anybody. We had known they were taking films, because we had seen them doing it. They'd had special places built to protect them from shells.

## Sergeant Charles Quinnell
### 9th Battalion, Royal Fusiliers

I'd always been a great lover of the country and before the war I used to do a lot of cycling. Pretty well every weekend in the summer I'd be out cycling. And one of the first things I did, when I was home on leave, was to resurrect my old bike, pump the tyres up, oil it and clean it, and I rode round the old country visiting the old scenes that I knew in peacetime. That to me was the most enjoyable thing.

### Sergeant Frederick Goodman
### 1st London Field Ambulance, Royal Army Medical Corps

One day, my colonel said, 'You know, I can't give you any Blighty leave, but if you and your pal want some leave, I'm quite prepared to give you a fortnight's leave here in France. Would you like to take it?' 'My dear sir,' I said, 'I would! Of course!' 'Where would you like to go?' 'Sir, there's only one place I want to go! I want to go to Nice! The south of France!' I'd always liked the idea of the Promenade des Anglais. And they gave me a pass.

I wrote to Thomas Cook – they were in existence – and I told them that I wanted to go to a place where I'd be looked after in a hotel, but I didn't want to be subject to a lot of discipline from officers. In other words, I wanted them to put me in a sergeant's place, somewhere appropriate to me. Well, they did. They fixed me up with a private flat, attached to an English restaurant. A girl used to come in every day, and make the beds and do the chores, and my pal and I would go downstairs to have our meal. I went to Monte Carlo where I sent my parents a card, and we joined up with some Women's Institute-type ladies who invited us to their homes, and we met a couple of girls . . . We had a wonderful time. Why not? Wouldn't you?

### Corporal Jim Crow
### 110th Brigade, Royal Field Artillery

At one point, there were a number picked out of each battery to go to the seaside. We had a rest. There were no other duties at all – just to keep the camp clean. We got there by train, in open trucks, and as the train chugged slowly up a hill, we jumped off and picked apples, but – my God – we didn't do that after we'd reached the top, because the train did sixty downhill.

### Corporal H. Tansley
### 9th Battalion, York and Lancaster Regiment

It was continual misery. We would come out of the trenches, out of the line, for a 'rest' at a place called Hardecourt Wood, behind the town of Albert. Our beds were chicken wire nailed on stakes. And there was more work for us there – carrying parties up to the line, and working parties – than there was when we were manning the trenches.

## Captain Maberly Esler
### 9th Battalion, Border Regiment

Out of the line, the mental condition was a condition varying between depression, and relief at being out of the thing. The men were frightened, they were timid; they didn't want to go back any more to war.

## Lieutenant William Taylor
### 13th Battalion, Royal Fusiliers

During the rest period, out of the line, we stayed in farmhouses. There was a company mess. I shared a room with another officer. In some cases, there were real beds, in others, wooden and chicken-wire beds, with a straw mattress. The mess was an ordinary room in a farmhouse. The next room was the kitchen, where the cook would prepare the officers' food. There would be four platoon officers, the captain commanding the company, and sometimes a second in command. There was one mess waiter and a cook. Then, you had your own servant, but he wouldn't be in the mess. He would be with the other men.

The men were accommodated in barns. It was all farming country, and each platoon would have its own barn. They had bunk beds made of wood and chicken wire. That was the standard bed in France in those days.

The mood was very friendly. Entirely different to the mood in England. There was an association of officers, usually very friendly. One inspected men's kit. One inspected their rifles. They had plenty of time to clean themselves, and to clean their rifles. We used to go to divisional baths, and one generally got fit again. The baths might be in the next village, or quite a long way away.

A number of men would be detailed to return to the line for a day only, to do a particular fatigue or to carry out some trench stores. Occasionally, working parties had to return to the line during rest periods. We had parades during rest periods – PT parades. We always had those in the morning, to keep them fit. There would be physical exercises. Not much else apart from kit inspections and rifle inspections. There might be one of each during the rest period.

For the men, football was the main recreation. We used to play bridge, whilst the men played Housey Housey [bingo]. There was a divisional concert party, but we saw them very rarely. We never saw them during our usual six days out of the line. We only saw them when we went out for a longer period, between battles. One of our company commanders was Captain Bliss who, afterwards, became Master of the Queen's Musick, Sir Arthur Bliss, and he always tried to find a billet where there was a piano. I can remember sitting in his billet one day, listening to him playing.

### Sergeant Frederick Goodman
### 1st London Field Ambulance, Royal Army Medical Corps

We had the Bow Bells Concert Party which became very well known in the division. And we had our own concert party. We'd find a hall, or a barn, out of the line, and we had large audiences. We had one chap who played all the women's parts. He'd take the part of Ethel Levy, and he was astonishingly good at it.

### Corporal Tommy Keele
### 11th Battalion, Middlesex Regiment

People didn't always know I was a man dressed up as a woman. Some officers from one of the regiments came to see our show and they teased their colonel that one of the girls in the show was a real girl and the other one was a female impersonator and they bet him fifty francs that he couldn't pick out the real girl. Dolly Clair, the other 'girl' appeared first. He was much fatter than me. I didn't come on stage until the end of the show. I walked on in a very low-cut evening dress. Halfway down my chest I used to put a dark red line and then shade the line off so the side was a little pink. It looked like a cleavage and when he saw me the colonel said, 'That one is the female.' So I had to go along to his barracks to prove I was a little lance corporal in the Middlesex Regiment. He was disgusted.

### Sergeant Charles Quinnell
### 9th Battalion, Royal Fusiliers

We always had at least one bath whilst we were out of the line. In pretty well every large-size French village, there was a brewery, a *brasserie* as they called it, and in these brasseries there were great vats, twelve feet in diameter and about three feet deep. Well, in the boiler house there used to be some old soldiers, men in their fifties, and they'd been given the job of stoking up the boilers and filling these vats with hot water and then we, the infantry, would be marched up to this *brasserie*.

We would take off all our things in one room, and leave our dirty shirts in a heap there, and then we'd go into the room where these vats were. There was plenty of soap lying about, but before getting into these vats, there'd been another battalion in there before, and there was an inch of scum on top of the water, which you gently scooped off and flung on to the floor. The floor became like a skating rink so you had to walk very, very carefully or else you were down.

We'd get into these vats and you could actually swim in them. We used to lather ourselves and we used to really enjoy that. And then we'd get out of the vats, and go to the room to the other side and pick up a clean shirt. Well, the old soldier who was in charge there, he didn't have time to see what size you were, you had the first shirt that came to you.

### Sergeant Frederick Goodman
### 1st London Field Ambulance, Royal Army Medical Corps

I had a chap in my section – a very fine stretcher-bearer – but he was renowned for giving an awful lot of trouble. Because he was such a nuisance, to make him take note that I wouldn't put up with his behaviour, I put him on latrine duties. And soon after that we played a football match, the men versus the NCOs. I was in goal for the NCOs, and this chap decided that he was going to get his own back on me. He ran the ball down the field on his own. They didn't attempt to get the ball off him, so it must have been prearranged. He got to my goal, and he shot the ball – and me – bang into the net. If I'd been in his place, I'd probably have done the same.

### Private Reginald Glenn
### 12th Battalion, York and Lancaster Regiment

At Colincamps, in the rest areas, our billets were broken-down houses, in amongst the ruins. We got tarpaulins and pieces of corrugated iron. We never went right out of the line – we were always within shelling range. When we came out of the line, the first thing we had to do was to get all the mud out of our clothes and boots, with a scrubbing brush, before we were given a meal. It wasn't full spit and polish. Just tidy.

## Sergeant A. S. Durrant
### 18th Battalion, Durham Light Infantry

Out of the line, about half a dozen of us were billeted in the loft of this farmhouse. It had a lovely soft 'bed' of hay, and we were very comfortable. We noticed a couple of rats in the rafters, and we became friendly with them. They used to come down, and we gave them morsels of food. They became our pets. There was a great box full of bully beef tins in the loft, and we helped ourselves to that. We were continually opening tins of the stuff, eating a bit, and throwing the rest away.

## Corporal Tommy Keele
### 11th Battalion, Middlesex Regiment

I was asked by a bandmaster whether I had a spare billet for him. He had just come out of the trenches. I told him I hadn't but that I did have a very nice bedroom with a double bed, if he didn't mind sharing. So, the first couple of nights, quite good, yes, we shared it and slept quite comfortably but, on about the third night, I woke up with a funny little movement round my bottom. I thought, 'Oh, he's having a dream,' so I sort of brushed his hand away and dropped off again. A little later, the same thing again, I felt a hand around my bottom again and I pushed the hand away quickly and said, 'Don't you dare!' He sorted of muttered in his sleep, or so I thought, and I dropped off again. Then he went even further and he was almost raping me. So, I turned round and I hit him. I knocked him out of the bed. I stood him up and I punched him with my fist. I really battered his head and face for trying to bugger me. Anyway, he said to me, 'You know what you've done?' I said, 'Yes, I do. And you know what you've done?' He said, 'I haven't done anything.' I said, 'You tried to bugger me.' He said, 'I shall report this. You'll be court-martialled.' I said, 'Fine! You report it tomorrow morning and you see who wins. You're a top NCO, I'm a lower NCO. Buggery is a crime in the army and it carries the death penalty. You'd be shot if I opened my mouth because you tried to bugger me.'

And he never opened his mouth except to say that on his way to his billet, he'd slipped over and got gravel rash down one side of his face. I was sorry for him afterwards, because everybody was sex-starved. There was no such thing as real girls around. He was probably in that mood and anything was good enough. But if I was good enough, I didn't want to be . . .

**Corporal Jack Critchley**
*Royal Artillery attached to Guards Division*
One day, one of the drivers behind the lines, said, 'There's a prisoner-of-war camp just across the way, German prisoners they are.' Out of curiosity, several of us went along to see these German prisoners. We found them in a compound, with nowhere to shelter, just huddled up in a ball, diving on to each other for warmth. There were probably two or three hundred of them.

Of course, to us, it looked a bit inhuman. As we were watching, one of these Germans shouted across to us, 'Is anyone there from Birmingham?' We found a lad from Birmingham, and this German called out, 'Do you remember me? I had a barber's shop on Salter Street?' No, he didn't remember. Anyhow the German then said, 'One of our chaps here will give his Iron Cross if you've a French loaf.' So, of course, somebody found a French loaf. He must have gone miles behind the line to get it. The point was that this Iron Cross would be a nice souvenir to take home. So when we thought that the little French guard – who was about sixty, by the way – had got to the other end of the alley and couldn't see us, somebody threw this loaf over. There were two rows of barbed wire and, unluckily for this German, it hit the top wire and fell back into the mud on the other side. And the splash drew the attention of the guard.

**Lieutenant Norman Collins**
*6th Battalion, Seaforth Highlanders*
The night when the witches walk. Hallowe'en. We were in a barn behind the lines, and the pipers were piping, and there was a lot of heavy drinking, and the colonel asked the pipe major what he would like to drink, and the pipe major ordered crème de menthe. And a tankard of the stuff was brought to him, which he drank in one gulp. I wasn't a drinker at all, but that night I was breaking my rule, and I was thumping the table. There was a bit of broken glass around, and a very kind major restrained me in case I thumped on the glass. And later that night, I had to go up the line with a sergeant, to do a reconnaissance in front of the line at Beaumont Hamel.

**Second Lieutenant W. J. Brockman**
*15th Battalion, Lancashire Fusiliers*
Ten miles behind the line, you wouldn't have thought there was a war on at all. The hotels stayed open. You could go into one of the hotels, or one of the

local *estaminets*, and have a jolly good meal. The French men were all gone, of course, but the women weren't . . .

## Private Philip Cullen
### 4th Battalion, Oxfordshire and Buckinghamshire Light Infantry

The French *estaminet* was an ordinary house with a bar. Lots of *vin blanc*, *vin rouge*, and beer – but we never drank beer. That was kid's stuff. One night, we were marching off to the front in the morning, so we went there at night, and we boozed, and we ate, and we boozed until we faded away, drunk as lords. On champagne. I walked out of the back door and fell down the stairs, and lay there. I wasn't bothered. It started to pour with rain, but I still lay there. The night went on, and my platoon lads were missing me: 'Where's the sergeant? If he misses the morning, he's going to get shot!' They found me in the back-yard, picked me up, dragged me back, covered me with blankets, took my clothes to the cookhouse and dried them off, and at six in the morning we fell in for a twenty-mile march. I found out that getting drunk off champagne's nothing too bad. I finished off at the front of the platoon, where I should be, and not only that, the last mile or so, I carried one of the men's rifles. I was feeling fine. Ever since, I've thought champagne's the drink to get drunk off.

## Private Reginald Glenn
### 12th Battalion, York and Lancaster Regiment

The *estaminets* were very good – if you could afford them. They always had the coffee brewing on the stove.

## Private William Holmes
### 12th Battalion, London Regiment

The *estaminets* were wonderful. The British have never had them. They would be beautifully warm, and they had different things that I've never seen in British restaurants. They had coloured lights and artificial flowers. The whole atmosphere was good. It was such a wonderful change from what we'd been through. The serving girls at the counter would be gaily dressed, and there'd always be music, sometimes a small band, and you could sing the popular songs of the day. The food was so good. I remember one of the delicacies was frogs – and they were quite enjoyable. We used to drink wine – they wouldn't stick to just tea, and the wines were so cheap.

### Sergeant Frederick Goodman
#### 1st London Field Ambulance, Royal Army Medical Corps

We used to frequent a little *estaminet*, run by a little French lady, a very pleasant woman, who could find cakes and what have you. We used to go in there and buy whatever was going. One day, a shell came over, right bang on to the *estaminet*. She was very badly hurt, and we brought her into our dressing station, but it was apparent that she wouldn't live. As she died, she said, 'C'*est la guerre, monsieur.*'

### Private Frank Turner
#### Army Cyclist Corps

One night, we found an *estaminet* with a piano. It was a fair size, and there were four or five soldiers having a quiet drink. We asked the madame if we could play the piano. '*Mais oui, monsieur!*' So I started. In no time the place was bursting at the seams with troops. It was a wonderful experience. There were all these drinks lined up on the piano for me – in all colours of the rainbow – but I didn't drink half of them. I wasn't used to it. Eventually, the madame got the wind up and she called the redcaps, who chucked us all out. And then someone handed me a concertina – I don't know where it came from – and I can knock a tune out. One old soldier was holding my right arm, another was holding my left arm, and we passed through the artillery lines. It was a quiet night; there was no firing going on, and chaps were coming out of the artillery dugout, yelling, 'What the –'s going on?' We didn't get nicked, but I couldn't look at a thing the next morning.

### Private Fred Dixon
#### 10th Battalion, Royal West Surrey Regiment

In one *estaminet*, a very kind old French lady was dispensing coffee from a jug and two girls in their late teens were dispensing pills which they assured us would give us additional power in our amorous exploits. Colonel Hayley-Bell was our colonel at the time. He was the grandfather of the actress Hayley Mills, and he was greedy. He took two.

### Corporal George Ashurst
#### 1st Battalion, Lancashire Fusiliers

We were drinking *vin blanc* in the *estaminet*, and it was absolutely crowded. There were five women in there, and it was five francs to go up the stairs and into the bedrooms with them. One night, the padre walked in. The stairs leading up to bedrooms were full; there was a man on every step, waiting his turn to go in with a woman. I was sat at a table with my friend Tom, when the padre came in. He dressed us all down. 'Have none of you any mothers? Have none of you any sisters?' I didn't fancy the prostitutes at all. They were so common. Tom said, 'Are you going up there?' 'No,' I said, 'not with them *things*!' They were all sorts of ages. Fellows could probably tell you what it was like going in; the first thing she does is grab your five franc note. Put it there! And then she unfastens your flies, and has a feel, and *squeezes* it, to feel if anything's wrong with you. And then she throws her cloak off, and she's on the bed. Ready for you. And when she's finished, she has the kettle boiling with some herbs in it, to give you a bit of a swill. For safety's sake. There was an old Frenchman upstairs, bossing the place, and he was shoving the men into the rooms, when they were empty, and shoving the men away, who'd been in. I didn't go for it – not with that lot. But most of the troops did. The stairs were lined with men.

## Anonymous

I went to a knocking shop. They were great big women, most of them, and they were all sitting round a big table, waiting for opening time. When I came in, 'Ah! The blue-eyed garçon! Ici!' I was so embarrassed by the time I got to the bedroom, I couldn't get a stand at all. I was – what do you call it? – impotent. It was the first time I'd had *that sort* of woman. We'd heard all these tales of disease, and I was a bit apprehensive. But I went once or twice afterwards, and it was all right. She'd be wearing a thin kimono, to give you the feeling, straight away, and she fleeced you for about ten francs. I picked the youngest one every time, and it was all very quick. In and out.

## Private Albert Day
### 1/4th Battalion, Gloucestershire Regiment

We would look for girls, but if you were a private you'd have no chance. The sergeants and the good-looking NCOs – they naturally pinched the girls.

## Private William Holmes
### 12th Battalion, London Regiment

We were always chatting the French women up. The French girls knew how to make the best of themselves. More than my own sisters. Our girls never had that '*petite*' business, and they never put all that colour on their faces, the way the French girls did. It was an art with them. Virtually every girl you met was beautiful. They wouldn't be above putting flowers in their hair.

**Anonymous**

I made up my mind to make the best of the war, and enjoy it. I used to take my washing to a girl behind the lines, and I used to do it when she was leaning over the ironing board, ironing. My first time had been at sixteen or seventeen, at Whitley Bay, lying on the sands, and the tide swept over us, but my first French girl was when we stopped at a station. There were some girls there, and they were very pretty. I was talking to one, and we started doing it on the platform. It wasn't much of a platform – more of a grass verge. The best one was the last one. I was billeted with her family – unofficially – and her grandfather ran the power station. She used to bring me coffee every morning, and get into bed with me. The grandfather never knew. He was a nice chap; I was sorry to do it – from that point of view. But she was very, very nice.

**Private Thomas McIndoe**
*12th Battalion, Middlesex Regiment*

When we arrived in France a memo was issued by Lord Kitchener. It said that in recent months quite a number of the Expeditionary Force had rendered themselves unfit for duty through negligence in contracting venereal disease. This must stop forthwith as the War Office takes a very poor view of this in view of the number that's been rendered unfit for duty.

**Anonymous**

I went to bed with one woman, and she was so fat I couldn't find anywhere to go.

# The Fight Goes On

*Why did I survive? I have thought about it over and over again.*

I n the wake of the bloody first day, British attention became focused on consolidating the gains that had been made to the south. Haig underlined to Joffre his plan to launch a major attack on Longueval. Joffre initially argued that the British should concentrate on attacking at Thiepval and Pozières, where British troops had just been so badly mauled. After a heated discussion, Joffre – for once – backed down.

## JULY 2 – JULY 14

On July 2, Fricourt – which had been abandoned by the Germans – was taken. Five days later, attacks were mounted on the villages of Ovillers and Contalmaison, and on Mametz Wood. These attacks were intended to consolidate the left flank in advance of the major thrust. In an assault on Ovillers, the 8th and 9th Battalions, Royal Fusiliers, together with the 7th Battalion, Royal Sussex Regiment, took the first three lines of German trenches. The 16th Battalion Welch Regiment was torn apart by machine-gun fire in its failed attack on Mametz on July 9. The wood was taken five days later, but only after the deaths of almost four thousand officers and men. On July 9, the 17th Battalion, Manchester Regiment took part in an attack on Trônes Wood, in order to consolidate the right flank. The wood was won and then lost, and had not been secured in time for the assault on Longueval.

**Anonymous**

Behind Fricourt, there's a ridge, and running along the ridge was a line of trees, and the Germans still occupied that. My company had the task of clearing them, as part of a mopping-up operation. We attacked the wood from a sunken road running parallel to it. Before the attack, there was – the only time I saw it – an unrestricted issue of rum. There was a large jar of rum being passed round, and men were holding out their mess tins for it. At the request of the artillery, the attack was postponed by an hour, and the rum was still being passed round during that hour. I just had a sip, but a lot of the older soldiers were walloping it down. When we eventually went over, they were a mob of waving, screaming maniacs. Some of them even forgot to take their rifles. But what could have been a stark tragedy turned into a black comedy, because the artillery had done a lot of damage, and there was just one German machine gun left, and two of our bombers silenced it. When we got to the trench, there were a lot of dead Germans inside it, and we could see the others running away. One man said to me afterwards, 'I don't remember a lot about it, but we must have frightened the bloody daylights out of Jerry.'

**Sergeant Wilfred Hunt**
*9th Battalion, Devonshire Regiment*
On July 2, we were called up to join the Devons, who'd been badly mauled between Fricourt and Mametz. We reorganised as best we could – I was made from lance corporal to sergeant, and we were taken straight to Death Valley. We went over the top, and our objective was a road. We were supposed to stay at the road, but somebody said, 'Come on! We're going further!' So we went through to a cornfield. When we got to the other end of this cornfield, we found some Germans busy digging. They saw us at the same time as we saw them, they brought their machine guns out, and we had to look sharp back to where we started from, to the road, where we should have stopped.

**Sergeant Alf Razzell**
*8th Battalion, Royal Fusiliers*
We went over on July 7, in the morning. Just before we went, the colonel climbed up one of the ladders and looked over. Each company was to go over separately, with a space of two minutes between each. I was going with the

third line – the 'Headquarter Company' as our colonel called it. He was going with the third line too.

Well, just as the first line were going, the colonel turned to the adjutant, who was alongside him, and he said, 'It's a gift, Bobby!' After just a few moments, it was our turn to go, and over we went.

The people who had been over on July 1 were lying there. The casualties were lying everywhere; there was a body every few yards, all the way down the valley. It was a horrifying experience, even for somebody who'd been out there quite a while. When we had gone about eighty yards, I saw the colonel stagger and put his arm around his orderly's shoulders. He staggered on for a few more steps, then sank down on to the ground. He was obviously badly wounded. Of course, you carry on, but I noticed that there were very few men still standing in the two lines in front of me. We were being enfiladed from either side from the high ground left and right, because when I went to use my rifle afterwards, there was a hole through the butt at right angles to the direction in which we were advancing.

With seven hundred yards to go to the German trench, we came to a road which cut obliquely across our line of advance, and I noticed that every man that got on to the road went down. They obviously had a fixed machine gun – or guns – a few inches above the road. I saw then the cutting power of a machine gun, because within a few seconds every man that went down was just a mound of bloody cloth with bits flying off. Naturally I didn't cross that road. I went along a slight ditch along the side of the road, until I came to the German wire, which was impassable.

The wire was breast high, and probably fifteen feet in depth, so I dropped into a shell-hole under their wire. I was immediately joined by another man, and we both thought that the attack had failed. For about an hour, the Germans were throwing bombs at us; we were just out of their range, but we were near enough that we could feel the displacement of the air when they exploded.

After an hour, we saw Mills bombs being thrown in the opposite direction, so it was obvious that we had a bombing party in their trench. And after a bit, the Germans in front of us got out of their trench and disappeared, so we made our way to the left until we found a place where we could get through the wire by picking our way carefully, and we joined the Tommies in the trench.

We stayed with them all that day, and we advanced up the German communication trenches and took over their support trenches, and various saps and little trenches. We more or less took it all that day. That night, we expected a counter-attack – which didn't come.

We discovered that the colonel, the adjutant and all four company commanders had been killed. Every officer in the battalion had been killed or wounded. There was one sergeant – myself, one corporal and one lance corporal. We were annihilated. Our battalion, that we were so proud of, was annihilated in the time it takes you to walk seven hundred yards.

The next morning, I had to take a squad of men with me to collect the pay books from our dead. It's a picture that's been in my mind ever since. Absolutely horrific. Every yard or so there was a dead man, and of course we had to sort our own men out from the others that had been there before. This was war at its worst. There were men with half faces, men with empty brain cavities, headless corpses, corpses without limbs. We were tripping over intestines, where men had been disembowelled. That was all the way up to the German wire.

Why did I survive? I have thought about it over and over again. How can anybody possibly walk seven hundred yards through those machine guns and not be hit? The only thing I can think of is that when I was a boy, I had been in the country and seen the old horse-drawn reaping machines. The people that I stayed with used to *glean* after the reapers had been over the fields. That means picking up the waste sheaves of corn. When the field was finished, here and there, odd stems of corn would be left standing. I can only think that just as they missed the reaper – so the survivors must have missed the machine guns.

### Private Tom Bracey
### *9th Battalion, Royal Fusiliers*

We moved into the line at Ovillers. We knew that the first days had failed because we could see the dead about, the wounded, hundreds of stretchers. It was late in the afternoon when we went in. We went back to Albert, and we were told that we would be making an attack at Ovillers. That was on the seventh. We were told to tear up all our writing paper. I tell you, I was scared. I'd seen all these bodies. But my friend Albert said, 'Now we'll show 'em what we're made of!' He was full of life, Albert, but the rest of us were very quiet. We just grinned at one another.

Royal Fusiliers after the attack of July 7.

Men of the Royal Warwickshire Regiment after an attack.

So we went up at eight o'clock at night, and we sat down waiting to attack. It was just about getting dark. I remember talking to a proper cockney – been in prison. The officer came up and told us that our machine-gun team was being taken out of the attack. They decided that our Vickers gun was too heavy for the attack. It needed six men. The gun itself was 38½ pounds, the tripod was forty-eight pounds, a box of 250 rounds was twenty-one pounds, there were four of those, and then there were all the spare parts. So they told us to return to the transport lines. God, that was a relief to me.

And then we heard the bombardment. Blimey, talk about thunder and lightning. After that, we were waiting for news of the men who attacked. We didn't hear anything, but the next morning we watched them coming out of the line. I could have cried. I asked about my friend Monty – he came from Hammersmith, he was always after the girls – and they said he was blown to bits. We lost fifty per cent of the battalion from shellfire before they even went over. They were very quiet.

**Sergeant Charles Quinnell**
*9th Battalion, Royal Fusiliers*
We were going to have a go at the village of Ovillers, and we were the third lot to have a go at it. Our objective was 250 yards away. Every man had a sandbag with twenty Mills bombs in it, and each Mills bomb weighs two pounds, so that was forty pounds of weight; we had two extra bandoliers of fifty rounds in addition to our 150 rounds in our pouches, and every alternate man had a shovel or a pick.

There was a four-hour bombardment. As soon as it started, the Germans' retaliation came and for four hours we had to sit there and take four hours of everything he slung at us. We lost twenty-five per cent of our men before we went over. I was in the second wave. My platoon officer was in the first wave: he took two sections over and I followed with the other two sections.

The first wave went over, and as soon as they had gone I gave the order 'Advance!' – up the ladders – over the top. The first wave, when I got through our wire, were down. Two machine guns played on them and they were absolutely wiped out. Everybody was either killed or wounded. We went through, we got halfway across, and then the two machine guns found us and they traversed. They played on us like spraying with a hose. At the finish I was the only man standing but I'm not one of those heroes who want to take the German Army on my own – so I went to earth; I got down behind the lip of a shell-hole.

I kept looking to see where these machine guns were. I couldn't see them but there was a German in the trench about a hundred yards away and he was standing up on his parapet and flinging bombs, so I shot him. The machine-gun crew spotted me and they opened up on me. I ducked my head down and I'm behind the lip of this shell-hole and the dirt was just spraying down the back of my neck. 'You bastard!' I said. He thought he'd got me and he played his machine gun somewhere else.

I put my head up again – he spotted it – and back came the machine gun, and down I had to go. I stopped there for about quarter of an hour. By this time the machine guns had stopped and I took one convulsive leap over into the shell-hole and there were seven wounded men in there. Well, we bound one another up, and there we stopped all day. When it was dusk, I brought them back to our own line.

Now, we'd paid the penalty – we'd taken the machine-gun fire of those two machine guns – but the companies on our right had got through, and they took Ovillers. Our company went into the line 193 strong on the night of the sixth, and on the night of the seventh there was eighteen of us fit men, that was all.

But there you are, the mission was accomplished, we'd taken the machine-gun fire off the companies on our right and they'd got through, so that was our reward.

## Private Victor Lansdown
### 16th Battalion, Welch Regiment

The bullets were whistling past our ears. This man was holding up his hand. He had his rifle, but only the finger and thumb in it, because three fingers had been shot off. He said, 'Look what the bastards have done!' I said, 'Lie down! Make yourself as small as possible!' We kept going until the officer gave the signal to get down. We spotted a shell-hole, which we dived into head first. The tops of our bodies and our legs stuck up in the air.

Jack fixed up the gun and fired a blast into the wood – and that brought the revenge: a hail of bullets. I passed out. I was unconscious. It wasn't till later that we came to the conclusion that a bullet had hit my helmet and stunned me. At the same time, a bullet had gone through my leg, so Jerry had given me an anaesthetic, and I never felt any of it . . . But poor old Jack had a bullet through both his legs, and he felt both of them.

When I came to my senses, Jack asked if I could get at my water bottle, so I turned over on my back, and handed him my water bottle. And then I could see my leg. The bullet had ripped my puttee, and the two ends were hanging down, soaked in blood. There was nothing I could do about it. I'd lost so much blood, I was too weak to do anything.

**Private Albert Hurst**
*17th Battalion, Manchester Regiment*
About two o'clock on Sunday morning, we got into a position in Bernafay Wood, facing Trônes Wood. We had to take up a position in a trench occupied by about thirty dead South Africans, who'd been caught by enfiladed fire. We could also see dead men in the open ground between Bernafay and Trônes Wood, from a previous attack. Our objective was to take a trench in Trônes Wood.

As we attacked, a German machine gun was firing at us from further up Trônes Wood, but we seemed to have a charmed life; none of us were hit, as far as I could see. Before we got very far, one of our shells got there and killed the machine-gun team. Trônes Wood was still a wood – it had been behind the lines and the trees were still profuse. As we were moving across, we heard cheers coming from the bottom of the wood, which we concluded came from our sixth battalion. Once we were in the wood, the problem was keeping in touch with each other, through the trees and undergrowth.

We arrived at a T-shaped trench in the middle of the wood that had been abandoned by the Germans. We all agreed that this must be our objective, so we stopped. I thought we should have carried on to the edge of the wood. We could have gone further. It seemed like a daft position to take up, but we mounted our machine gun and stayed there. We stuck in the position that we'd been allotted to – and that was it!

Now, somebody had sent me some chocolate and I stood up to hand it out to the others. Just then, a shrapnel shell burst and it hit everybody except one of us. I got shrapnel in my foot. No one was badly wounded. We'd been ever so lucky, but the only chap who wasn't injured was too shocked to bandage us up. We started to make our way back through the wood, to a dressing station.

We went down a communication trench, but I decided to take a more direct route because I didn't know where this trench was leading. As I was going, I was joined by another chap of B Company who'd been shot in the shoulder. My wound was numb, but I was losing plenty of blood. We struggled on until we thought we were out of range of the Germans, and we stood up and tried to walk. I picked up a broken branch to help me. And then I heard two shots. One bullet flicked across my helmet and bounced away, and the other one hit him. I called out to two South African stretcher-bearers and told them that my friend was wounded, and they said they'd pick him up. I crawled the rest of the way to the dressing station, and my friend died in hospital the next day. At the dressing station my foot was dressed, and I was sent to a military hospital in Rouen.

## Corporal Harry Fellows
### 12th Battalion, Northumberland Fusiliers

It was twelve o'clock on the morning of July 12. We got the order, 'All Lewis gunners parade at once with guns, ammunition and two days' rations.' Mametz Wood had been captured, and our CO had orders to move our battalion. He couldn't move it in daylight, but he was sending in the Lewis gun section. We marched in fours as far as Fricourt, and then we went into single file until we entered Mametz Wood. We entered the wood, and about sixty yards inside the officer stopped us, told us to drop our packs and our guns, and the captain and the sergeant went forward to see if we'd arrived at our position. My mate Alf Templeford said to me, 'What about some souvenirs?' There were loads of dead Germans lying about, and we started looking for Iron Crosses, watches, things like that. We'd got about a hundred yards, when a shell dropped just where the other lads were resting. I ran over. I never saw such carnage in all the time I was in France.

## Private Philip Cullen
### 4th Battalion, Oxfordshire and Buckinghamshire Light Infantry

In July and August the flies and the stench were terrible. It was piteously hot, and the dead don't stay very long before they start to smell. If it hadn't been for Bill Healey, our second sergeant, I don't suppose I should have been here. He saw me laying and panting. I couldn't breathe. The stench had got into my throat. I don't know where the hell he got it from, but Bill always had a water

Destroyed German barbed wire with Mametz in the distance.

The shattered remains of Mametz.

bottle full of rum. He poured it down me. I was spluttering, and it cut whatever was in my throat. I was able to breathe again.

# JULY 14

On July 14, the planned assault (which came to be known as the Battle of Bazentin Ridge) was carried out by five divisions, with the intention of securing the positions between Delville Wood and Bazentin-le-Petit. In addition, the 2nd Indian Cavalry Division was ready to advance quickly through any breaches in the German lines. In a change of tactics, the attack was preceded by a five-minute 'hurricane' bombardment of high-explosive shells. The lesson had been learnt that a shrapnel barrage did not cut wire. Other lessons had been learnt; in this attack, more emphasis was placed on a creeping barrage – moving forward fifty yards every minute and a half – and in addition, the troops crept forward under cover of darkness to assume starting positions close to the German lines. The element of surprise that this provided would prove crucial. The German defenders were still climbing out of their dugouts when the trenches were stormed by the British attackers. As a result, the attack was a success. Four miles of German second-line trenches were taken. The cavalry, however, could not exploit the success, and was withdrawn on the following day.

### Private William Holbrook
#### 4th Battalion, Royal Fusiliers

Before the attack on Bazentin-le-Grand, I felt a little bit shaky. I was always worried about being blinded. I'd seen people killed and wounded, and it didn't worry me, but I was afraid of being blinded. One fellow, a bit older than me, he started crying out during the shelling. I thought he was going mad; crying and shouting. There were people who were so shaky, they couldn't hold their rifles.

The fellow next to me was killed before he got over the top. He fell dead on the parapet. The battlefield was pretty flat. There were some factories on the right, and houses on the left, but we were concentrating on what was in front of us. There was some shelling, but the machine-gun fire was deadly. We had to hop from shell-hole to shell-hole. We couldn't make one run at it. A lot of the Germans had gone back to another line, so we didn't get much resistance when we got there. When we got into the dugouts, we found a general and his staff inside, and they were in their pyjamas. They'd been asleep. We took prisoners and sent them back.

### Corporal Henry Mabbott
### 2nd Battalion, Cameron Highlanders

After an attack, I brought a very young German boy, who had no uniform. When we got into our own front line, I piggy-backed him to the dressing station, and I got into trouble for it.

### Signaller Leonard Ounsworth
### 124th Heavy Battery, Royal Garrison Artillery

We were out all day. We stuck the flag up at times to send messages through, and we got shelled. We went further along, and there were some parties of Jerries coming along with their arms up; well, we didn't want them. 'Go on! Bugger off out of here!'

And so we went on and on and night came. Well, we got no orders and we'd no water. We'd given it all to wounded men. So I found a field battery, and begged the sergeant major to let me fill up these water battles. I said, 'We're on forward observation about a mile up in front.' So I got them filled and then when I got back, the next thing I knew was a shell burst. It knocked the lamp out of my hand, and I'm left with the sending trigger, and that was the end of the lamp. I thought it was a bloody good job that we didn't have to do any more signalling.

We were out all that night, and the next day we'd no more rations, so we set off to come back. On the way, we picked up a field artillery lad; he'd got himself lost. So we walked on with him and it was reasonably quiet, but suddenly they started shelling us and we flung ourselves down, only we didn't get down quick enough, I suppose, because when we got up, the lad didn't get up. I could see a dull glow, and I said, 'Go and see if that's a dressing station,' and it was. It was an advanced field post, and we got a stretcher for the lad. I picked him up, and I thought, 'He feels funny,' and the captain in charge just put a blanket over his head. He was gone, and his blood had run off the stretcher on to my britches.

Well, it was a misty, dull morning, thick ground mist, you see, and we got into Montauban. There was a dyke alongside the road, there were some fallen trees there, and we were under a big tree across the dyke. A blooming shell hit this tree and split it in half. Nobody got a scratch and we were covered with pulverised wood. It wouldn't come off your tunics. A yard or two either side, if it had missed the tree trunk and exploded in the dyke, we should all have got it.

We set off again. We were walking over this open ground and we heard a voice yelling to us, 'Get down, you silly so-and-sos!' So we dropped flat, and crawled up a bank, and we saw some infantry. It was the 8th East Yorks. There was about two hundred of 'em left out of eight hundred. They'd lost seventy-five per cent from machine-gun fire.

A little later we were in a shell-hole, and somebody was making a run behind, and he was hit right in the ear, and he pitched up amongst us, and just for a few moments – I suppose his heart was still beating – blood was spurting out of his ear, then gradually died away.

Well, then, the next thing was Jerry put a box barrage down, to cut off that section, so I said to this officer, 'We'd better get out of this, there'll be a counter-attack in a minute!' He wouldn't move, so I said, 'You bloody well stay there! I'm going!'

So we started crawling out. We had some rations with us. I had a sandbag with some tins of bully, and I put that across the back of my neck, and we were crawling flat on our faces to get through this barrage. It was shrapnel, fortunately, most of it going in the ground, not doing much damage.

Suddenly there's a terrific clout on the back of my head, knocked me out for a moment, and then I felt something move. What had happened – a big clod of earth had dropped on the back of my head as I'm crawling along, and bashed me. My nose was bleeding, my chin was cut, and we crawled on and got out of it.

We established another observation point, on a slope, for collecting information, and then on the far side we saw some infantry transport come up. There was a lieutenant quartermaster there, a man about fifty, not a fighting man at all. I went over and he said, 'How are you off for grub?' so I said, 'We've only got biscuits and bully,' and he gave us some bread and butter, jam, tea and sugar. He'd brought up all the rations, and he was practically in tears. He said his lads didn't need it. You see, the Army Service Corps in the back had sent up rations for so many men, and he'd lost half of his. What happens to all that grub? You live like fighting cocks on what's left – for a day or two.

After that, I watched a French monoplane that kept diving down on to the corner of a field, as our cavalry – the Deccan Horse – approached. The plane kept on diving towards this corner and, suddenly, the officer in charge of cavalry cottoned on and he stood up in his stirrups, waved his sword above his head and charged across the field. The two outer lots of cavalry split, to make a pincer. The next thing we saw, they had encircled thirty-four Jerry soldiers, some of them with heavy machine guns, and taken them prisoner. The Jerries had been waiting, while the cavalry got nearer, and the plane had drawn their attention to the Jerries. It was over in a matter of seconds – but if it hadn't been for the plane – my God, it would have been slaughter.

After that, I saw some more Jerry prisoners coming back. Terrible really. There were about two hundred of them, and a score of our chaps, guards, on the side and in front. There was a big German officer out in front, a proper square-head, a bloke about six foot three, and he's walking behind one of our corporals, who was leading. The Jerry suddenly grabbed the corporal's rifle from behind. The corporal turned round and yelled to the other guards, who ran back a few yards and started shooting at the Jerries. That quelled the mutiny, but it was a stupid thing to do. The Jerries were all disarmed.

Mr Noble, Mr Robbins and myself went into Trônes Wood. Well – good God – there were no trees intact at all, just stumps, tree tops all mixed together, barbed wire, bodies all over the place, Jerries and ours. Robbins pulled some undergrowth up, we were having to fish our way through it, you see, and there was a dead Jerry, shot away right up his hip, and all his guts were out, and flies on it, and Robbins just had to step back. This leg that was up in the tree became dislodged, and that leg fell across him on his head. Good Lord, he vomited on the spot, terrible.

We were walking across this open ground between Bernafay Wood and Trônes Wood, and there's a big communication trench goes right across it, and I'd stopped to cut some brass buttons off a dead man's coat – I mean, he won't want them any more. We were getting by with composition buttons at the time, awful things, so I thought, 'I'll have those brass buttons,' and I cut them off, and I've just got them in my pocket when I heard Jerry was sending over harassing fire. I thought, 'God! This one's coming close!' You always marked the nearest hole to dive into, so I dived for this trench and flung

The Deccan Horse at Carnoy Valley on July 14.

Refreshment caravans for the use of walking wounded during the Battle of Bazentin Ridge on July 14.

myself into it. And at that moment, a blooming shell landed in a corner of the trench. I'd have been better if I'd stayed on top.

Well, the blast blew me out of the trench. I bruised my hip on the edge of the trench as I flew out, and I landed two or three bays away. Mr Noble and Mr Robbins were in front, and they'd both dropped, and there was a huge cloud of smoke. 'By God,' I thought, 'that was bloody lucky.' They said, 'Are you all right?' I said, 'Yes,' and I started to walk after them.

I walked on a bit, and I felt my hand was wet, so I wiped it on my britches. There was blood running off my hand, so I thought, 'Oh hell!' I shouted to them, 'Half a mo' – I am hit after all!' and we sat down in a hole, and I got a field dressing from my tunic, and Mr Robbins started to bandage me up round my neck. I said, 'It's my arm,' and he said, 'No! it's here!' I didn't know it, but I'd got one through my jaw and one in the throat, just missed the jugular. I'd got another one in the back but they didn't find that till I got to hospital at Rouen. I'd stopped four pieces and never felt them. You feel it afterwards, mind you, but just at the moment you don't feel anything at all.

So then the two officers took me to an advanced field post, a dressing station in Bernafay Wood, and I was rebandaged there, and while we were there, there was a man brought in on a stretcher. They had to tie him down with wire on a stretcher; he'd got shell shock. God, he was raving mad.

When it got dark, I was put into a horse ambulance, a pair of horses, a covered wagon sort of thing, with two stretchers at the bottom and two stretchers at the top, and I was in one of the upper stretchers. From that point, we had to cross what had been no-man's-land for twenty-two months. Well, the road was in a hell of a state and this thing was lurching all over the place, and before long myself and the other lad on the top stretcher we were thrown into the floor. There was nothing we could do about it, and the driver got us to Billion Wood.

From there, we were unloaded and put on to a motor ambulance. There was no room inside, so I was put on the front with a blanket round me, and the driver was told to hold on to me so that I didn't fall out. From that point we were taken – this is still during the night – down to Dives Copse, where we were just laid on the bare grass. They gave us an injection in the chest, for tetanus, and then we were left. I wanted to piss like hell, and so I crawled away on my elbow and my knees, and I laid on my side and had a pee, and crawled back again.

In the morning, some of the old Tin Lizzie ambulances came along – the ancient T-model Fords. One took me down to Corbie, and I was taken to a school there and laid on the bare boards. Nobody came near me all day. Nothing was done whatever.

I had some secret codes on me – I crawled to a fireplace and put a match to them and burnt them – and then in the evening we were taken to the station and loaded on a train for Rouen. That was the first time I saw any nurses. We got to Rouen and the first thing was I was undressed, and I felt rather embarrassed with this girl undressing me. She used a towel and did it discreetly, and as she was pulling my shirt up at the back, there was a sudden sharp stab of pain. 'Ouch!' I said. 'What's the matter?' she said. She was smoking a cigarette, so I said that she must have dropped some ash on me. 'I haven't,' she said – and when she pulled my shirt up, she found the other wound in my back. She said there was a piece of shell in there, a shell splinter, and she threw it in the grass. So bang went my souvenir.

By then, my jaw was locked tight and I thought I'd got lockjaw. But a doctor – Dr McNeill – came round and looked at me. 'You've no got lockjaw, laddie,' he said, 'you've got a piece of dirty German iron wedged in your hinges . . .'

## Corporal Harry Fellows
### 12th Battalion, Northumberland Fusiliers

On July 14, I helped to bury about five hundred Welsh, English and German bodies. We dug graves about eight foot long, six foot wide and two foot deep. First you removed the man's equipment. If the body was badly damaged, you cut it away. Then you took the man's pay book out of his right-hand breast pocket. This pay book contained all his details: his religion, his next of kin, his regimental number and the will that we all had to make. His wallet was in his left-hand pocket. Then we cut the identity disc from the man's neck, and we put the pay book and the wallet together and tied them with the string from the identity disc. We then buried the men, six to a grave, head-to-tail, and we stuck a bayonet above each man's head. On the bayonet, we hung the little parcel we'd made, with the man's steel helmet over the top to protect it from the weather.

**Lieutenant Norman Dillon**
*14th Battalion, Northumberland Fusiliers*

We were sent up to clear a pathway through Trônes Wood, so that stretcher-bearers could carry their stretchers unimpeded. The route through the wood was very pocked with shell craters and some filling-in was necessary, and we were sent to do it. My platoon was no sooner on the job than the Germans began an 'area shoot'. In other words, they got every available gun in range, and put every shell they had on the area. It was extremely nasty. There was no cover. I got my chaps to sit down with their backs to the bigger trees – to get some protection. It was very frightening. In a wood, the noise of shellfire is amplified, and shrapnel bursts go through the leaves and make a terrific rending noise. The howitzer shells, which come down almost vertically, were responsible for killing several of my chaps. I got a lot of my chaps out of the wood, and went back with some stretcher-bearers to salvage what I could of the remainder. I'm afraid their lives were wasted. I was disillusioned by the waste of such a number of men without any just cause.

## JULY 15 – SEPTEMBER 15

Following the success of July 14, the British were now poised before the German third-line defences, and the villages of Flers and Gueudecourt. Before they could be attacked, however, Delville Wood and High Wood had to be taken. On July 15, whilst the 13th Battalion, Royal Fusiliers was taking part in an unsuccessful attack on Pozières, the first of a series of bloody assaults was being mounted on Delville Wood. Over the next four days of fighting, the South African Infantry Brigade suffered almost 2,500 casualties. Delville Wood would not be finally secured for another six weeks.

On July 16, the 11th Battalion Border Regiment took part in an attack which took Ovillers. Four days later, the 20th Battalion, Royal Fusiliers was part of an unsuccessful attack on High Wood. An attack by the 1st Battalion, Royal West Kent Regiment, three days later, also failed. The fight for High Wood would continue for almost two months.

Just after midnight on July 23, attacks began on Pozières Ridge. The 1st Australian Division captured most of the village of Pozières, but was then bombarded by the German artillery, suffering over five thousand casualties. Two days later, the whole village was taken, and attacks began on Mouquet Farm.

The battle was now descending into disorganised localised fighting, as is demonstrated by the 9th Battalion, Royal Fusiliers' attack on Pozières Ridge, on the night of August 4. Both sides were suffering heavy casualties, for minimal gains. In a confidential memorandum, circulated to the War Committee on August 1, Winston Churchill criticised the incoherent strategy and limited ambition of the campaign. In defence of the campaign, Haig argued for the importance of maintaining a steady pressure, and wearing down the enemy.

On September 3, an attack was mounted with the intention of securing the starting points for a coming major offensive. These starting points included High Wood, and Guillemont – positions that had already been the subject of fighting for several weeks. The 12th Battalion, Gloucestershire Regiment captured the German second line to the south-east edge of Guillemont. On the same day, Delville Wood finally came under British control.

### Lieutenant William Taylor
*13th Battalion, Royal Fusiliers*

We went into the line for our next attack, which was to take the village of Pozières. Pozières was beyond La Boisselle, off to the left, and it had been attacked by one of our other battalions in the brigade, and a new battle had been arranged where the 13th Rifle Brigade were to lead the attack and we were to support them. We knew that Pozières was heavily defended and we didn't relish the prospect. We knew it was a tough nut to crack. One just faced up to the thing.

When we took up our position, we had fairly good, deep trenches to assemble in, and we were there all night, under very heavy shellfire, before attacking in the morning. The attack began at about eleven in the morning. We were supposed to be supported by our artillery, but the Rifle Brigade led the attack, we followed them, and instructions came through – too late – that the attack was to be cancelled. So the artillery didn't open up at all. The Rifle Brigade had a terrible time, and we went forward about fifty yards when, suddenly, the message came through to us that the attack was cancelled. We'd seen what was happening in front with the Rifle Brigade being shot down, and we lay down about fifty yards ahead, stayed there about an hour, when we had the order to retreat. While we were laying there, we received all our casualties. That was frightful. Men that had been with you all the time. It was a complete shambles. The whole thing.

I have an extract here from a letter I wrote home three days afterwards. I said, 'I am still in the thick of it, and the shelling has been very heavy for the past twenty-four hours. I lost more than half my platoon, including both my sergeants, who were killed, and I now have only sixteen men left. I am still quite well, although somewhat shaken. A piece of shell hit my field glasses and smashed them beyond repair, and another piece hit my helmet. So I'm lucky to be alive.'

I was thankful that I hadn't been hit. If that piece of shell that hit my field glasses had hit me, I wouldn't be here now. Every time one went into action, one knew that one might not come out. It didn't affect my morale, but after a battle, one was exhausted. One only had a certain amount of resistance, and I suppose a certain amount of it was taken from one. The remaining members of the platoon took it as a matter of course. What could they do?

After that schemozzle, we were relieved by the 5th Australian Division, and we went well behind the line to a little village called Bresle, where we rested for about a week. About three or four miles behind the line. We had a quiet, restful time, while we received more men to make up our numbers, although we were still quite short of men. It was a peaceful farming village, which hadn't been shelled at all. Just the sort of place one wanted to recoup. We were there for about a week, and we were marched back to the line to hold a sector beyond Mametz Wood, on the edge of High Wood.

## Corporal Frederick Francis
### 11th Battalion, Border Regiment

We slept in a wood outside a village called Authuille, and at seven-thirty in the morning the colonel gave the command, 'When I blow the whistle, dash out of the wood, and try to get into the front-line trench.' So he blew the whistle and I remember distinctly, he patted us all on the back and said, 'Good luck! If things don't go well, I'll come out and lead you myself.' Well, they didn't go well; there were all these German machine guns focused on us, and he came out. He was shot through the head and killed immediately. I managed to get to our front line, but I couldn't see anybody about except one man, and I said, 'Who are you?' He said, 'My name's Joe Holgate, and I belong Workington.' I said, 'What are you doing in our front-line trench?' he said, 'I was in D Company and the commanding officer and his second were lying wounded and they told me to lead the rest of the company on.' But he found nobody else alive. So we shook hands with each other and we decided to rally anybody we could find, to come. I was just climbing over our barbed wire – I'd just got my right leg over – when I got this machine-gun bullet. It went right through my waterworks. It clung itself on to the wall of my bladder.

I was lying wounded, and I kept saying, 'Will somebody please come and get me in?' A voice replied, 'If I volunteer to come out, can you climb on my shoulder?' 'No,' I said, 'my left shoulder's badly wounded and my foot's practically hanging off.' So he said, 'Just a minute! I'll get help!' So he returned shortly, and between him and another man, they got me on to my back and on to a stretcher, and as they were lifting the stretcher up to get me back into our own front trench, the Germans sighted a machine gun on us. Luckily, they missed us. When I was back in our trench, the medical officer produced a big bottle of iodine and he poured it all over me, wherever he saw blood. Then he handed me to the stretcher-bearers. They took me as far out of the line as they were entitled to do, before handing me over to the Royal Army Medical Corps. I was taken to a field dressing station. There were British and German wounded lying next to each other. I can remember an RAMC man looking at me and saying, 'He won't live long . . .' and he took my watch out of my breast pocket – my official watch, suspended on a leather strap. Royal Army Medical Corps? Royal Army Robbing Corps!

**Private Donald Price**
*20th Battalion, Royal Fusiliers*
It was still dark, and we were taken out about five hundred yards, towards High Wood, with not the faintest idea what we were going to do. We lay down in the dark, ready for the final spurt. We came under an *enormous* barrage. God, it was appalling. Screams of death. Screams from fellows all over the place. By the time we got to the wood – we were nearly annihilated.

We made a big mistake. We had to go forward, and we kept to this big road because the undergrowth was so thick. The unfortunate thing was – that's what he had his machine guns trained on. And before we'd finished, I found myself completely alone. I was exhausted, carrying this load of shovels and ammunition, and I rolled over and I saw the dugout, and I rolled down this dugout – which was quite deep – and when I got to the bottom of the dugout, there were three seriously wounded Germans. They were sitting at the side, screaming away, and eventually I sat down next to one of them. And immediately, I went to sleep.

When I woke up, they were all dead. The lot of them had died. I was being held up by one of these dead fellows. I realised that I'd got to get out and get back to my regiment – if I could. Somehow. So I got to the top of this dugout and I remembered where I'd come from, I knew the way back, and I semi-crawled, crouched and ran back to the beginning of the wood, where I'd started from.

Much to my amazement, there was a sergeant major there with three other fellows, and the sergeant major said, 'Where the hell have you come from?' 'Up there!' I said. 'Is there nobody there?' 'No.' I got into the hole with them, on the edge of the wood. By that time, it was getting dark. The shelling had stopped – it was calm. At about midnight, somebody came to the back of the hole and said, 'Get out! We're your relief!' The sergeant major told us to make our own way back, and I got out with an Irishman named Terry, and we ran out towards Mametz Wood – but we missed our way. We started running past Delville Wood and there was a hell of a fight going on there.

So we turned right and made our way down Happy Valley, and Terry and I were so exhausted that we decided to stop. It was still dark, and we would find our way back in the morning. We found our way into a trench and, without any ado, we flopped down and went to sleep. When we woke up, we found that we'd been sleeping in a latrine. Covered in crap. And we thought nothing about it. We looked down and found that our battalion was back in the holes that we'd vacated. We went back there, and when we got back the people who'd turned up were minimum. We'd lost about four hundred men in that one night.

## Private William Holbrook
### 4th Battalion, Royal Fusiliers

We were sent to the trenches at Delville Wood on July 22, and as our company were making its way there, along the cart track, in the dark, an officer named Lieutenant Cook came and told us that this was a hell of a place. He said, 'Make very little noise. There's a German machine-gunner a hundred yards to your right. Any noise you make, you'll be under fire, so be as careful as you can.' He'd only just said these words, when a lot of Very lights shot up in the air. It was just like daylight. We didn't know what had happened, or where they'd come from. And the machine gun opened up on us, and they started shelling us, and about ten of us were killed. I went to help the wounded, and I saw one man lying on his back and I recognised him. I hadn't seen him since I joined the army, as a boy, back in 1908. And there he was, lying badly wounded. I bent down and he looked up – I know he recognised me – but he died. He was in my company and I didn't even know it. We found out what had happened. A fellow was carrying all these Very light pistols in his pack, and something hit his pack and set them all off. And turned everything to daylight.

When we got to the trenches at Delville Wood, we'd never seen anything like it. There was no entrance to the trench, and we had to slide in over the side. There was thick mud, and there were bodies lying everywhere. There were no duckboards, and the bodies squelched under you as you walked along. It was one hell of a place. I was orderly to our company commander, Captain Sparks, and when he saw that there was a fifty-yard gap between our lines, he said to me, 'I'll go along and see what I can do to close this gap.' I asked him if I should come with him, but he said, 'No, see what's been left behind. See if you can find anything to drink.' So he went off, and I looked around, and I found some concentrated cocoa and I started to make it up. Captain Sparks was a long time coming back, and I stopped someone and asked where he was, and I was told that he'd been killed. Killed by a whizz-bang.

We were holding the trench under heavy rifle fire, and I was told to take a message back to Carnoy Valley. So I left the Delville Wood trenches, and I was creeping along this ground when I met another fellow going down and we went on together. We came to a sunken road where we found over a hundred British troops, all lying dead. They were black from the sun. No one had ever found them. There was one man lying on a stretcher with one leg missing, and holding each handle of the stretcher was a dead man. All of them must have been killed by the same shell.

## Private Leonard Gordon Davies
### 22nd Battalion, Royal Fusiliers

Delville Wood was a beastly place. It was badly mutilated. The trees were stumps. The fighting was going on in the wood itself and it was taken, back and forth, several times. There were extremely heavy casualties, and I don't remember there being a proper line of trenches. There were bodies lying around the place – quite horrifying. I can remember stepping over them, in order to advance. I remember being given instructions to retire, and we having to move back several hundred yards.

## Lieutenant Duce
### 1st Battalion, Royal West Kent Regiment

We were detailed to go over the top, in an attack on High Wood, on July 23. I had Number Five Platoon, B Company, and we were detailed to go all the way through. I was darned annoyed because I was going over first. We were to go over at three-fifteen on Sunday afternoon, and while I was waiting there was nothing to do but go to sleep, and I found that I was able to sleep at the side of the trench. When we went over, I was quite fortunate. Of the three officers of my company, two were killed and I was only wounded. Out of 480 men, 160 were killed, 160 were wounded and 160 got through. It was rather extraordinary. As I was stepping over the wire, I was shot straight through the foot, which knocked me down. If I'd put my foot down before, I'd have got it right through the knee. I laid out there for some hours, and then as I started to crawl back, parallel to the German line, a German came over the top and stood, looking out, holding his machine gun. I just had to freeze. I can tell you, it's quite a nervous tension to lie there for ten minutes without moving, so that he thinks you're a dead body. Gradually, I turned my head round to look and saw that he had gone, and I crawled back. As I was crawling back, I followed a small trench and I came across a dead man in the trench. All I could do was crawl straight over him. It wasn't a pleasant thing.

## Private Frank Brent
### 2nd Battalion, 1st Division, Australian Imperial Force

Without doubt, Pozières was the heaviest, bloodiest, rottenest stunt that ever the Australians were caught up in. The carnage is just indescribable. As we

Delville Wood. A beastly and mutilated place.

were making our attack, we were literally walking over the dead bodies of our cobbers that had been slain by this barrage.

I can't imagine anything more concentrated than the artillery barrage of the Germans at that particular stunt. The bay on our left went in, two or three chaps were killed; the bay on our right went in. I said to this chap, 'It's our turn next!' I hadn't said it before we were buried. I was quite unconscious, buried in what had been the German front-line trench.

## Lieutenant William Taylor
### 13th Battalion, Royal Fusiliers

The woods had been very much knocked about. We took up a line of trenches – quite good old German trenches – on the edge of High Wood, waiting for instructions as to whether to attack or whether we merely had to defend. We were there for about a week. During that time, apart from being shelled, there was no action. The Germans did not counter-attack, and we were not ordered to attack further. One had no idea of the general strategy as to what was going on along the front. You might get orders to attack in the morning, or you might get nothing at all. One never knew. We couldn't see the German front line at all. We were facing the wood, about two hundred yards from the wood, and the German line must have been the other side of the wood, because we couldn't see them at all.

While we were there, we were improving our defence all the time. I can remember receiving a note from the adjutant one night, telling me that we had to work all through the night to strengthen the wire in front of our trench, and that it would be brought up by a fatigue party, dumped at a certain spot on our line, and we had to put this wire up during the night. We did it all night. After all, these were ex-German trenches and any wire we had was on the other side. We were wide open. It was barbed wire and concertina wire with the usual corkscrew stakes that we screwed into the ground, and trained the wire. I was commanding the company (my company commander had been hit) and I suppose that we had sixty or seventy men only. So we all worked on the wire, the whole night long. We weren't shot at. I don't think we had any casualties. We had no intention of staying there for a period, so the latrines weren't dug at all. There were plenty of shell-holes in the area, and we used those. Any dead bodies had been buried.

There had been severe fighting in High Wood early on, and every day we expected that there might be a counter-attack by the Germans. But nothing happened, other than shelling. We had a certain number of casualties, wounded by shelling, but I don't think we had any killed. I was promoted to acting captain, and I was commanding the company whilst we were in High Wood, but some weeks later, when we were behind the line, an officer came from another company, who was senior to me. He took over. I was disappointed, but I was still a second lieutenant, and he was a lieutenant. He'd been on the Western Front longer than I had. But there were other occasions when I was commanding the company, and a captain came out from home, who hadn't been out before, who had been promoted whilst at home, and I had to hand over to him. One was very upset about it. It happened again and again, and I rather resented it.

## Sergeant Charles Quinnell
### 9th Battalion, Royal Fusiliers

On the night of August 4, we moved up to what I now know was the Pozières Ridge. Just imagine a huge saucer, and the lip of the saucer was the ridge, the village of Pozières was over the top of the ridge and it was known as the Pozières Ridge. Whoever held that ridge – at that time it was the Germans – overlooked a huge part of the whole Somme battlefield so it was very, very important that this should be taken.

So that night, we were moved up into a newly dug slit trench. Our objective was uphill, somewhere between two hundred and three hundred yards. We lost a few men going up the communication trench – but not many. When we got into this assembled trench we settled down there, sat down on the bottom, and the order came, 'Platoon sergeants to come to headquarters.'

Company headquarters was in the same trench, and we went along, and there was Captain Cazalet, and this is the sort of order we got: 'It is now eight-fifteen, at nine o'clock we go over the top. We're going behind curtain fire.' Curtain fire was shrapnel bursts, and as you advanced the guns went farther in front. You advanced behind a 'curtain of fire', you see. Captain Cazalet went on, 'I will go over with the first wave, and Mr Firefoot, the second in command, will go over with you, Sergeant Quinnell. You'll be in the second wave. Now go along and tell your men to be ready and as soon as the curtain fire starts, we move.'

Back along the trench we went, and I told the men what to do. I gave them the tip, 'Run like hell, and catch up with the first wave!' That wasn't an order – it was just a tip because my experience told me that when you're out in no-man's-land, you're standing there naked, but if you catch up with the first wave, the sooner you'll get your job done and the fewer casualties you'll have. So that's what we did. We caught up with the first wave behind this curtain fire, and we were into the Germans with the first wave. We ran like hell, too.

When we got to the German trench, there was this German kneeling on the floor of the trench and the poor bugger was dead scared. While I'm standing, wondering whether to stick him or shoot him, a German jumped out of the trench away to my left, and another one to my right, so I jumped down on top of this German, pinned him down, knelt on his shoulders, shot the German on the left, worked my bolt, put another one up the spout and shot the German who was running away on the right.

By this time, all our men had reached the trench and I went along to report to the captain that we'd arrived. He said, 'Good, now let's have a quick roll-call.' So I counted my men and I'd only lost three coming over, which was a marvellous performance. It was the surprise attack, you see. The Germans didn't have time to drop their barrage down. But once we were in the German trench, the barrage came down behind us, and my tip of getting my men to catch up with the first wave paid off, otherwise they would have caught the barrage.

The battalion on our left had not got through, the companies on the right of our battalion had not got through, and we were the only battalion to get our objective. So we had a quick consultation, two platoon sergeants, Captain Cazalet and Mr Firefoot, his second in command, and it was agreed that we'd make a barricade on our right flank and a barricade on our left flank and hold it.

This we did, but all this time we were being sniped at from behind. We expected the shots from the front, but we were being sniped at from behind as well. We thought it was our own people sniping at us. In fact, there was over a hundred Germans in a little slit trench that we'd jumped over.

On the morning of August 5, we had our first experience of liquid fire. Over the barricade on our right flank came a German with a canister of liquid fire on his back, squirting it out of the hose. He burnt twenty-three of our chaps to death. I plonked one into his chest, but he must have had an armour-plated waistcoat on. It didn't stop him, but somebody threw a Mills bomb, which burst behind him, and he wasn't armour-plated behind so he went down. But he'd done a lot of damage. Plenty of our chaps were wounded, as well as those that were killed, and it practically wiped out Tubby Turnbull's platoon.

Then we got an order from the captain. I hope I never hear it repeated. He gave us an order to make a barricade of the dead – the German dead and our own dead. We made a barricade of them and retreated about forty yards back. I'd got a barricade on my left to look after, there were plenty of Germans to the front, and the sniping from behind, so we had to have our sentries facing both ways. And this barricade of the dead. We only had two bombs apiece, in our tunic pockets. Everybody handed their bombs in to the right-hand flank because we decided it was the danger point, and all our bombs were taken along to the barricade there.

Over the next three days, we would face five attacks either at dawn or dusk from over this barricade, but that afternoon the Germans in the trench behind us were winkled out, and that night our pioneer battalion dug a seven-foot deep communication trench, hundreds of yards, from the old British front line to where we were. As soon as that trench was dug, up came a Stokes trench mortar with plenty of rounds of ammunition, and a specially trained crew. As well as boxes and boxes of rifle grenades.

By this time Tubby was wounded, Mr Firefoot was wounded and that left Captain Cazalet and I. We were the bosses, so we had a consultation on where to site this Stokes trench mortar and we decided to put it about fifty yards back from the barricade. Well, the next time an attack came over this barricade – the usual performance, a man coming over with a liquid fire canister – he got a very, very hot reception. The Stokes trench mortar opened up and dropped the mortars just the other side of the barricade. I'd three men loading up these rifle grenades and I peppered the whole line. I couldn't miss, and, judging by the shouts and the screams, I was taking a very good toll.

All told we had five attacks. The first one was the disastrous one, which we paid very heavily for, but the other four we took a very heavy toll and we didn't lose a man. The strangest thing about this engagement was, although we were right in the thick of it, we didn't have a shell in the whole four days we were there. The artillery were so mixed-up, they didn't know where we were, and where their own men were.

## Rifleman Robert Renwick
### 16th Battalion, King's Royal Rifle Corps

We attacked Delville Wood on August 24. Just before we were due to go over the top, our artillery fell short and a few of our own men were wounded. The officer said, 'I'll be damned if I'll see my men knocked out by our own artillery!' and he took us out and led us into shell-holes before the attack began. That night was my first time over the top, and it was a very funny experience. No-man's-land was a mass of shell-holes. You couldn't see any growth at all. We were jumping from one shell-hole to the next, under machine-gun fire. I remember seeing a corporal, who had fallen, and I looked down at him and I saw that he'd covered his stripes so that he wouldn't be a target. That was a bit foolish. We attacked through the wood, but there weren't so many trees left and it wasn't too difficult to get through. As I was going, I had a vision of being back at school, and our schoolmaster was coming down the path to call us in, and I said to myself, 'If you ever see that place again, you'll be very happy.' The German line was at the back end of the wood and we got to it, but they'd retreated. They'd already gone.

We were sent back to bury the dead of our battalion. Our own pals. I thought a labour platoon should have done it. I've often wondered about that. It was mainly men from the new draft that were sent to do it, and I think they did it on purpose, to toughen us up a bit. One lad had a webbed belt, and a purse, and he had a golden sovereign in that purse. He'd shown it to me a few times and I didn't like the idea of taking it out. He was buried with the golden sovereign in his belt.

It was an upsetting job. When we buried them, the identity discs were taken off and brought back to headquarters. The bodies were buried individually: it wasn't a mass grave – although that *was* done sometimes – but the graves weren't marked. I often think when you see all these cemeteries in France with the names on the graves, I think in many cases the body's not there. But it's nice for the family to think that they're there.

After that attack, a lad who had gone home wounded wrote to my parents, telling them that I'd fallen. He said that I'd come across to see if there was anything I could do when someone was wounded in a shell-hole, and after that someone had shouted, 'Renwick's been killed now!' I remember the incident, but I wasn't killed! My father read it first, and then he handed it to my mother. She had a terrific shock, and my father said, 'Look. We've had a field card from him since this date, so it can't be right.' It's a bit of a mystery, that one.

### Private Harold Hayward
#### 12th Battalion, Gloucestershire Regiment

I was the colonel's personal runner, and after the attack on Guillemont on September 3, the colonel said, 'Can you take Bacon [the colonel's assistant], and go out to see if you can find the battalion?' So we set out in the direction that the battalion had attacked, in darkness, to see if we could get in touch with them, and find out from the different officers along the line what their situation was vis-à-vis the enemy.

We might very well have been walking into German lines. Alternatively, our chaps might have thought the Germans were coming for a night attack, to get them in the rear. Ours was not a pleasant position. I carried my rifle loaded, ready to fire at a moment's notice.

We walked through the night. We had to jump over trenches and communication trenches, and I thought we ought to have turned back. I didn't see or hear anyone the whole of that night. It was an eerie experience, being out on your own, and not knowing whether you had friends in front of you, or the enemy. The ground was very much cut up, and I was aware of the fact that my rifle was loaded – one up the spout – and I could have fallen into a trench and wounded myself.

When the sun started to rise, I decided it was sensible to get back, at least to tell the colonel that we hadn't caught up with the battalion. I really don't know how far around the radius I had walked – we might have been all over the place. Suffice to say we didn't meet anyone.

At about five in the morning, the colonel told us to have some breakfast and then we went off together. Of course, in the light, it wasn't difficult. We could see ahead, and the colonel said, 'This looks like the battalion!' but not only were there other brigade units mixed up with our chaps – who, of course, we didn't recognise by face – but there were odd chaps from other divisions.

People had become mixed up, but we did learn that the Germans had not made a night-time counter-attack. Our chaps were in small trenches, which they had dug with their trenching tools. I walked along to find my two friends. One – Hull – I found and he was in a bad way because a shell had burst near him. He was pretty badly shell-shocked, and he couldn't tell me about our mutual friend. But I did find a group of people from my old platoon. I asked what had happened to my other friend, and they said that a shell had dropped in front and buried him. He was in a poor way.

The thing that hit me was that every NCO in my company seemed to have been killed. Those were the days when ranks were distinguished by marks on the arm, and I feel certain that the Germans had people trained to look through field glasses to spot officers and NCOs and then shoot at them.

I was attached to the colonel, but he was in conversation with an officer, who was explaining the situation to him. There was a big gap on our company's right, which they couldn't spread out to cover, and the officer was afraid of the Germans getting in.

So the colonel told me to find out how big the gap was, and how far away the next troops on the right were. They were French, and I was to get in touch with a French officer and learn their plans, whether they had another attack planned, whether they were going to retire, whether the gap could be filled; it was a serious problem. I said, 'Yes, sir!' and wondered whether my fourth-form French would carry me through.

Just at that moment, I got a bullet. I was standing right next to the colonel, looking towards the rear. The colonel was facing the way the Germans were, and I was hit by a bullet that came from the rear, from the captured German trenches. A German had been left behind, in one of their deep dugouts, which hadn't been bombed; he had come out, seen the colonel – and let fly at him. As soon as that happened, he had walked down our reserve lines and given himself up as a prisoner of war. Nobody would have known.

I was wounded in the scrotum. The bullet had come up off the ground, carried dirt with it, gone through my tin of cigarettes, gone through my right low side, got into the crotch and was protruding from my left haunch. I was carried to the dugout that the colonel had decided to make his HQ. I never lost consciousness. The lieutenant put a field dressing on me, and he assured me that just as nature provides two eyes, it provides two of other things. Then he had to go back to see that his machine guns were set up well, and at sunrise the next morning, the stretcher-bearers came and put me on the stretcher and carried me out to where the Royal Army Medical Corps had brought their horse-drawn ambulance.

The ambulance was on very badly shell-pocked ground, and I did admire them for that. There were four of us inside – two Germans below and two

English above. On top, we took all the swing, of course. They took us back to the field hospital, and then from there by train down to a Canadian base hospital. My wound was dressed every four hours – and I broke into a sweat every time I heard that ward door open. The senior sister came up one night at ten o'clock, and she said, 'I want you to keep awake! I am coming to do something about that place down near your privates!' She came in with an orderly and they held one limb each, and she got her tweezers and pulled the shrapnel out.

It wasn't nice at the time, but – my goodness! – I was so pleased afterwards. It meant that they didn't have to come in every four hours to put the dressing on, and turn this *thing* over in my testicles …

## SEPTEMBER 15 – SEPTEMBER 22

The Battle of Flers-Courcelette, which began on September 15, marked the introduction of a new weapon which would – in time – change the nature of modern warfare: the tank. The aim of the battle was finally to wear down German resistance, to pave the way for a breakthrough between Morval and Le Sars. The tanks that were to achieve this aim had been conceived as caterpillar-treaded land-ships, which would combine the mobility of infantry with the firepower of artillery. They would be able to traverse trenches and crush barbed wire, allowing the infantry to follow in their treads. Their name reflects the conditions of total secrecy in which they were developed; they were transported to France, purporting to be mobile water tanks for use by the Russians. In this early manifestation, they were twenty-six feet long, travelled at two miles per hour, and carried a crew of eight. The 'male' tank was mounted with two six-pounder guns and three Hotchkiss machine guns. The 'female' had no six-pounders, but carried four Vickers machine guns.

For all its promise, the tank of September 1916 was a primitive affair. Visibility from it was poor, armour was thin, noise was so great that the crew had to communicate by hand signals, and the engine was intensely unreliable. Of the forty-nine tanks which arrived in France, only thirty-two arrived at their starting point ready to roll into action. Of those, fourteen broke down straight away and eight were disabled by shellfire. Two caught fire without any help from the enemy.

Supporting troops coming under artillery fire as they move up the line near Ginchy in September.

Nevertheless, when the first tank – D1, commanded by Captain H. W. Mortimore – appeared, German troops surrendered in panic, allowing two companies of the 6th Battalion, King's Own Yorkshire Light Infantry to take an enemy position. The village of Courcelette was taken, with the aid of a tank named 'Crème de Menthe'. Martinpuich was taken by the 15th (Scottish) Division, and High Wood was taken by the 47th Division. Flers was also taken, with the assistance of D17, commanded by Second Lieutenant Stuart Hastie.

One tank commander in action that day – Second Lieutenant MacPherson – died by his own hand. Having reported a 'broken tail' he turned back, and whilst waiting to give his report he shot himself, leaving a note which read, 'My God, I have been a coward.'

On their first day in action, tanks had probably failed to live up to unreasonably high expectations. Many had broken down and others had failed to keep pace with the infantry. On the other hand, they had inspired genuine terror amongst the enemy, they had bolstered British morale and they had contributed to the most successful advance since the start of the Battle of the Somme: a mile of enemy territory had been taken, over a six-mile front.

Corporal Jack Critchley
*Royal Artillery, attached to Guards Division*

One day, we were in the wagon line – quite a few of us – and somebody came along and said, 'The war is finished! Just go half a mile down the road, look in a field, and you will see!' He wouldn't tell us why. So we went down and there was quite a crowd there. We saw these 'tank' things that we had never seen or heard of, and the tank men were full of it: 'Oh this is *it*, boy!' and they were describing the tanks to us in full. 'This is a female tank, it has nothing but machine guns, but this is a male tank, it has cannon, and can fire this many shells, and these slots at the bottom of the door are where we point the revolvers through when we are going over trenches, and we kill them that way!'

After that, we thought, 'When we get a few of these lads over, the war is finished! We are going to be home by Christmas!' That was a feeling a lot of us had.

## Lieutenant Norman Dillon
### 14th Battalion, Northumberland Fusiliers

I was sitting with my platoon, waiting to follow the front-line troops, who had just advanced into the village of Flers. I was sitting with my sergeant by the roadside, when all of a sudden there was an almighty noise, when a huge crater opened about three feet behind us. Fortunately, it was a gas shell, not a high-explosive shell – which is why I'm still here. At that moment, I turned round and I saw a strange thing looming up through the darkness. This enormous thing crossed the road in front of me and ambled on behind the troops. I was watching one of the first tanks going into action.

## Lieutenant Cecil Lewis
### 3 Squadron, Royal Flying Corps

One afternoon the commanding officer said he wanted me to go off on a special job, and he gave me a designation on the map, and I and my observer went off. And when we arrived, we saw these curious sort of heavy-looking iron vehicles, and they were lumbering over the ground at about two miles an hour, with a whole lot of chaps standing round, and a kerfuffle going on. And these vehicles were, of course, tanks. And so, from that moment on, we started doing mock attacks with them – in order to get them to light their flares, note where they were and take back records to the brigade headquarters.

## Private Leonard Gordon Davies
### 22nd Battalion, Royal Fusiliers

I was in a long, narrow trench, waiting to advance, when all of a sudden these tanks rose out of the ground behind us. They were terrifying-looking things, and they came over and went right over our heads. When the Germans saw them coming over, they didn't know what they were, they got scared. Superstitious race, the Germans. They turned tail and ran, and we chased them right back.

## Captain Philip Neame VC
### Headquarters, 168th Infantry Brigade

We had been allotted one of the first tanks to land in France, to do some training with our brigade, and everybody was staggered to see this extraordinary monster crawling over the ground. We did what training we could with this one tank: one or two sections of the infantry – a platoon or less – following the tank, because we knew it had to make gaps in the enemy barbed wire, and a little column of infantry had to follow through the gap. It was a very limited amount of training you could do with one tank. Everybody thought it was a terrific thing, but then my brigade rather lost our faith because only one managed to get across our front line, and it broke down before it reached the German front line. But just to the north of us there was a tank that had a great success, at a place called Flers.

**Second Lieutenant Hatton**
*D Company, Heavy Branch, Machine Gun Corps*

On September 15, 1916, at approximately five-thirty in the morning, a barrage of terrific intensity opened up in front of Flers. Assembled in front of Flers were twenty-five tanks of D Company, all commanded by lieutenants who had been volunteers for this mission. They were assigned to launch an almost direct assault on Flers. Three tanks were given orders not to deviate, but to go straight to Flers. These three tanks, were D9 – commanded by myself, D14 – commanded by Lieutenant Court from South Africa, and D16 – commanded by Lieutenant Hastie from Edinburgh.

We were warned that the barrage would be something – *and it was.* Jerry fled but it was surprising how many Jerries were alive in spite of the previous bombardment, which had gone on for two or three days. On the previous day, we had been taken to the front line and shown what we had to go through. It was terrifying. There were shell-holes there that you could put houses in. They were running one into the other, and most of them were full of slime and water. The rain had been incessant, and the land was practically impassable. We decided amongst ourselves that we should never get there. But we had volunteered for the job, and we had a go, and so we three tanks who had been given these special instructions started up.

Court in D14 started. Before he had gone two or three hundred yards he attempted to cross a disused support trench, and as he crossed it, the tank – weighing twenty-eight tons – crumbled the parapet beneath him, and the tail end of his tank disappeared into the trench. He scrambled out of the tank, quite a job, and came to me. Now, we had been equipped with very large hooks on the stern of our tanks, and we had wire hoses coiled on the roof, and Court was a particular friend of mine, so I manoeuvred alongside of him

A C Company Mark I tank photographed on September 15 – the day that tanks first rolled into action.

The new and the old: a carrier pigeon is released from the porthole of a tank on the Somme.

and attempted to tow him out. But in manoeuvring alongside of him, my sponso (which was a protrusion on the side of the tank) got tangled with his and the tw tanks were locked together. Hastie, behind us, crossed the same support trench but he was successful; he didn't attempt to come near us, and Hastie on that love ly September morning went on.

Court and I climbed out of our tanks, and we turned our crews out to attempt t dig a tunnel. Both the crews dug with entrenching tools, which were in the tank and attempted to free the belly of the tank, which was trapping the fly wheel an immobilised the engine. When we gave up, Court and I climbed to the top of ou tanks and watched the remaining tanks of D Company attempting to get to Fler by various routes. The last I saw of Hastie was as he headed in a straight line fo Flers.

**Second Lieutenant Stuart Hastie**
*D Company, Heavy Branch, Machine Gun Corps*
It was up to me to carry on alone. Having crossed the front German line, I coul see the old road down into Flers which was in a shocking condition, having bee shelled by both sides. At the other end of this road, about a mile away, which wa about the limit of my vision from the tank, I could see the village of Flers, more o less clouded with smoke from the barrage which had come down on top of it, an the houses, some of them painted white, some seemed to be all kinds of colours.

Across the front of the village, we could see the wire of a trench named Fle Trench and this formed a barricade in front of the village on the British side. We made our way down the remnants of this road with great difficulty. Just as we star ed off, our steering gear was hit and we resorted to steering by putting on the brak on each track alternately, and trying to keep the tank following the line of th Flers–Delville Wood road. When we got down to Flers Trench and were passir into the village, there was a great deal of activity from the eaves, under the roofs the cottages, and also from a trench which appeared to be further through the vr lage but which we couldn't just locate at that point.

The engine was beginning to knock very badly and it looked as if v wouldn't be able to carry on very much further. We made our way up the ma street, during which time my gunners had several shots at various people who we underneath the eaves, or even in the windows of some of the cottages. We went c down through the high street, as far as the first right-angle bend. We turned ther and the main road goes for a matter of two hundred to three hundred yards, ar then turns another right-angle to the left and proceeds out towards Gueudecourt. But we did not go past that point.

At this point, we had to make up our minds what to do. The engine was really in such a shocking condition, that it was liable to let us down at any moment. So I had a look round – as far as it was possible to do in the middle of a village that was being shelled by both sides. I could see no signs of the British army coming up behind me, so I slewed the tank round with great difficulty on the brakes, and came back to Flers Trench, and turned the tank to face the Germans again.

## Lieutenant Wilfred Staddon
### East Surrey Regiment

From this tank, the commander had opened a little door from behind the port gun, and he called out to me for directions. I told him – straight up the main street of Flers and bear right for Gueudecourt. I did mention that I didn't know where the flanks were but I don't know whether he heard that or not because the door was soon closed. My attention was then diverted by a group of Germans coming out of a cellar. There were a lot of them; my imagination made them nearly an army corps. Anyhow, I saw almost at once that they were unarmed. I went along to them, and I formed them up into a platoon. There were exactly eight times four. I reluctantly spared a corporal and sent them back.

My attention then was diverted by a slow-moving plane coming across from the direction of Les Boeufs towards Thiepval. I think I was the only man who possessed a red flare in my pocket, and I put it on a wall and it ignited at once. The observer in that plane could hardly help seeing it. I have no doubt he saw the tank, and in spite of all the smoke and brick dust he probably saw this group of Germans.

I found myself approaching the wire. I think it must have been about an hour after zero hour. There were very few officers left. I only saw one other company officer. The wire was hardly cut, or at least, shall we say, half cut. My companion, Lieutenant Chesters, was urging his men forward with conspicuous gallantry really, and paid the penalty. He was too conspicuous and I saw him die in the wire. The method I adopted to get through the wire was to get on my back and pull it over me, and my fellows did the same. We got through the wire and, of course, there was quite a considerable approach to the trench.

It was a sunken road actually, and we gathered together and rushed it. I had already seen a white handkerchief; perhaps it gave us a little courage.

Anyhow, we got to the trench. There was not a little slaughter, mostly the Germans, which we were not a little bit pleased about, given the casualties which we'd incurred on the way. I found myself chasing the German commander. I took aim at the German commander, but he spotted me, dropped his revolver and ran. I found myself chasing him. He made for a dugout and dived into it, and threw a phosphorus bomb after him. I forgot there was an exit, and he came out, dodging behind walls again.

At that moment my attention was drawn to a shout that a tank was proceeding up the high street of Flers, with a group of laughing Tommies behind it. This was not true. Those laughing Tommies were actually a group of Germans with chattering teeth. I had never seen chattering teeth before but I did then. The tank, in the meantime, had gone further up the road. We followed, peering behind walls, not knowing what we were going to meet. We were rather slower than the tank, but then he had a nice steel waistcoat, and I hadn't. Eventually, we got to the exit of Flers. There was nobody around but my little group who were with me. A Lewis gunner all of sudden said, 'Look sir!' I looked – and there was my opposite number again – the German commander – walking towards Ligny with his sergeant major. I took aim and I missed him. I should have gone for the sergeant major. They fell into the ditch, and I advised my Lewis gunner not to be lavish with his ammunition.

**Second Lieutenant Hatton**
*D Company, Heavy Branch, Machine Gun Corps*
On the morning of the sixteenth, an attack had been ordered on Gueudecourt, which was a fortified position. I had orders to report to an Australian division, and when I reported I was told, 'Take your bloody stink box out of it, you are drawing the enemy fire on the Australians!' I went back to Lieutenant Court, who commanded D14, and told him our attack was cancelled. We were jubilant that it had been cancelled, but Major Summers, our commanding officer, came along and told us that though the main attack had been cancelled, those orders did not apply to the tanks. Furthermore, as the four other tanks that should have attacked with us had become ditched, therefore Major Summers had no option but to order our two tanks to carry out the attack on Gueudecourt, unsupported and alone.

Court and I had a conference, and we drank a considerable amount of rum, and Court started up. He led up the high street of Flers. I followed him up the high street but I had in my path about two thousand dead British and German soldiers. Any attempt to clear the dead from our path was impossible because of the shelling, and we ploughed over the lot of them. Court put his nose out of Flers and the Germans concentrated their fire on him. I followed, and soon I was being covered by shellfire, and every prismatic mirror in that tank was shattered.

My driver, Archer, called and said, 'I cannot see sir,' and I swept him out of his driving seat and called for Corporal Saunders to take his place. 'Where to sir?' he said. 'Follow Lieutenant Court!' We lifted the small armoured flap, and we saw Court's tank and it stopped. There was a small dense column of smoke arising from it and then it exploded. I ordered Saunders on. He was shocked at what had happened – so were we all who were inside D9 – but we were then almost astride 'T' trench and our starboard guns were trained on about four hundred bewildered Germans who were burrowing down like rabbits, seeking cover from our machine guns.

When we had finished on 'T' trench we went towards Gueudecourt – but I had noticed that my port guns had not fired a shot. I went over to the two gunner boys. They were huddled over their machine guns. I kicked them but I got no response – they were dead. Machine-gun bullets had penetrated the tank. We struggled on, with nothing to fire at, but we had to get to Gueudecourt. Jerry slapped shell after shell into us, until one shell penetrated the forward part of the tank, and D9 caught fire. What happened then, I cannot tell you.

I believe there was an explosion, and I was on top of my corporal, who had his shins sticking out in the air. There were two other survivors. Saunders was shrieking with pain, but fortunately I had been provided with morphia so that I could quieten a wounded man. I plugged Saunders with morphia, and I sent the two other survivors to try and get help. They were never seen again. I remained with Saunders in a shell-hole, in the German lines. I bandaged him and gave him more morphia. All he could say was, 'For God's sake, shoot me, sir!'

The Germans had turned their machine guns on us, and I had to get Saunders from that shell-hole. I fastened my Sam Browne belt to his belt, and I crawled a very short distance into what I considered a better hole. The

Guards and the Durham Light Infantry rose up – there appeared to be hundreds of them – and they captured 'T' trench, and, later that day, they came over and got Saunders and I in. I was probably in a very bad way, and I was sent to a clearing station. Saunders was taken through our lines and was immediately sent to England. I had the pleasure of visiting him in a Kentish hospital. All the wounded were lined up on the drive – and Saunders was in a special place.

**Captain Philip Neame VC**
*Headquarters, 168th Infantry Brigade*
In September, we began carrying out patrol work between the different offensives in the Somme battle; we were going out in front of our front line to lay out and prepare assembly trenches for the next attack. We needed a suitable line to start our next attack from, because the last advance might leave a very irregular line with our troops just dug into shell-holes. The form of attack of those days, you must start off from a fairly straight line, to give your troops a chance in a dawn or pre-dawn attack of going off in the right direction.

## SEPTEMBER 22 – SEPTEMBER 30

The Battle of Flers-Courcelette had not achieved a breakthrough for the British, but it had pushed the Germans back. Haig's strategy was now to seize control of the Thiepval Ridge, attacking along a front from Courcelette to the Schwaben Redoubt, before pushing east towards Serre. On September 26, Thiepval was taken, along with Mouquet Farm, the scene of intense fighting earlier in the battle.

Two days later, an attack was mounted on the Schwaben Redoubt, which had briefly fallen to the 36th (Ulster) Division on July 1, before they had been forced to withdraw. Fighting was again fierce, much of it hand-to-hand with bayonets, the infantryman's most unpleasant job. The redoubt changed hands repeatedly. It was not finally taken until October 14.

## Private Leonard Gordon Davies
### 22nd Battalion, Royal Fusiliers

I had the misfortune to meet another chap with a bayonet. I was on the top, and he was down in the trench, and I think he must have been the sort of man who funked things a bit, because he put his hands up and threw his gun down. So I didn't shoot. It was lucky I met that sort of chap. Thank God, I never had another opportunity to murder someone. I must have killed several people with gunfire, but a bayonet was different.

## Corporal Henry Mabbott
### 2nd Battalion, Cameron Highlanders

We went through to the support trenches, in order to clear them. I'd been through two or three bays and found nobody, and I came round a corner – and a German was standing there with his rifle. I had a rifle, and we looked at one another. He shook his head, and he threw his rifle down. I do believe that my knees were shaking more than his. It was a case of cold steel ...

## Private Basil Farrer
### 3rd Battalion, Green Howards

A bayonet is grooved. If you bayonet a man, and try and withdraw it, very often it is very hard because the flesh closes. You've got to give it a twist. If you withdraw without giving it a twist, the outside could close and it wouldn't bleed. Let air into it and the blood flows freely.

## Second Lieutenant Tom Adlam VC
### 7th Battalion, Bedfordshire Regiment

We were down at Thiepval, and things had been held up – especially on one flank – and our battalion was put in, to try and straighten out the line. And just before we went up, my commanding officer was called away and I was in charge of the company. I was briefed at headquarters, and it was impressed upon me that we had to do this at night, while it was dark, because they'd tried several times in the daytime and they'd been held up at strong points. We must get into the trench at night, and then bomb our way to these strong points.

But as things happened, the guides that were taking us up all got lost, except in my company. I thought, 'Yes, it would be us!' Luckily, just before we started the attack, my company commander came and took over. It had taken us so long to get into position, that it was quite daylight. I knew that we weren't supposed to do this in daylight, but he said, 'Well, get along!' And we got over. I was lucky, because the part my platoon was opposite was only about a hundred yards away. We got a certain way – then the machine guns started, and we all went in the shell-holes.

So I thought, 'Well . . . we've got to get in this trench somehow or other. What are we going to do about it?' So I went crawling along from shell-hole to shell-hole, till I came to the officer in charge of the next platoon. 'What do you think about it, Father?' I said. We always used to call him 'Father' – that was his nickname. He said, 'I'm going to wait here till it gets dark. We can't go forward.' I said, 'Well, I think we can. Where I am, I'm not more than fifty yards from the trench. And I think I can get in!' I remember he shook hands with me solemnly. He said, 'Goodbye, old man.' I said, 'Don't be such a damn fool. I'll get back all right. I'm quite sure I can get back.' It didn't worry me.

Of course, I was abnormal at the time. I didn't feel that there was any danger at all at that moment. I got back to my platoon. I went across to them. I said, 'You all got a bomb?' We always take two bombs with us. And I said, 'Well, get one in your hand, pull out the pin. Now hold it tight. As soon as I yell "Charge!" stand up, run two or three yards and throw your bomb. And I think we'll get into that trench! There's practically no wire in front of it . . .'

And they went like a bomb. They did. They all up and ran, and we got into our little bit of trench. There was no trench on the right of us. They'd been all blown away. And we were in this narrow bit of trench; by this time we had no more bombs. There were bags of German bombs – looking like a condensed milk can on the top of a stick. And on there was written '5 secs'. You had to unscrew the bottom, and a little toggle ran out. You pulled that, and you threw it. I'd noticed that the Germans were throwing them at us. And I'd see them coming over wobbling about as they did, pitching a bit short, luckily. And I could count up to nearly three before the bang came. So I experimented with one. I pulled the string, and I took a chance and I said, 'One, two, three.' My servant was beside me, and he was looking over the top of the trench, and he said, 'Bloody good shot, sir! Hit him in the chest! Hit the bugger!'

I think that when the Germans found their own bombs coming back at them, it rather put the wind up them. I don't know whether they thought I was picking up the ones they'd thrown, and was throwing them back, but there were bags of them in the trench. So with my few men behind me I got them all to pick up bombs.

Another thing I did was to dump all my equipment except my prismatic compass. I thought, 'I bought that myself and I don't want to lose it.' And I kept that over my shoulder. The men all brought these bombs along, an armful of them. And I just went gaily along, throwing bombs. I just counted every time I threw it, 'One, two, three.' And the bomb went, and it was most effective.

Then we got up close to where the machine gun was. And that was zipping about. We daren't look up above. But I got a whole lot of bombs ready, and I started throwing as fast as I could. And my servant, who was popping up every now and again, said, 'They're going, sir, they're going!' So I yelled, 'Run in chaps! Come on!' and we just charged up the trench like a load of mad things. Luckily they *were* running.

We never caught them, but we drove them out. Then we came to another machine-gun post. And they were keeping down, the other people behind, that had the longer journey to go over. By the time we got him out of the way, the others followed in behind us. And they did the cleaning-up of the dugouts. All we did, as we went along, was to throw a bomb down, and go on. Well, in the end, with these few men I had, we'd won the objective that the battalion was put out to do. But they came in behind us, and they took nearly a hundred prisoners, from the dugouts. It was lucky that the Germans didn't come up behind us. They were more frightened than we were – and I was frightened, I don't mind telling you.

So then we got to a certain point and the commanding officer saw two trenches leading up towards Schwaben Redoubt, and he said, 'It would be a good idea to get an advance post up there.' So they started off, and a man got killed straight away. I said, 'Oh, damn it! Let me go. I've done the rest of it – I can do this bit!' So I went on. I bombed up the trench, put some men to look after it, and bombed along this one there. It wasn't much of a trench at all. It was an easy job. Then I got to the other corner, bombed them out of there, and then bombed back down the way. We took more prisoners from the dugouts, and now we had our two advance points out towards the enemy.

There was a job to be done, and you just got on and did it. I was more frightened going up to the trenches, sitting, waiting to start. I was very frightened then – very frightened indeed. But when we got going, you've got a group of men with you. You're in charge of them. And we were all taught we had to be an example to our men. If you went forward, they'd go with you, and you sort of lost your sense of fear..

When I heard that I'd been awarded the Victoria Cross, I was back in Colchester. I'd been in the town for an evening out, and when I got back to the mess at night, the orderly room porter said, 'There's a lot of telegrams for you, sir, up in the mess. I was told to tell you.' So I went up to the mess and there were about a dozen telegrams. 'Congratulation!' 'Heartiest Congratulations!' 'Congratulations from all at home!' 'Congratulations from the regiment!'

So I went down, and I said, 'Can you get a wire off to my father?' And they said, 'Yes, if you like.' And in this wire, I said, 'Why congratulations. I know nothing.' And I sent that off to my father. And he wired back, 'Have heard papers are asking for a photograph of you as you've been awarded the VC.' That's how I heard.

**Corporal Don Murray**
*8th Battalion, King's Own Yorkshire Light Infantry*
Three months later, we had come back to the same place we'd been on July 1. We were *still* attacking Mouquet Farm. Haig was sending man after man; thousands were piled up like carcasses in a slaughterhouse, just rotting away. That was the Battle of the Somme.

**Second Lieutenant Stewart Cleeve**
*36th Siege Artillery Battery, Royal Garrison Artillery*
Mouquet Farm was an awfully difficult place to find, because it was rather low down in a valley, but it was a hive of iniquity, and a terrible source of trouble to the infantry. They had tried time without number to capture this wretched Mouquet Farm and they couldn't do it. They were decimated every time they went. So, finally, it was decided to blow the place to hell, and I was observation officer. I went up, got into the front line. They'd had an attack that morning that had failed lamentably, and that's why I was sent for. I asked the infantry, 'Where is Mouquet Farm?' and they said, 'Just over there. But you can't see it from here,' so I said, 'Well, where can I see it from?' They said, 'Between us and Mouquet Farm is a little ridge. You might be able to see it from there.'

The shattered remains of Mouquet Farm. Pronounced Mucky Farm by the British, and Moo-cow Farm by the Australians.

There was a terrific amount of shelling going on. Then there came a lull, and we decided to go to this ridge. We crouched down as low to the ground as we could, he carrying his telephone and telephone line, and we dashed into this little valley in front of no-man's-land.

The valley was filled with dead and dying, who had failed in their assault that morning. It was *pathetic*. I remember, particularly, a sergeant. He was lying on the ground, dead, and he had his hand on his Bible. Open. It was a Douai Bible, and from that I knew he was a Catholic. There was shrapnel pouring over our heads. It didn't matter. I took his address from that Bible, closed his eyes, closed the book, put it in my pocket, and then we crawled back to the front line.

I sent that Bible home to his widow, and I kept up with her for quite a long time.

## Second Lieutenant Tom Adlam VC
### 7th Battalion, Bedfordshire Regiment

The attack on Schwaben Redoubt was going to be, I believe, at one o'clock. Our company had done most of the fighting the day before. They put us in the last line of the attack. And three other companies were in front. But we got in position at twelve, and we chattered away to keep the spirits up. You see, waiting for an hour for an attack is not a very pleasant thing. We told dirty stories and made crude remarks. I remember quite well that there was a nasty smell about. And, of course, we all suggested that somebody had had an accident. But it wasn't. It was a dead body, I think. Well, we joked in that way, in a rather crude manner, to just keep alive.

And then when the shells started they put everything in. You'd never think anything could have lived at all in the bombing that went on at Schwaben Redoubt. And the old earth piled up. And we went forward. And you'd see one lot going to a trench. Then another line going to a trench. Three lines had all met and mingled together. Some of them were killed, of course, so they weren't so strong as when they went in. And then we caught up with them, and by the time we got quite close to the Schwaben Redoubt, there was a huge mine crater there, about fifty feet across. And it was all lined with Germans, popping away at us. So I got hold of the old bombs again, and started trying to bomb them out.

After a bit we got them out of there, and we started charging up the trench, all my men coming on behind very gallantly. And we got right to within striking distance of Schwaben Redoubt itself. Just at that minute, I got a bang in the arm and found I was bleeding. So having been a bombing officer who could throw with both arms, I used my left arm for a time. And I found I could bomb as well with it as I could with my right.

We went on for some time holding on to this position, and working our way up the trenches as far as we could. And when we were going along the trenches, the men would lose all control. There was a German soldier just at the dugout. He'd been wounded. He was in a bad way. He was just moaning 'Mercy *kamerad*! Mercy *kamerad*!' And this fellow in front me – one of the nicest fellows I had in my platoon – said, 'Mercy, you bloody German? Take that!' And he pointed point-blank at him. But he jerked, and he missed him. And I gave him a shove from behind, and I said, 'Go on! He won't do any harm. Let's go and get a good one!' But it was so funny, the fellow said afterwards, 'Sir, glad I missed him, Sir.' It was just in the heat of the moment, you see.

And then my commanding officer came up, and he said, 'You're hurt, Tom!' I said, 'Only a snick in the arm.' And he said, 'Let's have a look at it.' And he put a field dressing on it. He said, 'You go on back, you've done enough.' And so I sat down for a time. And the fight went on. But what happened afterwards, how they did actually catch Schwaben Redoubt, I don't know.

## Major Alfred Irwin
### 8th Battalion, East Surrey Regiment

We were to go and occupy the Schwaben Redoubt on the night of September 29. We went on to ground that was utterly unrecognisable. Staff officers, back in comfortable offices, had detailed us to certain parts of the line that simply weren't there. There was a quarter moon, and very little light at all. Whiteman, one of my best subalterns, was commanding his best company, and when he'd got into what he thought was the correct line of trenches, he was heavily attacked by the Boche with flame-throwers, and driven back for some distance, but he led a counter-attack himself. He was a powerful man and a very good bomb thrower, and he got it all back again.

A German soldier's overcoat hangs suspended from a tree.

A dead German soldier lying outside his dugout.

**Second Lieutenant Tom Adlam VC**
*7th Battalion, Bedfordshire and Hertfordshire Regiment*
My commanding officer said, 'You've got to go back. Take this batch of prisoners back!' So I took about a dozen prisoners back with me. They filed in front of me. They were all unarmed. And I just had my old gun. I came to a little dugout, and there was a body lying on the floor there. I said, 'Why is that stiff down there? Why don't you get him out of the way?' 'He ain't a stiff, sir. He got at the rum jar. He's tight as an owl.' He looked dead.

**Private Nathan Pizzy**
*Suffolk Regiment*
You know they say the shell-holes were full of water? Well – they were full of blood and water. Everywhere was crimson, you see.

## OCTOBER 1 – NOVEMBER 19

Haig had never lost sight of his hope for a breakthrough to end the attrition. The enemy third-line trenches had now been taken and, believing in an imminent German collapse, Haig planned a sweeping advance on Bapaume, and from there on to Cambrai to join up with a simultaneous advance to the north. At the beginning of October, however, heavy rain started to fall, which within days had turned the ground to glutinous mud. As conditions became difficult, so casualties continued to mount. And whilst the Germans were being pushed – slowly – back, and their morale was undoubtedly low, they continued to fight doggedly. The resistance encountered in the Schwaben Redoubt is testament to the German soldier's tenacity. The weather and an unreasonably obstinate enemy forced Haig to delay his plans.

Nevertheless, the offensive momentum was maintained. Prisoners were taken, and Le Sars was captured on October 7. The next day, however, the 1/5th Battalion, London Regiment was cut to pieces whilst attacking west of Le Transloy. As the weeks passed, and the weather worsened, so British morale fell and continued attrition seemed inevitable.

Nevertheless, on October 26, Haig formulated plans for another offensive. He would have to wait until the weather improved, but attacks continued in the meantime. On November 5, the 16th Battalion, King's Royal Rifle Corps attacked near Le Transloy, achieving its objective. Three days later, Haig set the date of his final push for November 13. His objective was no longer a breakthrough – he would now settle for an advance of a thousand yards. With an eye on an upcoming Allied military conference, he wanted the British army to give a good account of itself.

The Battle of the Ancre lasted five days. On the first day, the Hood Battalion of the Royal Naval Division took Station Road, south of Beaumont Hamel (which was also taken – almost five months after it had been first attacked on July 1), and the Seaforth Highlanders captured Y Ravine within the German lines. Beaucourt was taken on the second day, by the 63rd Division.

As the battle drew to a close, so the temperature fell. The final assault of the battle was launched in whirling sleet. The 8th Battalion, East Surrey Regiment, the battalion that had punted footballs towards the German lines back in July, now attacked the snow-covered Desire Trench. On the following evening, the 19th Division failed to take the village of Grandcourt and, with that final action, the Battle of the Somme came to an end.

## Corporal Don Murray
### 8th Battalion, King's Own Yorkshire Light Infantry

On October 1, there was a lot of German prisoners coming down, and they'd built a special marquee for them. And this fellow said, 'Hey, Yorkie, there's a lot of Germans coming down, and they've been out in no-man's-land for a long time. They're nearly all wounded. Get jugs of hot tea and coffee, but don't give a drink to anyone with a body wound! Only to those with superficial wounds!' So I went into this marquee, and the place stank! Oh, it was awful! You know when you've had a sore finger, and you've bandaged it, and it's white when you take the bandage off? Well, they were like that, all over! Their face and everything. Wrinkled and white, from being out in the open. They were saying, 'Kamerad! Kamerad! Trinken! Trinken!' And I didn't look whether they had body wounds, or what; I gave them their hot drink.

The next morning, I was told that they all had to have their boots taken off. They had no socks on – just rags on their feet. I said, 'I'm not doing that!' I was told, 'No, you don't do it! Get a big German out, and get him to bend down, and the one with the boots puts his foot on his backside, and a third one pulls the boot off!' 'How do I tell them that in German?' I asked. 'Oh, it's easy. Just say, "*Stoopen! Stoopen!*" ' I believed it, too!

Anyway, there was one man who'd been mouthy all night. He'd been shouting, and going on, and I didn't know what he was on about. I called him out, and he came and stood to attention, and I said, '*Stoopen!*' '*Stoopen?*' he said. In the end, I bent him over and showed him what I meant, then I called the smallest one out and demonstrated what I wanted. Every time he pulled a boot off, he turned round to me; I thought he wanted to eat me! He was shouting at me, and going on, and all the prisoners were laughing. For all that they were so ill, they were laughing their heads off. Then, the parson came in the door, and he started laughing as well. 'Look, padre,' I said, 'there's such a joke going on here, and everyone's having a good time, but me!' 'It's no wonder!' he said. 'You've got the colonel pulling their boots off!'

**Sergeant Sidney Amatt**
*1/5th Battalion, London Regiment*
The night of October 8. As we went towards the front line, there was literally hundreds of bodies we passed, of all different regiments. You could tell from their uniforms and regalia. They had died on the first few days of the July advances. We went up though the communication trenches, up to the front line, and you saw dead men and pieces of limbs sticking out of the trench. To us young soldiers, it was very disconcerting.

So we went up. Each of us was taking it in turns to do sentry duty. That's staying on the fire-step, while the others lay about in the trench, best they could, and tried to get as much rest as they could.

I was resting on a box, and I woke up with a shot. I looked round, and there was a corporal laying down in the trench, with one hand hanging off, his face was spattered with pock-marked pieces of shell, and one ankle almost severed. I looked round and I saw another chap, who'd been sitting at the end of the fire bay. His head was blown off.

What had happened was that one of Jerry's shells had come through just where this chap was sitting, come straight through the parapet, taken his head right off, and burst in the trench. There were several other people wounded as well, but I was astounded because I wasn't touched.

I'd had training in first aid, as a stretcher-bearer, so I started patching this chap up. I made a tourniquet and stopped the bleeding. Then an officer came along and gave him a tablet of morphine. Officers used to carry these things in their pocket. Anyone who was wounded, to take the pain away, they'd put this little sweet on their tongue, and they sucked it, and it sort of sent them off into unconsciousness. We got this chap on a stretcher, but we had to leave him there because word got around that, at three o'clock in the afternoon, we was going over the top.

At about two o'clock, the runner came up with a jar of rum. The officer dealt off the rum to every soldier. They gave us two Mills grenades to put in our overcoat pockets, plus another fifty rounds of ammunition, strung round our shoulders. That meant we had 150 rounds of ammunition, besides our rifle and equipment, and a respirator across our chests. How we were expected to go along, I haven't the faintest idea.

At three, the officer looked at his watch, blew a whistle and we went over the top. The order was that the guns would start firing five minutes before we went over on to the barbed wire and their front-line trench, so that when we got there, everything would be clear. Their front-line trench would be decimated.

We'd gone about a hundred yards, when machine-gun fire opened up from both flanks. I was with a pal of mine, called Ted Freeman. Big feller, he was. There were plenty of shell-holes about, and Ted said, 'Let's jump in this hole!' To get out of the fire. We turned round in the shell-hole, with our rifles over the top, facing the Germans, and Ted said he could see a German. He put his rifle up to fire. I was right alongside of him, and I felt him give a bit of a jerk and a shudder. He'd been shot right through the heart.

I turned him over a bit, to make sure what had happened. I more or less knew – from my medical knowledge – that he was dead. I crawled up the rim of the shell-hole to look around, and I saw a couple of officers who'd just come up. They told me I was to join another party that had come up from the reserve trenches.

The casualties I saw were terrific. There was 140 in my company to start with, but at the roll-call afterwards I was the only one of B Company on parade. Several others joined us later, but there was only about half a dozen of us. All the rest was either killed, wounded, or missing.

**Rifleman Robert Renwick**
*16th Battalion, King's Royal Rifle Corps*

A tremendous number of men went sick through the month of November. It was very wet. It seemed to rain night and day, and the Somme front became a bog. Men and horses were sinking into it. And trench foot was a problem. You got your feet wet to begin with, and then the frost came, and there were a lot of casualties. I remember once when we came out of the line, we were put into tents, and I got three parcels all in a heap. One from home, one from my nan and one from my old master at the shop. They had sent cold chicken and sausages, and I shared it out with two or three of my mates and we had a terrific dinner that night. But I woke up in the early hours of the morning, and I had a terrific pain. I was reported sick and the doctor came, and I had a chill in the kidneys. Nothing to do with the food.

**Lieutenant William Taylor**
*13th Battalion, Royal Fusiliers*

As soon as you got rid of one battle, it was only a question of time before you had to go into another. The Battle of the Ancre was the last battle on the Somme, and I've discovered since that it was postponed three or four times. The weather was very bad – it was very, very wet.

**Rifleman Robert Renwick**
*16th Battalion, King's Royal Rifle Corps*

Conditions were deplorable. We went up the line on the third, and we hadn't a dugout of any description, and the next day a few of us went away looking for sandbags and duckboards to make a little bit of shelter for the next night. We got to this dump and we grabbed sandbags and duckboards, and we were making our way when the sergeant major in charge of the dump appeared, and he fired his revolver. But we ran and we had some shelter made for the next night.

On the Sunday morning, just before the attack, a shell came over and buried fourteen of us in a slit trench. There were six men killed on the left of me, and seven wounded on the right of me. Some of them very badly. And I came out unscathed. I pulled the live ones out and reported to the stretcher-bearers, who took them down to a dressing station.

After that, we went over at midday. On the way over, it was just a case of

British troops wearing sheepskin coats.

Mules stranded in mud.

jumping from one shell-hole to another. Two of us were in a shell-hole, and I must have eased up, out of the water, because a sniper put a bullet through the top of my steel helmet. The helmet didn't fit too well, and there was a tiny bit of space between my head and the tip of the helmet. The other man was slightly wounded as well, but he didn't go back. We went forward after that. We came across two men of the Scottish Rifles, who had been in no-man's-land since the last attack, a few days before. They were badly wounded, and they were just able to crawl about and take biscuits out of dead men's haversacks and water out of their bottles. They had a fearful appearance. They were blue in the face. I hoped that our stretcher-bearers would get them out that night. I've often wondered about those fellows.

We went on, and it was dusk before we obtained our objective. We advanced beyond the German line and dug in, as well as we could. We were so exhausted. Two men were digging themselves in, one minute, and they fell down asleep, the next, flat on their faces. I wasn't quite as bad as that – but I was very tired. After we were relieved the next day, men were just lying on the floor, caked in mud, and the brigadier appeared and a few men began to get up to salute him. He said, 'Lie still, men! I'm proud of you!'

### Leading Seaman Joe Murray
#### Hood Battalion, 63rd (Royal Naval) Divison

It was still raining, raining like hell, wet through. The whole battalion were on parade, all there, and Major General Shute inspected us. He starts off, the usual stunt, you know, 'Blah … blah … blah … ' What wonderful men we had, both on Gallipoli and in France, he'd done this, he'd done that, he was reliable. He says that the place we were going to attack now was one of the most formidable parts of the firing line of the whole of the Western Front. The Germans had been there umpteen months. We know it was all honey-combed with dugouts. We know this. We know that. We've had five different attempts – but we must get that ridge *at all costs* – because if we don't, the whole advance on the Somme would be in danger of being encircled like a pincer movement.

He said, 'I'm going to tell you this much. You know what you have got to do! The more prisoners you take, the less food you'll get – because we have to feed them out of your rations … '

## Lieutenant William Taylor
### 13th Battalion, Royal Fusiliers

We marched to a village behind the line, and we were told that we were to attack Beaucourt, next to Beaumont Hamel, which was going to be attacked at the same time. The attack took place on the morning of November 13. It was the practice to leave the second in command of a company out of the line on the first day, to take the place of the commanding officer of the company going up to the line on the next day. So I was left out of the first day's fighting. I might not be here had I gone in that first day, because the captain of the company was wounded, and I went up the next day and commanded the company for the rest of the battle. It was actually a very successful battle. It went on for a week, and the casualties were rather more than usual.

The conditions were frightful. There was so much water, everywhere. I remember a broken-down railway station, shelled for months, and it was one of the most unpleasant times in my experience. The terrain was simply a mass of shell-holes. Men marching along flooded roads, with broken-down trees and mud.

I missed the first day, but the battalion took their objective, and we held on to it. After that, conditions were extremely unpleasant. Trenches were all knocked to hell. There was constant shelling. I went in about seventy strong, and I brought out thirty-six a week later. We were living in funk holes, scooped out of a bank by the side of the road – there were no trenches. We were in the open for a week, day and night. There was no trench system. There was no accommodation at all. We would drape a groundsheet over the front of these funk holes. It rained and it snowed. We were extremely cold, and it was one of the most unpleasant times in my experience. The doctor had an aid post in a large shell-hole. We were expecting a counter-attack any moment, and I was very glad to get away a week later.

That was the end of the Battle of the Somme, and we marched north and finished up at a part of the line where they had breastworks, as opposed to trenches. These breastworks were built up with sandbags from the ground. Instead of going down, the trenches were built up. They were a much better target for shells than a trench. I never felt safe for a moment. They couldn't dig trenches there because of the low-lying country. You dug down a foot and you were in water. Actually, there were a few communication trenches of a sort, but you had to keep very low because if you stood up in them you were head and shoulders above them. We went into the line at Neuve Chapelle, where there'd been a battle earlier on in the war, but the line had been held since then and it was now a quiet sector.

## Lieutenant Norman Collins
### 1/6th Battalion, Seaforth Highlanders

At Beaumont Hamel, no guns were fired beforehand, except for ranging purposes, and at six o'clock in the morning of November 13 the guns opened up. It was terrific. I think there might have been two thousand guns, almost wheel-to-wheel. When they opened up, the noise was so terrific that one couldn't hear separate explosions, or gunfire. It was a continuous drumming. The shells fell on the German front line, and they'd had no previous warning. The first wave of the battalion moved forward under a canopy of steel. When they arrived at the German front line, some of them were killed by their own guns. I wasn't in the first wave. After a few minutes, the guns stopped and there was dead silence. The silence was terrific. The contrast. For a space of about two or three minutes there was silence, and then they opened up again, simultaneously. During that period of silence, the gunners were changing the trajectory of their guns. The second bombardment fell on the German second and reserve lines, and our troops occupied the front line.

We were excited, but never having been over the top before, we were not particularly afraid – even though we knew the chances were that we'd be wounded or killed. The bravest man was the man who'd never been in the trenches before, because he didn't know what he was getting into. The officers carried a cane, a 45 revolver, and a few Mills bombs. The cane was no use whatever. Just a bit of show. I carried a 45 revolver but it wasn't until afterwards, when I went on a revolver course, that I was taught how to use it. It kicks so heavily, that most people couldn't hit a barn door at ten yards with it. The infantry had their Lee-Enfield rifles with bayonets fixed.

I had to go into Y Ravine, which was an extension of the German front line, where a couple of platoons had a job to do. We had to clean out the dugouts – to make sure that no Germans came out of the dugouts, or if they did, that they were taken prisoner. The dugouts in Y Ravine were very deep, with a lot of steps down to the bottom, and at the bottom there were wire beds, and even a row of little brass servants' bells which privates or batmen had to ring before they entered the final compartment. No shell could penetrate them; Beaumont Hamel was like a fortress and the Germans would keep the machine guns in these dugouts during the shelling, and bring them up when the shelling stopped. That was fine during the old style of continuous bombardment, but there was no time to bring them up during the creeping barrage because the troops were only a few yards away when the barrage stopped. Anyway, this was a success, and the village of Beaumont Hamel was taken. My men performed magnificently in the attack. I saw one man kneeling, with his rifle in his hands. I went up to him – and he was stone dead. He'd just dropped to his knees like that, facing forward.

We took prisoners, and we detached a lance corporal to take them back out of the line. I remember a young German prisoner, using a piece of wood as a crutch. I could speak a few words of German and I asked him how he felt, and I wasn't popular because I had him put on a stretcher and taken back behind the lines with the British wounded. It was probably the wrong thing to do, but he was a young fellow, not more than eighteen, badly wounded, and I suppose I felt sorry for him. There were a lot of British wounded, and others felt I was using up a valuable stretcher in looking after a German at the expense of a British man. Actually, I did hear stories of German prisoners being killed on the way back, so I don't know that he survived. I only know that I saw him set off from the trenches, to be taken back to the cages.

After the battle – I don't know why – I was made burial officer. The Newfoundland Regiment, all volunteers, had come to France and taken part in the attack of July 1. They had been chosen to attack Beaumont Hamel, which had been a fortress with its deep ravine and dugouts – and they were decimated. Some of them had been lying out here in no-man's-land since July 1, four and a half months previously, and I had the job of burying these dead, who were skeletons in uniform. The shape of the leg was quite round, with the shape of the puttee, until one stepped on it and one saw that the flesh was gone. A rat's nest was in the cage of each chest. The rats ran out as we shovelled them into shell-holes. We took the pay books off them, but left their identity discs on, so that they could be identified later and given a decent burial. In the pay book, you might have the soldier's will, or pictures of his father, mother and sweetheart. We carefully put these pay books into sandbags, and shovelled the corpses into shell-holes, and covered them up as well as we could. We put up a bit of wood and made marks on it, to identify the place. The whole area had a sweet smell. The sweet smell of decaying flesh. I can still remember it.

A machine-gun officer outside a German dugout captured in November.

After that, I went down the line with the sandbags full of pay books to Brigade Headquarters. There were two or three fellows carrying the bags, and we went down a communication trench to a very deep dugout, dug into the chalk. That was Brigade HQ, and it was very clean, and it was full of very smart staff officers with red tabs and well-polished Sam Browne belts. I was asked, very politely, to have a cup of tea, and they handed me some cakes which had come from Fortnum & Mason in Piccadilly. I was feeling a little under the weather, and it seemed strange that a short distance away the war was going on, but in this dugout you were back in London. They were all so clean, and I was dirty and lousy in my Tommy's uniform. I was treated very kindly by the supermen, but I wanted to get back. I handed over my pay books, said goodbye and went back up the communication trench with my little crew, and went back to the line.

I had two particular friends in the battalion, a lieutenant called Smith and a lieutenant called MacLean. MacLean was a divinity student – and what he was doing in the front line was anybody's guess. Smith was a dentist, who was going to go sick after the attack – if he survived – because he had a hernia that badly needed attention. He wouldn't go sick before the attack, because that would have been cowardly. Well, both men were killed in the attack. We buried the newly killed men from our battalion at a village called Mailly Wood. We buried them in one long trench, each one wrapped up in an army blanket, laid side by side. They were given a decent burial – we had the reverse arms, the bugle, the Last Post. I saw MacLean and Smith buried there, side by side. Later on, Mailly Wood cemetery was built, and they were all properly identified and properly laid to rest, with headstones.

**Private Reginald Glenn**
*12th Battalion, York and Lancaster Regiment*
I used to play the organ for little religious services. One day, after our troops had gone forward and taken Serre village, the chaplain and another officer took me into what had been no-man's-land on July 1. We stood there, with all these skeletons lying around, and the officer said to the chaplain, 'Can we sing a little hymn over these bodies?' The three of us stood there and sang 'On the Resurrection Morning', and the next morning it snowed heavily and it covered all the bodies over. That was the start of the terrible winter.

Gordon Highlanders in a reserve trench at Bazentin-le-Petit in November.

Working parties of British troops – photographed in November – inside one of the mine craters carved out by the explosions of July 1.

**Major Alfred Irwin**
*8th Battalion, East Surrey Regiment*
On November 18, 1916, I was wounded in the assault on Desire Trench. In the morning, before it got light, I went up to look round this new ground we'd taken, and I went round with the company commander and was very pleased with the arrangements he'd made. Just as it was getting light, I started back to my battalion headquarters, and I hadn't gone more than a few yards when I was shot in the thigh. I fell into a shell-hole full of water and ice. It was freezing hard, and every time I raised my head the sniper had another go at me. So I had to lie in the water and wait for help, which came in the form of Canadian stretcher-bearers, later in the morning. When I was hit, I'd told my orderly to carry on back, but the unfortunate man was hit and died.

**Corporal Jim Crow**
*110th Brigade, Royal Field Artillery*
We had a direct hit on a signalling dugout at Mouquet Farm. After that, the brigade medical officer said that every man in the division was unfit for service. That was at the end of November, and that's when I got out.

# Looking Back

# Looking Back

*Half of the men, I'm sure, had no idea what they were fighting for.*

By the end of the Battle of the Somme, 419,654 British and Dominion soldiers had become casualties, of whom 127,751 had been killed. There had been no Allied breakthrough, and 1917 would bring renewed bloody attritional struggles on the Western Front, at Arras and Passchendaele.

### Second Lieutenant W. J. Brockman
*15th Battalion, Lancashire Fusiliers*
The people at home did not understand the conditions under which we were fighting. I don't think they wanted to. Just as it's not fashionable now to talk about war – it wasn't then. It's a very strange thing. I've never told any of these stories to anybody before; people just don't want to know.

### Major Murray Hill
*5th Battalion, Royal Fusiliers*
I've read the poems of Owen and Sassoon. I thought they wrote nonsense. Writing poetry about horrors. No point. It goes without saying. No need to write it up. Sassoon went off his head. He threw his medals into the sea. But he wrote a very good book about fox hunting.

**Private Leonard Gordon Davies**
*22nd Battalion, Royal Fusiliers*

I wasn't at all a brave man. I wasn't one of those who volunteered to go over the top, whenever there was a chance. It was an experience that you knew nothing about. You just jumped up on to the trench and hoped that you wouldn't meet a bullet. Actually going over, and seeing one man drop, and another man drop, and you'd wonder why you were still going. I always put it down to the prayers of my mother and father. But I didn't deserve to get through it all.

**Private Donald Cameron**
*12th Battalion, York and Lancaster Regiment*

I wasn't frightened. I was bloody petrified.

**Corporal Frederick Francis**
*11th Battalion, Border Regiment*

A pal of mine was blown into a shell-hole and there was already a German in there. And they started to fight each other. To kill each other. But in the end, they gave it up and shook hands. They decided it was just a waste of life and they started talking to each other.

**Corporal Wilfred Woods**
*1/4th Battalion, Suffolk Regiment*

You didn't hate them as individuals, no, no, you felt sorry for them. I remember, on the Somme, in a German dugout there was this poor little drummer boy, about sixteen. He had been left behind in this dugout and he was scared stiff. We felt sorry for the poor little chap.

**Private Harold Startin**
*1st Battalion, Leicestershire Regiment*

There were no bitterness at all. There's many a German that helped our wounded people down the communication trenches, even carried them down. There were no hatred between the forces. Although we *were* shooting at one another.

### Private Leonard Gordon Davies
*22nd Battalion, Royal Fusiliers*

The trenches were very close together. Vimy Ridge was a very important vantage point, and both the Germans and us were at the top of it. The idea was to get the Germans off it. The fighting was extremely fierce, when it was on, but when it was off, it was very quiet. We were just fifteen yards from each other and we used to speak to them. They spoke quite good English. We agreed a ceasefire and we got out of the trenches and met each between the two trenches in no-man's-land. It wasn't very easy to get across, because there was wire in the way. I was smoking in those days, and they gave me some tobacco and we rolled it up into cigarettes. Then we got back into our trenches and we started to fight each other again. It had only lasted about five minutes. But we didn't shoot to kill, because we liked these people and they liked us as well.

It was a most extraordinary experience. It wasn't common. We must have been lucky to have particularly friendly opponents at that time. These were not military people by desire – one of them told me that he had been a waiter in London. The stupidity, the absurdity of war really struck me then, that this could happen, and the next moment you're trying to kill the man you've just been talking to. I began thinking it then, and I still think it. War is ridiculous.

### Private William Holmes
*12th Battalion, London Regiment*

I look upon the war as an experience. I got just as much pleasure out of it as I did the bad times. I saw horrific things, but we were so disciplined that we took it all for granted, as though it was normal. When I came back, I was no different from when I went.

### Private Stanley Bewshire
*11th Battalion, East Lancashire Regiment*

I never regretted joining the army. We had some good times and we had some bad times, I remember every minute of it. Every night I go to bed and I think about it.

**Private Fred Dixon**
*10th Battalion, Royal West Surrey Regiment*

While I was on the Somme, life was absolutely miserable. After that, I was never the same man again. I was always looking to see how I could get away from the dangers. I wanted to live. I was never the same man again.

**Second Lieutenant Edmund Blunden**
*11th Battalion, Royal Sussex Regiment*

How did we get through? Partly the fear of fear. The fear of being found afraid. Another factor is the belief in human beings – your colleagues. Any one day, you say, 'My job is to be at the crossroads at such and such a time with whatever I'm carrying, and old so-and-so will be there expecting it and there'll be no letting him down.' Also, there was the interest in what would come out of this extraordinary, titanic, fatal performance, and interest in how it was being done. During the Passchendaele battle, I was walking with one or two signallers, in front of the Germans. The Germans had a bang and it was beautiful shooting. One of our lads, a tall, handsome youth, said, 'I never did see such shelling!' It was like he was applauding a conjuring trick in the music halls, or a piece of fast bowling in a Test match. He was really looking at a remarkable feat of skill on behalf of another human being. Of course, after a time nobody cared any longer. Even a drama could go on too long. That was what we felt. This one went on far too long.

**Corporal Don Murray**
*8th Battalion, King's Own Yorkshire Light Infantry*

There was a chap in my carriage on the train home from the war, and he said, 'Let me come to the window! There's something I've wanted to do ever since I've been in the army!' 'All right then,' I said. So he stood at the window, and at the end of the platform was a military policeman, and this bloke waited until the train had pulled level with him and he spat straight in his face. And then the train was off. 'God!' he said. 'That was good!'

**Signaller Leonard Ounsworth**
*124th Heavy Battery, Royal Garrison Artillery*

The officer in charge back in England – he'd been retired God knows how many years and come back into the army – he was all spit and polish, parade and that kind of thing. He came on parade one day – I've forgotten what he had to tell us, but he marched up and down like Napoleon for a minute or two, with his hand across his chest like this, you see, and then he suddenly turned round, he says, 'You men fought with honour and glory in the field of battle in France and Flanders, gad! How I wish I could have been with you.' He banged his fist like that. We gaped open-mouthed at him, silly old devil.

## Corporal Don Murray
### 8th Battalion, King's Own Yorkshire Light Infantry

I'd always imagined the end of the war: we'd come marching through the streets of Bradford, and there'd be flags flying. Well, when the time came I was all by myself, it was pouring with rain and I got a tram home. I knocked on the door, and Sissy's mother answered. 'I'm so glad you've come. Dad's just dying . . . ' That was some homecoming.

## Private Albert Day
### 1/4th Battalion, Gloucestershire Regiment

When I came back from the war in March 1918, the Bristol tramway gave me back the office job I'd had before I went in. It was all chaps when I went, but when I came back it was full of girls. I'm scared stiff of girls. So I became a bus driver, a navvy, a labourer, you name it. I did it for eighteen months. Then I went to Canada, but I came back because I couldn't get a job as a Turk over there.

When I was back here, I wasn't very happy about the way they treated the chaps. I mean, Lloyd George said that when the war was over, he'd make this a land fit for heroes. Two years afterwards, and there's fifty thousand men out of work in Bristol, nearly starving. They stopped these men's dole and they stormed the Bristol Board of Guardians offices, demanding relief. Able-bodied men couldn't get relief, but they soon altered that. So then I saw this job and that's when I went home and wrote a letter, and I became an Assistant Relieving Officer. And I took the full law examination of England and Wales.

## Sergeant Frederick Goodman
### 1st London Field Ambulance, Royal Army Medical Corps

After my time in the Royal Army Medical Corps, my parents wanted me to become a doctor. But it wasn't for me. I'd had quite enough on the Somme, and I thanked them very much – it would have been quite an outlay putting me through medical school – and I told them that, if they didn't mind, I would much prefer to become a chartered accountant.

**Private William Holmes**
*12th Battalion, London Regiment*

My wife was a very good artist, in watercolours. We were living in Broadstairs, and I used to go round with a pedlar's licence, door-to-door, selling birthday cards, which I'd sell for sixpence each. I was making a living. One Christmas, I sold 1,500 Christmas cards around Margate and Ramsgate. And even with a bullet still inside me, I never had any sickness.

**Reverend Leonard Martin Andrews**
*Chaplain, attached to Royal Fusiliers*

Half of the men, I'm sure, had no idea what they were fighting for. But they went and gave their lives.

**Private Frank Lindlay**
*14th Battalion, York and Lancaster Regiment*

We used to say, 'If your name's on it – you get it.' That was the philosophy.

**Private James Snaylham**
*11th Battalion, East Lancashire Regiment*

General Haig wanted shooting. That's what I thought because there was no support at all. When I called back to our trenches there weren't a person in, not one. They were all out there wounded or dead.

**Private Tom Easton**
*21st Battalion, Northumberland Fusiliers*

I have a great respect for Douglas Haig. I believe that his idea was correct.

**Corporal Harry Fellows**
*12th Battalion, Northumberland Fusiliers*

Haig was a man who never cared for men's lives, and he became known to us as 'The Butcher'.

### Captain Philip Neame VC
*Headquarters, 168th Infantry Brigade*
I don't think I ever came across any – what shall I say? – defeatist feeling in the brigade I was with, nor did I ever hear or feel any disgruntlement at our high command.

### Lieutenant Phillip Howe
*10th Battalion, West Yorkshire Regiment*
I would say that I enjoyed the war more than any other period of four years I have ever had.

### Corporal Henry Mabbott
*2nd Battalion, Cameron Highlanders*
There is one spot in France – Contalmaison – where there are eight hundred Cameron Highlanders in four graves. That's what we lost, eight hundred out of a thousand in taking Contalmaison, and losing it again.

### Private Russell Bradshaw
*11th Battalion, East Lancashire Regiment*
In those days, there were just stumps in the copse, but today it's a thick, wooded area. A mass of trees. Far different to those days, when there was nothing about.

### Private Tom Easton
*21st Battalion, Northumberland Fusiliers*
Today, on visits to the Somme, I often go back to the line of graves where these men are. Some of these men were old enough to be my father, and they treated me like a son – even in those circumstances.

### Private William Holmes
*12th Battalion, London Regiment*
We were all just a band of brothers. No brothers were ever more united than we were. But, after the war, we never kept in touch ...

## Private Arthur Pearson
### 15th Battalion, West Yorkshire Regiment

The Leeds Pals have a very strong association. We meet about once a month. There's about twenty people who turn up. We used to have dances and whist drives – of course, those days are over – but it's nice to see the old faces, and talk about the old days; we can't forget them …

## Private Frank Lindlay
### 14th Battalion, York and Lancaster Regiment

I can only remember faces and first names. I can remember them one after another. I have photos in my house, and I look every day. It's a thought that's in my mind all the time. Has been for years.

## Private Donald Cameron
### 12th Battalion, York and Lancaster Regiment

About a month before the sixty-fifth anniversary of July 1, I wrote to the Mayor of Sheffield, asking her if she would invite the few surviving members of our battalion to her parlour, for a talk. She wrote back, and refused. Such is life. But you'd expect the mayor to remember that it was the mayor who appealed to the young men of Sheffield, in 1914, to join up and make one of the best battalions in the world.

## Second Lieutenant W. J. Brockman
### 15th Battalion, Lancashire Fusiliers

I'm eight-six, but as I've got older I've avoided the company of older men. Men my own age. They get into that lazy, slurring way of speaking, which I determined not to do. I go down to the golf club every week, and play poker with men about fifty years of age. That keeps my mind active. And I don't lose *a lot* of money. I win a bit more than I lose, but this isn't what we're here to talk about …

## Private Joseph Pickard
### 4th Battalion, Northumberland Fusiliers

I got hit by a shell. When I came to myself, I was lying amongst a load of dead men. I found out where I was hit, and I tore my trousers down, and I thought if I stop here it's either a bullet or a bayonet. So I got the first-aid packet out;

all that was in there was a lot of gauze and a little tube of something. I was hit underneath the joint of the leg, and it cut the sciatic nerve, it chipped both hip joints, it smashed the left side of the pelvis, I had three holes in the bladder. I lost my nose. Ha-ha. I was a bloody mess. Oh dear. I crawled along the road on my hands and knees, and I saw a fellow I knew and I gave him a shout, and someone or other got a stretcher. They carried us through the barrage, and I got into a wagon, and I remember a fellow said, 'You'll be all right now, chum.'

I reckon if anything like this happens, and you're shocked, it takes a lot of the feeling away from you. The ambulance took us to an old farmhouse, where the roof was blown off. I wanted a drink. Well, they wouldn't give us any water, you see, abdominal wounds – you never get water. I asked a fellow to take my boot off, and I remember being in this advance clearing station, and when I come round it was dark. I was lying in a stretcher and I didn't know what was the matter with us. It turned out there was a blanket over the top of us. I was left for death.

I got rid of this blanket and I shouted at an orderly, and two of them came down and had a look at us. They wouldn't give me a drink, of course. Picked the stretcher straight up and put us on the hospital train. I knew there was something the matter with my face, but I never bothered about it. In cases like that, you want to live, and to hell with what you look like. So I got on the hospital train and I began to know what was the matter, because I got on me side on the hospital train, but I had to get the sister to pull me back. I couldn't shift myself. I lay on me back all the time until I got to Rouen.

They shoved us on the Red Cross wagon there, and Rouen is a lot of cobbles, you know. The wagon had a bit of speed on. I was calling the driver everything you could think about. I finished up with my hands through the slats at the top, and the fellow was saying, 'I am trying to get you there as quick as I can!' When I got to Rouen, they left us outside the hospital.

I was lying there and the doctor came and said, 'What's the matter with you then?' I says, 'It's not bloody hard to see, is it?' He walked away. They can get nippy when you are like that, you know. So later on they took us inside and, believe it or not, every bed was full, stretchers six deep across the floor. You could hardly get moving. An orderly came up and said, 'Had any dinner?' I said, 'Son, I have had nowt to eat for ten days.' He fetched me a plate, and God, I scoffed the lot. He fetched some rice pudding in a basin, I scoffed that; he fetched something to drink and I scoffed that.

I don't suppose they knew what was the matter with us, and I didn't care. Shortly after, they put somebody out of a bed and put me into it. They cut all my clothes off. There was a mixture of chalk, wet, blood, God – everything. They cut everything off of us, and they took us up to X-ray. I mentioned I had shrapnel behind the joint in my leg, but they couldn't find it. The X-ray couldn't find it, and they slashed us in the operating theatre, and they couldn't find it. The sister used to come every day to change my dressing, and I'd tell her it was still there. She got hold of the flesh and opened it – and there was the piece of shrapnel, just like that, stuck underneath the joint. I got the last rites in that hospital. They came and laid this thing out in front of us, and I thought, 'Oh God, I can't be as bad as that.' Ha ha.

I was in Rouen for six weeks. The sister did her damnedest to get us out, and back to England, but the doctor used to come and look at my graph every morning, and say, 'Oh, it's not down yet.' My temperature. Eventually, he gave in, and I was sent home with a tube from my thigh, right up into my bladder. I was sent to the Ford Western General in Glamorgan. I was there for about eight months, in the abdominal ward, with the doctor working on my pelvis.

When I was there, I always had blinking bandages over my nose. I was chatting away with the sister; one day I said, 'Give us a loan of your scissors.' And I cut all the blinking bandages off, to have a look at it. It didn't bother me. The sister asked if it bothered me. 'What do you think about it?' she said. 'Off it's gone!' I said. 'And I don't think I'll be travelling along the line to look for it!'

I was let out to a convalescent place because – well – I guess I was improving. It was in this place called Baglan, near Aberavon. I was on crutches, and I couldn't do very much. Sometimes the local doctor would come up and take us out to a tea house, and I would sit with my leg stuck out, like a wooden leg, and his daughter would come and have her tea, sat beside us.

In the end, I was sent up to Newcastle. I was still on crutches, and I had to start all over again with my leg. I had severed my sciatic nerve. I have still got a dead foot, and I have always got to wear boots; I cannot wear shoes. They opened my hip up, cut the two ends and sewed them together. Not so long after that, I was walking along the side of my bed, strapped into what they called an 'elephant's foot'. It was an enormous boot. And I made it quite clear that, no matter what happened, I had to be sent to Sidcup for the plastic surgery.

So then, I got sent down to the Queen Mary's hospital in Sidcup, to have a new nose put on. That took about two years, in total. Professor Kilmer was the man I was under. First of all they took photographs. I had to go to a small hut, and I was smothered with plaster of Paris. They made a mask, and when that came out, it showed up every little blemish. Then, they cut down my ribs and they took a lot of cartilage out, and then they buried it in my stomach, to keep it alive. Then they put in into the bridge of my nose, to build it up. The first lot went wrong. Professor Kilmer said, 'What have you been doing? It shouldn't have gone like that!' I said, 'Well . . . *you* did it!' You could talk to the doctors like that. They would do anything for you.

So eventually Professor Kilmer said, 'What do you want? A Wellington nose, or a Roman Nose?' I said, 'I don't care, as long as I get one.' I went into the operating theatre at nine o'clock the next morning, and the next thing I remember is the middle of the night, the next night. All the night staff used to come down and have a rub of the nose, that was what they used to say, they would have a go at the lucky nose: I couldn't raise my head off the pillow. I had two black eyes, a square chin, and a pal went away and fetched a mirror so I could look at myself, but he showed me the magnifying side, and the blinking nose seemed to fill the whole mirror. I was happy with my new nose. I didn't care much, so long as I had one. Have you ever imagined being without one? I was down to nine stone, and the nose used to stand out like a piece of marble. They kept a piece of cartilage, in case anything got knocked off, or broke.

One day, I walked past some kids playing about, and as I went past they got up and galloped past me. I passed two or three streets, and when I got there all the kids in the blinking neighbourhood had gathered. Talking, looking, gawping at me. I'd just had this thing put on! I could have taken a crutch and hit the whole blinking lot of them. I knew what they were looking at, and I turned round and went straight back into the hospital. But then I thought, 'Well it's no good! I could be stuck like this for the rest of my life! I've got to face it sometime,' so I went out again after that; I just walked out. Anytime I wanted to go somewhere, I just walked out. And if people stared, I turned around and stared back.

I never really got my sense of smell back. One nostril is pretty well closed. I got a pair of silver nostrils that I wore for a long time to keep them open, but I got careless. I kept them out for so long, that I couldn't get them back in again. I always thought if I get another two of them, I could have a pair of cufflinks.

After a time, I was walking without crutches. I had a spring across the front of my boot that lifted the foot, otherwise it would scrape. Gradually, it got better, until I got the lightest boots it was possible to buy; my mum got them in Freeman, Hardy & Willis. In the end, I learnt to walk without it. But I couldn't do very much in the sporting line. That was impossible.

When I got back to Newcastle, I was discharged from the army, and put on a twelve-month outpatient for electrical treatment and massage on my leg. I was thinking, 'What the devil will I do, now?' I didn't want to be like some of them, walking the street with a stick and trying to live on a pension. I found out what the government was able to do. I found what they called an 'Instructional Factory' in Durham, for veterans, and they had a list of things you could go in for: tailoring, cobblering, that sort of thing. I thought if I went for watchmaking, I could sit down. I couldn't stand at the bench, you see. I had to go in front of a board of watchmaker's people, who had shops up in Newcastle, to find out if my fingers were good enough, and next thing I was invited to start at the Instructional Factory. There was instructors there, and I started like an apprentice would, with a file and a square and a block of oak, and I had to square the block of oak. Towards the end, I had to go out and find a job on civvy street. So I went back to Alnwick, where I was from. Where I belonged.

I went to this shop where I knew this fellow, and I talked to him, and I served my apprenticeship with him. And by the start of the last war – believe it or not – I was running the shop. Doing the jobs on the bench, doing the office work, estimating and tending to the salesmen doing the orders. He tried to get me to run his bank account and I refused. I said no bloody fear. I was there thirty-odd years.

Looking back, it's hard to explain, but I look back on the war with a certain amount of satisfaction. I was determined to go to war, and I went. It made me a man. I was standing on my feet, and amongst men; I had to stand up for myself. I have had thirty-three operations, but I've never regretted anything in my life. I had a job, and I had a wage. My wife got all my wages, and I lived on my pension, backing horses and playing cards. I didn't do too badly over the years. No. I've never regretted anything – except the death of my wife. That is the only thing I regret. I don't care about anything else.

The casualty figures for the battle are shocking. They are very difficult to comprehend, and very difficult to excuse. Nevertheless, the fighting severely weakened the German army physically, mentally, in numbers, and in its ability to fight the war on its own terms. Had the Somme not been fought, Verdun would have been lost and the war could well have drawn to a quite different conclusion, just as General Falkenhayn had predicted.

Mistakes may have been made in the conduct of the battle by British commanders, but does that mean that it was necessarily a mistake to engage in the first place? Or to persevere at such a shattering human cost? Was the British leadership demonstrating unforgivable indifference to men whose interests it should have been protecting? Was it pursuing a pragmatic strategy when set against a seemingly inexorable enemy? Similar questions – relating to different conflicts – have arisen since 1916, and they will continue to arise in the future. The answers should concern us: they will always divide us – but the questions themselves may not always be as straightforward as they first appear.

General Joffre, President Poincaré, the King, General Foch and Sir Douglas Haig, photographed on August 12.

A chaplain tending a soldier's grave in the Carnoy Valley.

# Index of Contributors

Number in brackets denotes IWM Sound Archive catalogue number.
Page numbers in **bold** refer to photographs.

# General Index

Page numbers in **bold** refer to photographs.